Ovid

Heroidum Epistulae XIII

Ovid

Heroidum Epistulae XIII

ISBN/EAN: 9783337186821

Printed in Europe, USA, Canada, Australia, Japan

Cover: Foto ©Thomas Meinert / pixelio.de

More available books at **www.hansebooks.com**

P. OVIDII NASONIS

HEROIDUM EPISTULAE XIII.

P. OVIDII NASONIS

HEROIDUM EPISTULAE XIII

EDITED WITH NOTES AND INDICES

BY

EVELYN S. SHUCKBURGH, M.A.

FORMERLY FELLOW AND ASSISTANT TUTOR OF EMMANUEL COLLEGE, CAMBRIDGE; LATE ASSISTANT MASTER AT ETON.

London:

MACMILLAN AND CO.

AND NEW YORK.

1896

First Edition 1879.
Reprinted with corrections 1885.
Reprinted 1896.

PREFACE.

The object of this edition is to provide the higher classes in Schools with a useful edition of Ovid's Epistles, which should contain some information as to their Author, as to the materials on which he worked, and the spirit in which he used them: and at the same time one in which an intelligent study of the language should not be neglected, nor the history of the text passed entirely over.

The book contains 13 of the 14 Epistles, the genuineness of which has not been refuted by modern criticism. At the same time no one can fail to be struck with the inferiority of the Laodamia; and I must record a strong suspicion that the Episode in Ep. 9, from v. 67 to 102, and that in Ep. 14, from v. 85 to 108, bear marks of interpolation, or at any rate of having been inserted after the completion of the rest.

My plan has been to illustrate the Poet from his own works; which is particularly proper in the case of Ovid, who so often repeats his own words. I have, when quoting from his other works or from other writers, usually given the quotations in full, knowing how likely mere references are to be passed over. References however to other parts of the Epistles are generally given with the number of Epistle and line only. Those who will not take the trouble to turn to another part of a book in their hands are not likely to use notes of any sort with much interest or profit. As to grammatical information I have decided to refer to one Grammar only, that of Mr Roby. No doubt references might have been profitably given to Madvig and others. But nearly everything is to be found in Roby's work; and it is perhaps more in the hands of English Students than any other, as it well deserves to be; taking rank as it does with Mr Munro's Lucretius, and Professor Mayor's Juvenal,—the three great works which have in our day done most to vindicate the honour of Latin Scholarship in England. I have also referred my readers from time to time to Ramsay's *Roman Antiquities*, and to Rich's *Dictionary of Roman and Greek Antiquities*.

It only remains for me to express my thanks to the Provost of Eton for his kindness in putting the Eton MSS. into my hands: and to my friend and colleague the Rev. F. St. J. Thackeray for kindly reading over the proofs of some sheets of the notes, and aiding me with valuable suggestions and corrections.

ETON, *August* 11, 1879.

INTRODUCTION.

The knowledge which we possess of the life of Ovid is drawn for the most part from his own writings. Not only has he left us a poem professedly autobiographical[1]: but the *Tristia* and *Letters from Pontus* abound in references to the circumstances of his past life; and though no doubt often composed with a view of their being seen by the Emperor, they yet contain as complete a self-revelation as any perhaps existing in Poetry. The art with which he set forth his feelings of sorrow and despair, his hopes and affections, had become a second nature to him; and, however embellished, the thoughts in the Poems of his exile have for the most part the appearance of genuineness. While reading this part of his works we gradually learn to feel a kindly interest in the character of a man, who if he did not possess any heroical virtues, was yet free from a spark of littleness or spite: and who if he did not meet misfortune with high courage, at any rate was not utterly crushed or driven from his natural tastes by it. His generous admiration for the poets who were his immediate

[1] *Tristia* 4, 10.

predecessors[2]; his affection for his wife[3] and daughter[4]; his warm feelings toward his friends, and the delicacy with which he refrains from putting too severe a strain upon their friendship by connecting them publicly with a man under the frown of the Emperor[5]; are

[2] *Temporis illius colui fovique poetas,*
Quotque aderant vates rebar adesse deos. *Tr.* 4, 10, 41.

[3] In *Tr.* 1, 6 is a tribute to his wife for her devotion and fidelity *si quid adhuc ego sum muneris omne tui est.* Amidst the miseries of his exile the loss of her society is the chief, *Tr.* 3, 3, 15

Omnia quum subeant vincis tamen omnia, conjunx,
Et plus in nostro pectore parte tenes.
Te loquor absentem, te vox mea nominat unam,
Nulla venit sine te nox mihi, nulla dies.

If when on the point of death some one should announce to him that she was come, *resurgam, Spesque tui nobis causa vigoris erit.* Like the hero of Tennyson's *Maud* 'My heart would hear her and beat had it lain for a century dead', he declares (ib. 83) *quamvis in cineres corpus mutaverit ignis Sentiet officium maesta favilla suum.*

[4] *Tristia* 3, 7 has been generally set down as addressed to his daughter. And her name Perilla rests on the authority of that elegy. Mr Church has expressed some doubt as to this: and indeed the expressions in it are not so warm as one would expect from a father to an only daughter. The recollections which he calls up are chiefly literary. He reminds her of the interest he had taken in her culture and her attempts in poetry. He urges her to keep up all innocent and liberal tastes, and declares that amidst all his own sorrows and losses poetry has been a comfort of which no Caesar could deprive him.

En ego cum patria caream vobisque domoque,
Raptaque sint adimi quae potuere mihi.
Ingenio tamen ipse meo comitorque fruorque,
Caesar in hoc potuit juris habere nihil. *Ib.* 45.

He says that this daughter was twice married and had offspring by both husbands *Tr.* 4, 10, 75. And in *F.* 6, 219 he mentions her marriage, and the precautions he took as to selecting the proper season for it. None of these passages however would preclude the possibility of the person he calls *filia* being really the daughter of his third wife by her former husband, see *Pont.* 4, 8, 9. Cf. *ib.* 90.

[5] *Vos quoque pectoribus nostris haeretis, amici,*
Dicere quos cupio nomine quemque suo.

indications of a loveable and generous nature, which go far to incline us to forgive him many faults and extravagances; and to indulge the fancy that much in his writings which none can approve, and which I believe shocked his own generation, was, in his own words, more an error than a crime.

His lamentations over his fate as an exile, his humble, sometimes abject, intreaties to the Emperor for pardon or some relaxation in the strictness of his punishment, have fixed on him the reproach of unmanliness and servility[6]; but, in mitigation of these hard terms, we should try to conceive what that punishment was to Ovid. He was past middle age[7]; devoted to Rome[8]; to society; to his literary

Sed timor officium cautus compescit, et ipsos
In nostro poni carmine nolle puto.

. . . .

Quod quoniam est anceps, intra mea pectora quemque
Adloquar, et nulli causa timoris ero.
Nec meus indicio latitantes versus amicos
Protrahit: occulte si quis amabat amet. *Tr.* 3, 4, 63.

Afterwards he becomes less scrupulous, or finds that less danger is involved than he imagined; and names his various friends.

[6] Ovid does not however refrain from hinting respectfully that Augustus has made a mistake in his case. *Fas ergo est aliqua caelestia pectora falli; Et sunt notitia multa minora tuâ. Tr.* 2, 213.

[7] Ovid was 51 years old at the time of his banishment,

Postque meos ortus Pisaeâ vinctus olivâ
Abstulerat decies praemia victor equus.
Tr. 4, 10, 95.

There would really have been twelve Olympic contests in his life. But he confuses a Greek Olympiad (4 years) with a Latin Lustrum (5 years). According to the Greek reckoning Ovid was born in the 2nd year of the 184th Olympiad and was banished in the third year of the 196th. He shows this confusion plainly in *Pont.* 4, 6, 5, *In Scythia nobis quinquennis Olympias acta est, Jam tempus lustri transit in alterius.*

[8] *Ante oculos errant domus, urbs, et forma locorum,*
Acceduntque suis singula facta locis. *Tr.* 3, 4, 57.

In another place (*Tr.* 1, 1) he directs his book as to the way

friends[9]. He was banished to a spot on the very extremity of the Empire[10], barely protected from the raids of warlike barbarians[11]; the climate was odious to him after that of Italy; the food disgusted him; he was often ill, and no proper medical aid was at hand[12]; the society was provincial or worse than pro-

it was to take through Rome, and dwells fondly on every object and building.

[9] Ovid seems to have especially felt the want of intellectual companionship: *Non liber hic ullus, non qui mihi commodet aurem, Verbaque significent quid mea norit, adest.* Tr. 5, 12, 53. Again he complains *Non qui soletur, non qui labentia tarde Tempora narrando fallat amicus adest.*

Tr. 3, 3, 11.

[10] *Haec est Ausonio sub jure novissima, vixque*
Haeret in imperii margine terra tui.

Tr. 2, 199.

[11] *Protinus aequato siccis aquilonibus Histro*
Invehitur celeri barbarus hostis equo.
Hostis equo pollens longeque volante sagitta
Vicinam late depopulatur humum.

Tr. 3, 10, 53.

He describes the effect of these raids. Some of the people are killed with poisoned arrows; some sold into slavery; cattle are driven off; cottages burnt; the implements of the farmers are taken, the whole wealth of the district destroyed; so that for fear of these incursions the fields are left uncultivated. Cf. also Tr. 4, 1, 77 sq.

[12] *Aeger in extremis ignoti partibus orbis,*
Incertusque meae poene salutis eram,
Quid mihi nunc animi dira regione jacenti
Inter Sauromatas esse Getasque putes?
Nec caelum patior nec aquis adsuevimus istis
Terraque nescio quo displicet ipsa modo.
Non domus apta satis; non hic cibus utilis aegro,
Nullus Apollinea qui levet arte malum.

Tr. 3, 3, 2.

Again, *Ut tetigi Pontum vexant insomnia, vixque*
Ossa tegit macies nec juvat ora cibus.

Ib. 3, 8, 27.

Nec caelum nec aquae faciunt, nec terra nec aurae.
Hei mihi, perpetuus corpora languor habet.

Ib. 3, 8, 23.

vincial; there was no one to sympathize in his favourite studies; the language of the people was unknown to him[13]; he was separated for ever from his family; and he felt bitterly that his punishment was more than he could possibly have deserved, although I think he never really cherished a hope of recall.

It is to be set down to Ovid's credit that he did not yield entirely to these depressing influences. He always declares that though his writings had been loose, his life had been pure. And in his exile he might well have pleaded that, though his verse breathed only sorrow and despair, his life showed signs of a manful attempt to master them. He worked at his poetry, if not with energy yet with interest; he learnt the language of the country so well as to be able to write some verses in it which were popular with the Barbarians[14]; he even served in arms at times to help to beat back the attacks of the hostile border tribes[15]; and made himself by his courageous bearing and genial disposition so beloved by the Tomitae, that

[13] *Nesciaque est vocis quod barbara lingua Latinae*
Graiaque quod Getico victa loquella sono est.
Tr. 5, 2, 67.
Per gestum res est significanda mihi.
Ib. 5, 10, 36.

He however conquered this difficulty by learning the language:

Ipse mihi videor jam dedidicisse Latine;
Nam didici Getice Sarmaticeque loqui.
Ib. 5, 12, 57.

[14] He pretends to be ashamed of this (*Pont.* 4, 13, 19).

Ah pudet, et Getico scripsi sermone libellum,
Structaque sunt nostris barbara verba modis.
Et placui, gratare mihi, coepique poetae
Inter inhumanos nomen habere Getas.

Perhaps these verses were in a language something of the same nature as that with which Hans Breitmann has made us familiar.

[15] *Aspera militiae juvenis certamina fugi,*
Nec nisi lusura movimus arma manu.

they voted him a crown of laurel, relieved him from all public burdens[*], and after his death erected a tomb in his honour. In regard to his servile language to Augustus and Tiberius, we must judge of it in connection with the manners and fashions of the day. Catullus had indeed assailed the Great Julius with a freedom and rancour which surpasses belief. But his were the last notes of Liberty. The courtier-like language of Virgil is so polished as almost to excuse its exaggeration. But a despotism was producing its inevitable consequences, and poet after poet vied with each other in using language to the Caesars which would be almost exaggerated if addressed to the gods[16]. Martial as far out-ran Ovid in this revolting practice as Ovid went beyond Virgil. Our own poets, of the Jacobean age for instance, have erred nearly as grossly, without nearly so good an excuse. Much of such language is to be regarded merely as conventional. Some of it is to be excused, or passed lightly though regretfully over, in consideration of Ovid's misery, and his feeling of the utter hopelessness of any escape from the power which he was trying to propitiate. Its lesson is rather to make us hate tyranny than despise poets.

Publius Ovidius Naso was born at Sulmo, about 90 miles from Rome, in the country of the Peligni, on

Nunc senior gladioque latus scutoque sinistram,
Canitiem galeae subicioque meam.
Nam dedit e specula custos ubi signa tumultus,
Induimus trepida protinus arma manu.

Tr. 4, 1, 71.

[*] *Pont.* 4, 14, 55 *Solus adhuc ego sum vestris immunis in oris, Exceptis si qui munera legis habent. Tempora sacrata mea sunt velata corona Publicus invito quam favor imposuit. ib.* 4, 9, 101 *nec mihi credideris: extant decreta, quibus nos Laudat et immunes publica cera facit.*

[16] Of course the official deification of the Caesars may be put forward as an explanation of much of this. But such deification *was* official, and could have had no real influence in the mind of any rational man.

the 20th of March[17], in the year B.C. 43: the year in which the two Consuls Hirtius and Pansa were killed at Mutina. The men of his family had for many generations been equites[b]. He had a brother born on the same day of the same month in the previous year. The two boys were well educated, and in due time went to school in Rome; and were, he says, under famous masters. Their teachers of Rhetoric were, we learn elsewhere, Arellius Fuscus and Porcius Latro. The elder Ovidius early showed a taste for Oratory: but our Poet from his boyhood betrayed the bent of his genius. Like Pope he 'lisped in numbers for the numbers came'[18]. His father however looked upon

[17] *Haec est armiferae festis de quinque Minervae*
Quae fieri pugna prima cruenta solet.
Tr. 4, 10, 13.

The *quinquatrus*, or feast of Minerva, began on the 19th of March and lasted perhaps five days; the Romans themselves supposing the name to be derived from that fact, whereas it is derived from the fact of the festival being on the fifth day after the Ides. See Paley on *F.* 3, 810. However the 19th was kept sacred from gladiatorial shows, as the reputed birthday of Minerva; and Ovid therefore dates his birth as occurring on the 20th.

[b] *Si quid id est, usque a proavis vetus ordinis haeres*
Non modo fortunae munere factus eques. *Ib.* 7.

For Ovid's own admission to the rank see Trist. 2, 89, 90.

Ovid elsewhere repeats the substance of these lines. He evidently thinks it a legitimate subject for pride. But we must be on our guard against supposing from the use of the word *haeres* that the rank of *eques* was hereditary in our sense of the word. Admission to the *ordo equestris* was simply a matter of money (subject to the *nota* of the Censor), and had been so since the lex Sempronia B.C. 122. It was the money that was hereditary, and that was a qualification for the rank.

[18] *Frater ad eloquium viridi tendebat ab aevo*
Fortia verbosi natus ad arma fori.
. . . . *Ib.* 17.

Sponte sua carmen numeros veniebat ad aptos
Et quod conabar dicere versus erat.
Ib. 25.

Poetry as an unprofitable pursuit and urged him with the usual arguments to continue his rhetorical studies. The two brothers accordingly went on with their education with the ostensible object of fitting themselves for the business of the Forum. In due time they assumed the *toga virilis*[19], and set out in the path in which civic distinction was to be won.

In B.C. 24 Ovid experienced his first sorrow in the loss of his brother, to which he refers with genuine feeling. He himself, about the same time we may presume, went to Athens, as was the custom with Roman youths of good means, to complete his education at its Schools; which occupied at that time a position akin to our Universities[20]. His active career should then have begun, and he did hold some of the

[19] This was done with a certain solemnity; and the ceremony was called *tirocinium fori*. It seems not quite certain at what year in a boy's life it took place, *i.e.* whether at the end of the 14th, 15th, or 16th year. Probably it depended on the judgment of the father, who decided in accordance with the circumstances of the case, the forwardness of the boy, and his position in life. See Bekker's *Gallus* p. 195. Ovid calls it *liberior toga* in reference to the freer and less restrained life of the boy after its assumption. The 17th of March was the usual day for this ceremony because it was the feast of Bacchus, the *Liberalia*, and the name was a good omen for the assumption of the *libera toga*. See *F.* 3, 777 and compare Prop. 4, 15, 3 *Ut mihi praetextae pudor est velatus amictu, Et data libertas noscere amoris iter.*

[20] It is somewhat remarkable that Ovid does not mention this in his account of himself (*Tr.* 4, 10) which we have been following. Our only information is a chance remark in another Elegy describing his melancholy journey to Tomi; *Tr.* 1, 2, 77 *Nec peto quas quondam petii studiosus Athenas.* Was it then so much a matter of course, that it might be passed over lightly in the account of a young man's life? It is not certain whether his visit to Asia and his stay in Sicily took place at the same time. These visits he enjoyed in the company of Macer, the Poet of the Trojan war (not Aemilius Macer who wrote on birds): cf. *Pont.* 4, 10, 21 *Te duce magnificas Asiae perspeximus urbes: Trinacris est oculis te duce nota meis.*

minor offices open to a man of his age[21]. But he never held any *magistratus*, which would have given him admission to the Senate[22]. Neither his health, nor his intellectual tastes fitted him for a political career; and his genius, as genius usually will, took its natural course. With the eager generosity of youthful admiration, he became a hero-worshipper. His heroes however were not political leaders, but men of letters. He made his way into a set of Poets, among whom the most conspicuous were Aemilius Macer of Verona, the poet of natural history; Propertius, the poet of passion; Paulicius the writer of Heroics, and Bassus of Iambics. He heard Horace recite; and once at least saw Virgil, though he appears not to have known him[23]; and for a few years was intimate with Tibullus, who died when our Poet was about twenty-five. He regards Gallus as the father of Latin Elegiac Poetry; and considers that he was succeeded by Tibullus,

[21] He mentions in *Tr.* 5, 10, 34 his having filled the office of *triumvir*, *i. e.* one of a board of Three, several of which existed; *e.g. triumviri monetales*, *capitales* etc. In *F.* 4, 384 *Inter bis quinos usus honore viros*, he refers to his having been one of the *decemviri*, *i.e. decemviri litibus judicandis*. These *decemviri* were presidents of the court of *centumviri;* to which Court therefore Ovid mentions that he belongs, *Tr.* 2, 93 *nec male commissa est nobis fortuna reorum, Lisque decem deciens inspicienda viris*. And in the two lines following these he says he had held the office of 'Judicial arbiter' (for which office see Cic. *Rosc. Com.* 4), *Res quoque privatas statui sine crimine judex, Deque mea fassa est pars quoque Victa fide.*

[22] The first *magistratus* which he might have held, and which would have admitted him to the Senate, was that of Quaestor, which he might have obtained at the age of 27, according to the *lex annalis*. But he says he could not endure the trouble, and *clavi mensura coacta est:* that is, he assumed the *angusticlavia* instead of the *laticlavia*, which he had worn as one of the *illustres equites*, a distinct class among the equites which had arisen since republican times, and consisted of men of senatorial descent or of senatorial fortune.

[23] *Vergilium vidi tantum*, *Tr.* 4, 10, 51.

Tibullus by Propertius, Propertius by himself[24]. His poems soon became popular; and like many of the early poems of young men were inspired by a passion for some mistress unknown, whom he chooses to call Corinna. He boasts, however, that though the morality of his 'Amores' was lax, his life was free from scandal. And it is natural when we compare these elegies with, for example, the Sonnets of Shakespeare, to suppose that the greater part of them were dramatic and not founded on actual experiences of the Poet.

Of his private life during this period we only know what he has chosen to tell us. He was thrice married. His first wife, given him when he was almost a boy, proved unworthy, he says, and was quickly divorced. His second was divorced with equal despatch, though he tells us that there was no fault to be found with her[25]. By the third, to whom he remained warmly attached to the day of his death[26], he is generally said to have had a daughter, Perilla. His daughter was twice married, he says, and had a child by each husband[27]. This third wife

[24] Caius Cornelius Gallus was born B.C. 66 at Forum Julii (Frejus) in Gaul, and died by his own hand in B.C. 26. He was a school fellow of Virgil, who addresses one of his Eclogues to him. He was with Octavianus at Actium, by whom he was afterwards made Prefect of Egypt. His principal work was a Collection of Elegies in four books. Quinctilian 10, 1, 93) says that he was less polished (*durior*) than Tibullus or Propertius.

[25] For the extreme facility of divorce at this time see Ramsay p. 253. Augustus tried in vain by the Lex Julia et Papia Poppaea to restrain it. Suet. *Octav.* 74.

[26] There are symptoms however of his feeling somewhat dissatisfied with his wife's exertions for his recall. See *Pont.* 3, 1, which is an exhortation to her to use more energy in his cause cp. Tr. 5, 2, 37—40. And Pont. 3, 7, 11 *Nec gravis uxori dicar; quae scilicet in me Quam proba, tam timida est, experiensque parum.* After which her name does not occur. But it is the inevitable result of such a position to make a man fancy that his best friends might have done something more.

[27] We hear of a certain Fidus Cornelius as a son-in-law of Ovid; about whom Seneca (*Dial.* 2, 17, 1) tells us that

was of noble birth, and belonged to the Fabian gens[28]. From this fact, and from the names of the friends whom Ovid addresses in the *Pontine Epistles*, we may clearly gather that Ovid was not only a popular poet, but that he lived in society of the better sort at Rome. He possessed, besides his ancestral property near Sulmo, a suburban estate or *horti* on the hills beyond the Milvian bridge, near the junction of the via Clodia with the via Flaminia; not far from which in a sepulchral cavern many inscriptions of the Nasones were found *. All he tells us of this part of his life is that his father and mother lived to an advanced age, dying one soon after the other, not long before his own exile.

In these circumstances, unusually happy and prosperous perhaps, Ovid lived till past the age of fifty. But a sudden and final change came upon him. In the year A.D. 8, he was peremptorily ordered by a rescript of Augustus to retire to Tomi[29] on the shores of the Euxine, the Capital of lower Mœsia. There was nothing for it but to obey; and accordingly after an affecting parting with his wife and friends[30], the Poet set out for his barbaric residence. His journey occu-

he wept in the Senate House because Corbulo called him 'a plucked Ostrich,' *Struthocamelus depilatus*.

[28] *Pont.* 1, 2, 138, to Fabius Maximus, *Ille ego de vestra cui data nupta domo*. She was also niece to Rufus, *ib.* 2, 11, 13. She had a daughter by a former marriage married to Suillius, *ib.* 4, 8, 9.

[29] Ovid only twice uses the name itself, in both cases he writes *Tomis*, *Tr.* 3, 9, 33. *Pont.* 4, 14, 59. Suetonius in the fragment of Ovid's life has *Tomos* (acc.). Strabo has two forms Τομέα (acc.) 7, 5. Τόμις (nom.) 7, 6. Elsewhere Ovid avoids the word and uses *Tomitae*, 'the people of Tomis,' or some substantive with the adjective *Tomitanus*, or *Pontus*. The name probably means the 'Cuts' (τέμνω) from certain Canals near it. But Ovid mentions the Mythological derivation from τέμνω as the place where Medea cut up her brother Absyrtus.

Inde Tomis dictus locus hic, quia fertur in illo
Membra soror fratris consecuisse sui. *Tr.* 3, 9, 33.

[30] Described in *Tr.* 1, 3.

* Tr. v. 4, 8, 27, cp. 1, 8, 41 *hortos flaminia Clodia juncta viae*. The road which branches from the *Flaminia* is properly the *Cassia*, of which the *Clodia* is a branch. This passage shews that the whole route was sometimes called *via Clodia*.

pied nearly a year; and according to his own account was exceedingly dangerous and fatiguing. There he resided till his death in A.D. 18. His punishment was not *exilium* but *relegatio*. That is, he did not forfeit property or citizenship, nor personal freedom, except in so far as his place of residence was concerned[31]. He was simply obliged to live away from Rome at a fixed place, during the will of the emperor[32]. But this meant for Ovid the loss of all that made life worth having, of wife and friends, of congenial society, of country, of habitual pursuits, of interest in his work[33] and the sweets of contemporary fame, of everything in fact except property; though he complains more than once of impaired means (Pont. 2, 7, 61; 4, 8, 32), and speaks gratefully of pecuniary help given him (*ib.* 4, 1, 23); and describes himself as *pauper* (*ib.* 4, 9, 122.)

The cause of his banishment has never been fully cleared up, and still remains, like the authorship of the letters of Junius, one of the mysteries of

[31] *Adde quod edictum, quamvis immite minaxque,*
Attamen in poenae nomine lene fuit.
Quippe relegatus, non exul, dicor in illo,
Privaque fortunae sunt data verba meae.

Tr. 2, 135.

It was no doubt the proper guardianship of his property which was the object of Ovid's wife, staying at Rome, and not accompanying her husband to Tomi. *Tu facis ut spolium non sim nec nuder ab illis Naufragii tabulas qui petiere mei.* Tr. 1, 6, 7. She wished to do so but gave in from prudential motives. *Vixque dedit victas utilitate manus.* *Tr.* 1, 3, 88.

[32] The punishment was entirely an act of the Emperor's will and not inflicted by any legal tribunal: *Nec mea decreto damnasti facta senatus Nec mea selecto judice jussa fuga est.*

Tr. 2, 131.

[33] Ovid often asserts that he has lost the energy or care to correct his poetry or make it worthy of him, e. g. *Pont.* 1, 5, 15 *cum relego, scripsisse pudet; quia plurima cerno Me quoque, qui feci, judice digna lini. Nec tamen emendo: labor hic quam scribere major. Mensque pati durum sustinet aegra nihil.* And again *ib.* 57 *Gloria vos acuat: vos ut recitata probentur Carmina, Pieriis invigilate choris. Quod venit ex facili, satis est componere nobis, et nimis intenti causa laboris abest.*

literary history. Mr Munro (*Catul.* p. 185) says: 'Dates and his own reiterated hints prove beyond any reasonable doubt that Ovid's disaster was connected with the detection of the younger Julia.' This Julia was the grand-daughter of Augustus and was banished in the same year as Ovid. The circumstances which led to her punishment were such as to make it quite possible that Ovid, or any one else leading a life of free pleasure in the higher society of Rome, should have been implicated more or less remotely in her crimes. But granting this, it is still an unsolved mystery in what way Ovid was involved, and what his particular offence to Augustus was. In the Classical Museum (vol. 4, p. 229, of 1847) Mr Dyer has laboured to show that his crime was that of having been privy to Julia's adultery with Decius Julius Silanus, and having concealed it.

His own language in speaking of the causes of his banishment seems to go through two phases. He first seems to wish to convey the idea that his youthful indiscretion in publishing his Amatory treatises was the sole cause. 'He is a poet destroyed by his own genius; his verses have been his undoing; they deserved punishment but surely not so heavy a one[34].' But presently he begins to own that there was another cause; not, he is careful to state, any political offence; no plot against the Emperor; no plan of violence against the state[35]. He had seen something that he should not have seen. He is ruined by his simplicity and want of prudence, combined with treachery on

[34] *Inspice, dic, titulum non sum praeceptor amoris*
Quas meruit, poenas jam dedit illud opus.
Tr. 1, 1, 67, and so often.

[35] *Causa mea est melior, qui non contraria fovi*
Arma, sed hanc merui simplicitate fugam.
Tr. 1, 5, 41.

Comp. *Pont.* 2, 2, 11.

the part of slaves and friends. The exact cause he dare not reveal, and yet it is well known in Rome[36].' The conclusion arrived at from these various hints of the Poet, at any rate must be that there was another cause of a personal nature affecting Augustus, which brought about the disaster besides the immorality of his poems. The ostensible cause however put forward in the Edict was this; nor can we say that it was not a plausible or *prima facie* a sufficient cause, in spite of the fact that they had been published ten years. No doubt much that was coarse and licentious had been written before and had found at any rate toleration, and much was being daily written of the same nature. But nothing had been written before, nor I think has been written since, which so deliberately and with such apparent seriousness systemizes vice and ignores all idea of virtue. It is surprising to hear pleaded that Horace was as licentious, or that Augustus wrote uncleanly epigrams.

[36] *Cur aliquid vidi? cur noxia lumina feci?*
Cur imprudenti cognita culpa mihi?
Inscius Actaeon vidit sine veste Dianam;
Praeda fuit canibus non minus ille suis.
Scilicet in superis etiam fortuna luenda est
Nec veniam laeso numine casus habet.

Tr. 2, 102.

The chief passages in the *Tristia* and *Pontine Epistles* referring to Ovid's banishment have been collected by Mr Dyer and Professor Ramsay. They are too numerous to quote at length. Dyer thus classifies them: (1) His offence was error not crime, *Tr.* 1, 2, 97; 3, 37; 4, 41. 4, 4, 43. *Pont.* 1, 7, 41. 2, 9, 71. (2) He had seen a crime committed, *Tr.* 2, 102; 3, 5, 50; 3, 6, 27. (3) Augustus would be offended by its revelation, *Tr.* 1, 5, 51. 2, 207. *Pont.* 2, 2, 59—62. (4) It was known at Rome, *Tr.* 4, 10, 99. *Pont.* 1, 7, 39. (5) His conduct, subsequent to his seeing what he saw, helped on his ruin, it was not only one act, *Tr.* 4, 4, 37. 3, 6, 13. *Pont.* 2, 3, 91. 2, 6, 17. (6) His own want of courage helped, *Tr.* 4, 4, 37. *Pont.* 2, 2, 19. (7) He acted from no mercenary motive and involved no one else. *Tr.* 3, 6, 33. *Pont.* 2, 2, 17.

The distinction is a wide one. Unbridled coarseness of invective, descriptions the most nauseous, jests the most filthy, might be passed over, or allowed some currency. But this handbook of seduction was, I believe, not less likely to shock decent Roman taste and feeling than it would those of modern times. From Rem. 361 sq. we see that this was the sentiment of many at Rome. Ovid himself felt this, and was fain to suggest what poor excuse he could[37]. Perhaps Augustus, alarmed at the growing corruption of manners, and determined for once to exercise the function of a Censor, looked upon this as a really good reason for sending Ovid from Rome: and at the same time as an excellent pretext, sure to find a ready acceptance, for getting rid of a man whom he may have discovered to be connected with his own family dishonour. However this may be, to Tomi Ovid had to go, and at Tomi he remained until his death in A.D. 18, neither Augustus nor Tiberius ever being prevailed upon to revoke the edict which relegated him[38].

[37] Thus in *Tr.* 2, 423 he goes through the list of Roman writers from Ennius downwards, who might have been charged with a similar transgression against morals. He asserts that no one has been made vicious by reading his lines, and that they were not intended for the perusal of the innocent. *Pont.* 3, 3, 51 sq. He also takes care to make the common distinction between what he writes and what he does, *vita verecunda est Musa jocosa mea*, *Tr.* 2, 354.

[38] One is glad to think that he behaved with some manliness there in spite of his abject letters. He even at last came to feel some affection for the place, in return for kindness and honour shown to him:

Quam grata est igitur Latonae Delia tellus
Erranti tutum quae dedit una locum
Tam mihi cara Tomis: patria quae sede fugatis
Tempus adhuc nobis hospita fida manet.
Pont. 4, 14, 57.

He only wishes, he adds, that it were a little further from the North Pole. His descriptions of the severity of the climate (especially *Tr.* 3, 10) are at variance with what we know of it

Up to the time of his banishment Ovid had only published, of his writings now extant, the *Amores*, the *Heroides*, and the series which proved fatal to him, the *'Ars Amoris'*, *'Remedium Amoris'*, and *'Medicina faciei'*. He tells us that the *Metamorphoses* were finished though not corrected; that in his anger and despair he burnt them, but that other copies were in existence, and that thus they were preserved[39]. He speaks of destroying much other work at the same time, but of this of course we know nothing. His other important work, the *Fasti*, was no doubt begun by this time, but was not finished even so far as we have it, until after his banishment, to which it contains two allusions[40]. In early life he wrote a tragedy called *Medea*, but though he thought himself fitted for this sort of composition he laid it aside for lighter work (Am. 2, 18, 13). Of this play Quinctilian (10, 1, 98) says: MEDEA *videtur mihi ostendere quantum ille vir praestare potuerit, si*

now; and Ovid found that he was not believed at Rome, *Pont.* 4, 10, 35 *qui veniunt istinc vix vos ea credere dicunt. Quam miser est qui fert asperiora fide!* cf. *ib.* 4, 9, 85. and 4, 7, where he appeals to the personal experience of a certain Vestalis. The probability is that there have been great changes in that respect.

[39] *Haec ego discedens, sicut bene multa meorum,*
Ipsa mea posui maestus in igni manu.

. . . .

Vel quod eram Musas, ut crimina nostra, perosus,
Vel quod adhuc crescens et rude carmen erat.
Quae quoniam non sunt penitus sublata, sed extant,
Pluribus exemplis scripta fuisse reor. Tr. 1, 7, 21.

Perhaps he remembered this fact when he put the book in the fire, like Pendennis and his novel Walter Lorrain.

[40] *Puppibus egressus Latia stetit exul in herba,*
Felix exilium cui locus ille fuit. F. 1, 539.

Sulmonis gelidi, patriae, Germanice, nostrae,
Me miserum Scythico quam procul illa solo est!
Ib. 4, 81.

ingenio suo imperare quam indulgere maluisset. His work during his exile, as far as we know, consisted of a revision and perhaps completion of the Fasti, and the composition of the Elegies known as the *Tristia* in five books, and the *Pontine Epistles* in four[41].

The *Heroides*, or *Epistulae Heroidum*, are imaginary letters from women of the heroic or legendary age to various heroes. They have all this common feature, that they are written in sorrow for the loss of his society to whom they are addressed. But their circumstances otherwise differ widely. Penelope, Hermione and Laodamia have suffered no wrong from the man whom they address; while Phaedra is a victim of irresistible passion, and Medea, besides the wrong done her by Jason, has upon her all the horrors of remorse for crimes she has herself committed. Briseis, on the other hand, has only violence to complain of from another, and supineness on the part of her lover. Ariadne, Œnone, Deianira, Hypsipyle, Dido have all got a clear case, and are able to utter direct and well deserved reproaches to their betrayers.

These Epistles have been perhaps the most popular of all Ovid's works. They were known and read throughout the middle ages. Immediately after the invention of printing editions of them appeared in quick succession; and they have maintained an almost undiminished popularity up to the present day. The reason is not far to seek. They are highly dramatic. Each heroine has distinct and striking characteristics; and yet the theme of them all, unhappy love, is simple and one which has ever, and probably will ever, command interest and awaken feeling.

[41] The latter he says were not meant to form a book, but consisted of separate letters to his various friends, afterwards collected without regard to their proper order. *Pont.* 3, 9, 51 *Nec liber ut fieret, sed uti sua cuique daretur Littera, propositum curaque nostra fuit. Postmodo collectas, utcunque sine ordine junxi.*

There are twenty-one of these Epistles which have been attributed to Ovid. But of these, the last seven have been now pretty generally pronounced to be by another hand. And without entering further into the question we may without difficulty acknowledge their inferiority in many ways. In this edition I have undertaken to deal with the first fourteen only, and of them have omitted the eleventh: not as being inferior,—for it seems to me to possess an energy and passion superior to most of the others,—but because its subject is such as to make its absence at any rate no matter of regret in a book intended primarily for Schools.

As to the title of the book there is much variation in the MSS.; and the fact perhaps is that it was commonly spoken of either as 'Epistulae' or 'Heroides', but that the full title was 'Heroidum Epistulae'; which indeed expresses the actual nature of the book, if the last seven letters, some of which are from the Heroes to the Heroines, are not genuine[42].

MSS. The text here given is founded on that of Merkel, in the Teubner series, of 1876, which has been formed by a Collation of the two best MSS. (1) The Codex Puteanus (P) of the ninth century, at present at Paris. To this MS. Palmer attaches an almost superstitious veneration. It doubtless is the highest authority we have, though not without many mistakes. Its great value consists in the fact that it was written before the recension of the text which took place some time in the 11th century, and which has affected all the other MSS. which we possess[43].

[42] The two passages in Ovid which seem to allude to these letters are *A. A.* 3, 345 *Vel tibi composita cantetur Epistula voce Ignotum hoc aliis ille novavit opus. Tr.* 1, 6, 33 *Prima locum sanctas heroidas inter habens.* The MS. ε, whose readings are given in the critical notes, has at the end of the Epistles *Explicat liber heroidum sive Ovidii Epistolarum.*

[43] *P* has three large deficiencies, *i.e.* from 1, 1 to 2, 14, from 4, 48 to 4, 103, and from 5, 97 to 6, 49.

(2) The Codex Guelferbytanus (G) of the 12th century, corrected and annotated in the 13th.

The readings of these two MSS. are given from Merkel's collation at the end of this introduction.

(3) But besides these two MSS. another of great antiquity has been long known to exist in the Eton College Library (*Codex Longobardicus*), whither it was probably brought by Sir Henry Wotton from Venice. Its readings have been from time to time examined, but it has never before been thoroughly collated. I have thought it worth while therefore to give a complete collation of it in the critical notes (E). It is pronounced to be of the 11th century; and it unfortunately presents many of the characteristic readings of the MSS. of the recension mentioned above, as having taken place some time in that century. It is in Gothic characters, and only contains of the Epistles from the beginning to 7, 157, breaking off abruptly in the middle of a couplet. It contains besides this fragment of the Epistles (1) Theoduli carmina, (2) Cornelius Gallus, (3) Statii Achilleis, (4) Ovidii Remedia amoris, and following the Epistles (5) Aratoris Carmina[44].

(4) I have also given the readings of another Eton MS. (ε). This is a beautiful French MS. of the end of the 13th or beginning of the 14th century. It contains all the usually received works of Ovid, except the Consolatio ad Liviam, and besides them some shorter spurious pieces *de Sompnio, de Pulice, de Cuculo, de mirabilibus Mundi.* I have given its readings, not as being of any special value, but because they serve as a fair specimen of the readings of the MSS. of this later age.

[44] This MS. has been collated for H. S. Sedlmayer, and described by him in his Prolegomena Critica, Vienna 1878. I think however in one instance at least he has been wrongly informed as to its reading.

Editions. (5) The Editio Princeps of the Epistles is that of Rome A.D. 1471. I have not been able to see it. But I have thought it worth while as a specimen of the state of the text shortly after the time of the invention of Printing to give the readings of a Venice Edition of 1491, which I had in my hands from the Eton Library, and which is accompanied by a commentary of Vossius. This I have marked V in the critical notes.

(6) In our own time the most important work on our text has been done by Mr Arthur Palmer of Trinity College, Dublin, in his edition of 1874. His notes are highly instructive, and his emendations always ingenious, and often convincing. I have, when I could not accept them, given them in the critical notes with the symbol Pa.

(7) The last emendations I have to notice are those of Madvig in his Emendationes Latinae 1873. His authority must always carry great weight. In several instances he has coincided with Mr Palmer. Some of his emendations I have admitted into the text. All others are given in the critical notes, with the letters MADV.

Of the various Editions of the Epistles I have found that of Loers (Cologne 1829) the most useful for illustrative matter. Van Lennep's Edition (Amsterdam 1809) is mainly critical, and contains much that is valuable. Jahn gives the readings of a great number of MSS., but his collations have been shown to be often inaccurate. I have also from time to time consulted the notes of Heinsius; and have frequently used Zingerle's '*Ovidius und sein Verhältniss zu den vorgängern und gleichzeitigen Römischen Dichtern*'. But as my plan has been in all cases if possible to illustrate Ovid from himself, I have found Burmann's very excellent index my greatest and best help. It is with this experience of the usefulness of a complete index, that I have joined to this edition an index of the Epistles it contains, which I have made as complete as I could, with an earnest hope that Students will avail themselves of this best help to understanding their author.

Epistulae. I 77 *quod sit* G.—103 coni. ed. *Hec faciunt* G.—105 *inutilis ar.. s* G.

II 10 coni. ed. *nunc et amore noces* G.—47 *quod me* G *fugit. haberes* PG.—50 *numin.* PG.—53 corr. Heins. *credid. quid iam* G. in P. ras. Heins. fals.—61 corr. ed. *quia...temeruisse* P *quia me mer.* G.—62 *Quaec. de merito* P.—83 ita PG.—84 e G. *Armifer.* P.—96 e G. *Quoque* P.—98 ita P. *fac* G.—100 *negateta* P.—103 *iam te* G.—111 e G. *letiss.* P.—114 e Guelf. 2. Helmest., P. ma. sec. *exit* P *exiit* G.—121, *fruticosaque litora* PG.—122 *litora nota* G.—133 *Hic* G.—142 corr. Heins. *iuuat* PG.—143 *neque* P.—148 *ipsam man.* P. *illa man.* G, P pro v. scr. ma. pr.

III 4 *tamen he lacr.* G.—6 *uiroqua queri* P.—19 *proregressa* G.—20 e G. *nuris* s. *nurus* P.—21 *data sum* G.—30 corr. Heins. *blandus* PG.—31 e G. *operosos ex aere* P.—48 e G. *quae mea* P.—57 *fulseri*[*s?*]......P hodie quidem. *fulserit hora* G.—58 corr. Micyll. *lintea vela* PG.—73 *nepoti* P; G a sec. ma. —76 *plenos* PG sub ras.—95 *Bello* G; P ma. sec.—115 *et quisquam quaerit* G. *Si quis quem quaerit* P, pleraque ma sec. in ras.—132 *admon. sinum l' suis* P *admon. sinu* G.—136 e G. *hospiciis p. ad arma tuus patris* P.—149 *At* G.

IV 1 *Quam* P sub ras. *salutem* P sub ras. G.—27 *carpis* PG. —46 ita G et fort. P sub rasura.—108 *patr. carior* G, var. scr. ma. pr. in P.—111 *nos* om. P.—115 *trinodis* P.—127 *nunc si* P (fals. Heins.) G.—155 e G. *relinquit* P.—157 ita PG, nisi quod G. fortassis *Quid.*

V 4 *ipsa* P. *ipse* G.—16 corr. Parrhas. *Depressa* P *Deprensa* G.—30 e G. *xanthum* P.—40 e G. *Longeuusque senex* P.—65 e G in P ras.—73 *yden* G *idam* P ma. sec. in ras.—75 e G. *Sic bene d. defectaque* P.—92 e G. *superba domos* P.—95 ita PG (falso notatur *censeat* e G).

VI 7 corr. ed. *signetur* G.—15 *Hoc* G.—32 *aeripedes* G.—51 ita PG.—54 coni. ed. *tam fortuna tuenda* P *forti uita* G, P ma. sec.—82 *exspectato* G, P ma. sec. in ras.—83 *meritis placet* P *carmine* G *mouet* P *mouit* G, P a corr.—90 *colligat* P.—91 e G.

figit P.—92 *tenues* G.—93 *mage* PG.—94 *Mo......*P *Nobilis* G. —103 *filia fasias ete* (*oetae*) G, P a ma. sec. in marg. Vetus scriptura in P erasa, lacuna est pro spatio emendationis Salmasianae, id quod Heinsius indicare voluit.—107 corr. Heins. *tanais* PG *undae* PG.—118 *quoque q......lis inter* P *quoque quod tales* G.—119 *etiam properi* P.—131 e G. *tamen* in P om.—140 *iratis* om. ma. pr. P *Quodlibet ad facinus ipse* G.—147 *per te* P. —156 *sit illa uiro* PG.—162 e G *expers* P.

VII 4 e G. *novimus* P.—5 corr. Heins. *merite fam.* P *meriti fam.* G.—16 *tenenda* P.—17 *tibi est habendus* P *tibi et exstat habenda et* G.—21 *Omnia......*(in parte eius ras. *si* a ma. sec.) *ueniant* P *Omnia si ueniant* G.—26 *Eneanque* G.—33 *aut ego quae* PG, nisi quod *Aut* non fuit sub ras. G.—45 *tanti quid non mereris* (*mer* incertum) P *quod non cenaris*, ut videtur, sub ras. G *censeris* G ma. sec.—71 *totum* G. *tutum* P, *dices* G.—82 e G. *plector* P.—85 *narraras a...me...nouere* P *narr. at me nouere* G.—86 *ure* P. *Inde minor* G *Illa* P ma. sec. *fut. tua est* G.—87 e G. *quin te te munera damnant* P.—97 *poenas uiole...te sycae...*P *penas uiolate sychei* G.—103 e G. *dedita* P.—104 *amissi* P *amisso* G.—106 e G. *derabit* P.—108 e G. *ded. uiri* P.—113 *in terras* PG.—138 *auferat* P.—152 *Namque* P sub ras. *Inque loco regis regia sceptra tene* G.—172 e G. *Scilleuisseiectam* P.—179 *dum tempteret......*(supra scr. *usum* ma. sec.) *dum forte tepescat* G.

VIII 9 *Surohos ille* P.—34 *posset* PG.—61 *flendo dispargimus iras* G.—69 *freta destinat* PG *dest. hemos* P.—72 *tyntaris* G.—73 *Tyndaris* G.—77 *phoebique* P.—79 *etiam...unc* P ma. pr. *tunc* ma. sec.—88 ita PG.—99 *helenem* P; G, ut videtur, sub ras.—102 e G. *pugnat* P.—103 *captam* G.—104 e G. *Et minus a nobis d. tr. dedit* P.—111 e G. *stuueo nerusqui obl.* P.—117 e G. *inf. oro* P.—120 *Quod se* P.—121 e G. *Ut ego prem. priorque exuar in* P.

IX 9 corr. Daumius. *ille uenis* PG *si cred.* G.—15 e G. *Si* P.—52 e G. *relicta tuo* P.—53 e G. *referentur* P.—55 coni. Heins. *Maeandros ter totiens erratur in* P *Menandros totiens qui terris errat in* G.—66. corr. Heins. *dedec. pudet* PG.—83 *pompas immania semina laudum* ma. sec. P.—88 e G. *Incubuit, laedat* P. —103 e vett. ed. *dardanis* PG.—106 e G. *Quem tu* P.—126 e G. *fassa tegente......*P.—129 coni. ed. *sublime sub herc.* PG.—133 *atque insani* G.—141 corr. Heins. *in letifero ueneno* P. *in letiferoque ueneno* G.—153 corr. Micyllus. *acrius*, posterior syllaba in ras. a sec. ma., P *acrior* G.—160 *uidear eat insidiata......*P *uidear titulis ins.* G.

X 9 *somno languentia* P.—10 corr. Heins. *prens.* (*press.* G) *semisopita* PG.—26 *Hinc* G.—31 *tanquam quae me* P sub ras., ut videtur, et G. *putaui* G.—46 *desieram* P.—69 ita PG.—106 ita G.

belua strauit P ma. sec. in ras.—112 *At* G.—126 G, *Dum turbae in ore. Cum steteris turbes celsus in aure* corr. urbis c. *in arce* P.

XII 1 *Ut* G.—17 *Semina.........totidemque et seminat et hostes* P ma. pr. *Sem sensisset* P ma. sec. *Sem. iecisset totidem quod seminat host.* G *totid. sumpsisset et host.* G ma. sec.—25 corr. Heins. *fuit* PG.—39 corr. Heins. *Dixerat* G *tibi rex* PG.—65 ita G ma. sec. *habebit* PG.—69 *fuer. cinctae* G var. scr.—71 e G, *N......*P *exciderant animo loca* G.—75 ita G, nisi quod *iuuat. posse......dest si* P.—99 ita P. *miserabile* G.—100 ita G. *Inter constrictas* P.—140 ita G. in P rasurae.—149 coni. ed. *pueris iussus* PG.—152 *Ducet* P.—170 *Nec tener in...abit* PG, sed *teneram misero, ram* P ma. sec. in ras.—185 corr. Heins. *Nam* PG *quod tu* G.—205 *potentem* G.

XIII 8 ita PG.—13 *mandatis* PG.—29 *Utque animus rediit* G.—37 e recent. libr. *murice uestes* G.—43 e recent. libr. *Dux pari* PG.—77 *tant. uoluore* P.—110 *querela tens* P.—113 *quaesare lucet* corr. ma. pr. *quis ara rel.* P *quae sparsa* G.—120 *tamerapites osc.* P.—122 *refere* P.—135 *quid ego reuoco......... omen* P supra ras. scriptum *teuocantis et* ma. sec. *ago reuocans? omen reuocanti abesto* G.—137 corr. Salmas. ex scr. P.

XIV 5 *dimitt.* PG.—11 ita PG.—18 corr. Nauger. *ossa* PG.—46 *sublato......etendit* P ma. pr.—91 *Conato.........mug* P. *Conataque* G.

ABBREVIATIONS USED IN CRITICAL NOTES.

E.	Eton MS. of 11th Century.
ε.	Eton MS. of 13-14th Century.
V.	Venice Edition of 1491 (Vossius).
M.	Merkel's Edition, 1876.
Pa.	Arthur Palmer, 1874.
Madv.	Madvig, Emendationes Latinae, 1873.

EPISTULAE.

I.

PENELOPE ULIXI.

HANC tua Penelope lento tibi mittit, Ulixe.
  Nil mihi rescribas. at tamen ipse veni.
Troia iacet certe, Danais invisa puellis.
  Vix Priamus tanti totaque Troia fuit.
O utinam tum, cum Lacedaemona classe petebat,
  Obrutus insanis esset adulter aquis!
Non ego deserto iacuissem frigida lecto,
  Non quererer tardos ire relicta dies:
Nec mihi quaerenti spatiosam fallere noctem
  Lassasset viduas pendula tela manus.
Quando ego non timui graviora pericula veris?
  Res est solliciti plena timoris amor.
In te fingebam violentos Troas ituros.
  Nomine in Hectoreo pallida semper eram.
Sive quis Antilochum narrabat ab Hectore victum,
  Antilochus nostri causa timoris erat:

1 Pa *haec.* EεV *hanc.* 2 E *sed tamen.* εV *attamen.* Pa *ut tamen; ipse.* 5 EεV *tunc.* *Telamone* sed *a* superscr. 6 E *insanus.* 8 EεV *nec.* 9 ε *non.* 10 ε *lassarent.* EV *lassaret.* 13 E *vilentos.*

Sive, Menoetiaden falsis cecidisse sub armis,
Flebam successu posse carere dolos.
Sanguine Tlepolemus Lyciam tepefecerat hastam,
Tlepolemi leto cura novata mea est.
Denique, quisquis erat castris iugulatus Achivis,
Frigidius glacie pectus amantis erat.
Sed bene consuluit casto deus aequus amori.
Versa est in cineres sospite Troia viro.
Argolici rediere duces. altaria fumant:
Ponitur ad patrios barbara praeda deos.
Grata ferunt nymphae pro salvis dona maritis:
Illi victa suis Troica fata canunt.
Mirantur iustique senes trepidaeque puellae:
Narrantis coniunx pendet ab ore viri.
Atque aliquis posita monstrat fera praelia mensa,
Pingit et exiguo Pergama tota mero:
'Hac ibat Simois, hac est Sigeia tellus,
Hic steterat Priami regia celsa senis:
Illic Aeacides, illic tendebat Ulixes:
Hic lacer admissos terruit Hector equos.'
Omnia namque tuo senior te quaerere misso
Retulerat gnato Nestor, at ille mihi.
Retulit et ferro Rhesumque Dolonaque caesos,
Utque sit hic somno proditus, ille dolo.
Ausus es, o nimium nimiumque oblite tuorum,
Thracia nocturno tangere castra dolo,

28 E *illic*. 32 Pro *mero* Sedlmayer *metro* E attribuit: falso ut videtur. 33 Sic EεM. Pa *haec*. V *hic*. E *sigeia porta*. 34 E *cella*. 36 Sic Pa ε. EVM *alacer missos*. 39 E *delonaque cesus*. 40 E *dolon*. Pa *vigil*. Mihi quidem placet illud Tyrellii *lucro*. Dolon enim non *dolo* sed *lucro* periit. Cf. Il. x. 401.

Totque simul mactare viros, adiutus ab uno!
At bene cautus eras et memor ante mei?
Usque metu micuere sinus, dum victor amicum
Dictus es Ismariis isse per agmen equis.
Sed mihi quid prodest vestris disiecta lacertis
Ilios, et murus quod fuit, esse solum,
Si maneo qualis Troia durante manebam,
Virque mihi dempto fine carendus abest?
Diruta sunt aliis, uni mihi Pergama restant,
Incola captivo quae bove victor arat.
Iam seges est, ubi Troia fuit, resecandaque falce
Luxuriat Phrygio sanguine pinguis humus:
Semisepulta virum curvis feriuntur aratris
Ossa. ruinosas occulit herba domos.
Victor abes. nec scire mihi, quae causa morandi,
Aut in quo lateas ferreus orbe, licet.
Quisquis ad haec vertit peregrinam littora puppim,
Ille mihi de te multa rogatus abit:
Quamque tibi reddat, si te modo viderit usquam,
Traditur huic digitis charta notata meis.
Nos Pylon, antiqui Neleïa Nestoris arva,
Misimus. incerta est fama remissa Pylo.
Misimus et Sparten: Sparte quoque nescia veri.
Quas habitas terras, aut ubi lentus abes?
Utilius starent etiam nunc moenia Phoebi.
Irascor votis heu levis ipsa meis!
Scirem ubi pugnares, et tantum bella timerem,
Et mea cum multis iuncta querella foret.

48 ε *Ilion.* Pro *esse* EεV *ante.* 50 E *erit.* 62 Sic εVPa. E *nota.* M *novata.* 63 E *ad Neleia.* 64 Om. E, additur a 2 m. 68 E *en.*

Quid timeam, ignoro. timeo tamen omnia demens,
Et patet in curas area lata meas.
Quaecumque aequor habet, quaecumque pericula tellus,
Tam longae causas suspicor esse morae.
Haec ego dum stulte metuo, quae vestra libido est,
Esse peregrino captus amore potes.
Forsitan et narres, quam sit tibi rustica coniunx,
Quae tantum lanas non sinat esse rudes.
Fallar, et hoc crimen tenues vanescat in auras,
Neve, revertendi liber, abesse velis!
Me pater Icarius viduo discedere lecto
Cogit, et inmensas increpat usque moras.
Increpet usque licet. Tua sum, tua dicar oportet.
Penelope coniunx semper Ulixis ero.
Ille tamen pietate mea precibusque pudicis
Frangitur, et vires temperat ipse suas.
Dulichii Samiique et quos tulit alta Zacynthos,
Turba ruunt in me luxuriosa proci:
Inque tua regnant, nullis prohibentibus, aula:
Viscera nostra, tuae dilacerantur opes.
Quid tibi Pisandrum Polybumque Medontaque dirum
Eurymachique avidas Antinoique manus
Atque alios referam, quos omnis turpiter absens
Ipse tuo partis sanguine rebus alis?
Irus egens pecorisque Melanthius actor edendi
Ultimus accedunt in tua damna pudor.

75 ε *hoc*. EPa *meditor*. 77 εV *narras*. 79 ε *tenues crimen*. 86 Eε *ille*. 91 E *pissadrum poliuumque*. 92 E *antinoris*. 93 ε *quidque*. 95 E *auctor*. εV *autor*. Sed Ovidius vertere videtur Hom. Od. xx. 173—4, ἦλθε Μελάνθιος, αἰπόλος αἰγῶν, αἶγας ἄγων αἳ πᾶσι μετέπρεπον αἰπολίοισιν δεῖπνον μνηστήρεσσι.

Tres sumus inbelles numero, sine viribus uxor,
  Laertesque senex, Telemachusque puer.
Ille per insidias paene est mihi nuper ademptus,
  Dum parat invitis omnibus ire Pylon.
Di, precor, hoc iubeant, ut euntibus ordine fatis
  Ille meos oculos conprimat, ille tuos.
Hinc faciunt custosque boum longaevaque nutrix,
  Tertius inmundae cura fidelis harae.
Sed neque Laertes, ut qui sit inutilis armis,
  Hostibus in mediis regna tenere potest.
Telemacho veniet, vivat modo, fortior aetas:
  Nunc erat auxiliis illa tuenda patris.
Nec mihi sunt vires inimicos pellere tectis.
  Tu citius venias, portus et ara tuis.
Est tibi, sitque, precor, gnatus, qui mollibus annis
  In patrias artes erudiendus erat.
Respice Laerten, ut iam sua lumina condas
  Extremum fati sustinet ille diem.
Certe ego, quae fueram te discedente puella,
  Protinus ut venias, facta videbor anus.

II.

PHYLLIS DEMOPHOONTI.

Hospita, Demophoon, tua te Rhodopeia Phyllis
  Ultra promissum tempus abesse queror.
Cornua cum lunae pleno semel orbe coissent,
  Littoribus nostris anchora pacta tua est.

101 E *ho juueant.* 103 E *hec.* eV *hoc.* Pa *hac* conj. Madv. *hinc.* E *longaeva conjux.* 105 EeV *annis.* 106 E *valet.* 110 EVM *aura.* e *arna.* Pa *ara.* 111 E *est ut sitque.* 115 e *en ego.* 116 E *redeas.* 3 E *cohissens.*

Luna quater latuit, toto quater orbe recrevit,
  Nec vehit Actaeas Sithonis unda rates.
Tempora si numeres, bene quae numeramus amantes,
  Non venit ante suam nostra querella diem.
Spes quoque lenta fuit. Tarde, quae credita laedunt
  Credimus. Invita nunc et amante nocent.
Saepe fui mendax pro te mihi. saepe putavi
  Alba procellosos vela referre notos.
Thesea devovi, quia te dimittere nollet:
  Nec tenuit cursus forsitan ille tuos.
Interdum timui, ne, dum vada tendis ad Hebri,
  Mersa foret cana naufraga puppis aqua.
Saepe deos supplex, ut tu, scelerate, valeres,
  Cum prece turicremis devenerata focis;
Saepe, videns ventos caelo pelagoque faventes,
  Ipsa mihi dixi 'si valet ille, venit.'
Denique fidus amor quidquid properantibus obstat
  Finxit, et ad causas ingeniosa fui.
At tu lentus abes. nec te iurata reducunt
  Numina, nec nostro motus amore redis.
Demophoon, ventis et verba et vela dedisti:
  Vela queror reditu, verba carere fide.
Dic mihi, quid feci, nisi non sapienter amavi?
  Crimine te potui demeruisse meo.
Unum in me scelus est, quod te, scelerate, recepi.
  Sed scelus hoc meriti pondus et instar habet.

6 E *Sithois un.* 7 Sic EPa. M *quae nos.* 10 Sic EεV (E *nocens*). Pa *invito nunc et amore noces.* M *invito nunc es amore nocens.* 11 Sic EεVPa. M *notavi.* 15 *nec dum.* 17 E *diis.* 18, 19 Om. EεV. 18 Pa *sum.* 20 V *ipse venit.* 21 εV *quanto.* 23 E *jurate.* 28 E *merui.* 29 E *in me unum.*

Iura, fides ubi nunc, commissaque dextera dextrae
  Quique erat in falso plurimus ore deus?
Promissus socios ubi nunc Hymenaeus in annos,
  Qui mihi coniugii sponsor et obses erat?
Per mare, quod totum ventis agitatur et undis,
  Per quod saepe ieras, per quod iturus eras,
Perque tuum mihi iurasti, nisi fictus et ille est,
  Concita qui ventis aequora mulcet, avum,
Per Venerem nimiumque mihi facientia tela,
  Altera tela arcus, altera tela faces,
Iunonemque, toris quae praesidet alma maritis,
  Et per taediferae mystica sacra deae.
Si de tot laesis sua numina quisque deorum
  Vindicet, in poenas non satis unus eris.
At laceras etiam puppes furiosa refeci,
  Ut, qua desererer, firma carina foret:
Remigiumque dedi, quo me fugiturus abires.
  Heu, patior telis vulnera facta meis!
Credidimus blandis, quorum tibi copia, verbis:
  Credidimus generi numinibusque tuis:
Credidimus lacrimis. an et hae simulare docentur?
  Hae quoque habent artes, quaque iubentur, eunt?
Dis quoque credidimus. Quo iam tot pignora nobis?
  Parte satis potui qualibet inde capi.
Nec moveor, quod te iuvi portuque locoque.
  Debuit haec meriti summa fuisse mei!

35 E *in undis*. ε *iniquis*. 37 E *jurasti mihi*. ε *falsus*. 39 E *uenire*. 40 E *alta tela faces*. 41 E *al maritis*. 45 ε *ah*. V *ha*. E *puppes etiam*. 47 E *quo tu fugiturus*. 49 E *copia est verbis*. 50 Sic EεVM. Pa *nominibus*. 52 E *juuentur*. Cf. I. 101. 53 E *quid*.

Turpiter hospitium lecto cumulasse iugali
   Paenitet, et lateri conseruisse latus.
Quae fuit ante illam, mallem suprema fuisset
   Nox mihi, dum potui Phyllis honesta mori.
Speravi melius, quia me meruisse putavi.
   Quaecumque ex merito spes venit, aequa venit.
Fallere credentem non est operosa puellam
   Gloria. simplicitas digna favore fuit.
Sum decepta tuis et amans et femina verbis.
   Di faciant, laudis summa sit ista tuae.
Inter et Aegidas media statuaris in urbe:
   Magnificus titulis stet pater ante suis:
Cum fuerit Sciron lectus torvusque Procrustes
   Et Sinis, et tauri mixtaque forma viri,
Et domitae bello Thebae, fusique bimembres
   Et pulsata nigri regia caeca dei,
Hoc tua post illos titulo signetur imago,
   'Hic est, cuius amans hospita capta dolo est.'
De tanta rerum turba factisque parentis
   Sedit in ingenio Cressa relicta tuo.
Quod solum excusat, solum miraris in illo.
   Haeredem patriae, perfide, fraudis agis.
Illa...nec invideo...fruitur meliore marito,
   Inque capistratis tigribus alta sedet.
At mea despecti fugiunt conubia Thraces,
   Quod ferar externum praeposuisse meis.

61 E *quae meruisse*, om. *quia*. M *demeruisse*. ϵV *te meruisse*. 65 E *dum*. 66 E *faciunt*. 69 E *dum*. *Chiron*. 72 ϵ *Et pulsata dei regia celsa nigri*. EV *Et pulsata nigri regia celsa Ditis*. 73 E *illo*. 75 E *tantisque*. 77 ϵ *solum hoc miraris*. V *solum imitaris*. 80 E *caput stratis—sedit*. 81 E *a*. 82 E *feror*.

Atque aliquis 'Iam nunc doctas eat' inquit 'Athenas:
  Armigeram Thracen qui regat, alter erit.
Exitus acta probat.' Careat successibus, opto,
  Quisquis ab eventu facta notanda putat.
At si nostra tuo spumescant aequora remo,
  Iam mihi, iam dicar consuluisse meis.
Sed neque consului, nec te mea regia tanget,
  Fessaque Bistonia membra lavabis aqua.
Illa meis oculis species abeuntis inhaeret,
  Cum premeret portus classis itura meos.
Ausus es amplecti, colloque infusus amantis
  Oscula per longas iungere pressa moras,
Cumque tuis lacrimis lacrimas confundere nostras,
  Quodque foret velis aura secunda, queri,
Et mihi discedens suprema dicere voce
  'Phylli, face expectes Demophoonta tuum.'
Expectem, qui me numquam visurus abisti?
  Expectem, pelago vela negante data?
Et tamen expecto, redeas modo serus amanti,
  Ut tua sit solo tempore lapsa fides.
Quid precor infelix? te iam tenet altera coniunx
  Forsitan et nobis qui male favit, amor:
Utque tibi excidimus, nullam, puto, Phyllida nosti.
  Ei mihi, si, quae sim Phyllis et unde, rogas.
Quae tibi, Demophoon! longis erroribus acto
  Threïcios portus hospitiumque dedi,

84 E*ϵ armiferamque.* Pa *armiferam.* 85 E *suce cessibus.* 87 *ϵ spumebant.* 89 E*ϵ*V *tangit.* 90 E *lababis.* Cf. I. 101. 98 EV *face.* *ϵ fac.* 100 Emend. Pa edidi: *data* tamen in fine versus vix placet. MEϵV *vela negata meo.* 103 E *jam tenet et*, 2 m. corr. *jam te tenet.* 105 Madv. *Atque tibi excidimus: nullam.* E *fillidam.*

Cuius opes auxere meae, cui dives egenti
  Munera multa dedi, multa datura fui:
Quae tibi subieci latissima regna Lycurgi,
  Nomine femineo vix satis apta regi,
Qua patet umbrosum Rhodope glacialis ad Haemum,
  Et sacer admissas exigit Hebrus aquas:
Cui mea virginitas avibus libata sinistris,
  Castaque fallaci zona recincta manu.
Pronuba Tisiphone thalamis ululavit in illis,
  Et cecinit maestum devia carmen avis.
Adfuit Allecto brevibus torquata colubris,
  Suntque sepulchrali lumina mota face.
Maesta tamen scopulos fruticosaque litora calco,
  Quaque patent oculis aequora lata meis.
Sive die laxatur humus, seu frigida lucent
  Sidera, prospicio, quis freta ventus agat.
Et quaecumque procul venientia lintea vidi,
  Protinus illa meos auguror esse deos.
In freta procurro, vix me retinentibus undis,
  Mobile qua primas porrigit aequor aquas.
Quo magis accedunt, minus et minus utilis adsto:
  Linquor, et ancillis excipienda cado.
Est sinus, adductos modice falcatus in arcus:
  Ultima praerupta cornua mole rigent.

109 ε *eunti.* 109—110 Madv. post 114 ponit et utrumque versum nota interrogationis distinguit. 110 E *plura dāta.* 111 E *letissima.* 114 E *amissas.* 116 Madv. *manust.* 121 E *mens tamen,* 2 m. corr. *mensta.* M *culmina.* EεV *litora.* 122 M *quaeque.* E *quaque.* EεVM *litora.* 123 E om. *die*, transponit *frigida sidera.* 127 E *udis.* 128 ε *quo.*

Hinc mihi suppositas inmittere corpus in undas
  Mens fuit. et, quoniam fallere pergis, erit;
Ad tua me fluctus proiectam litora portent,
  Occurramque oculis intumulata tuis.
Duritia ferrum ut superes, adamantaque, teque,
  'Non tibi sic' dices 'Phylli, sequendus eram.'
Saepe venenorum sitis est mihi. saepe cruenta
  Traiectam gladio morte perire iuvat.
Colla quoque, infidis quia se nectenda lacertis
  Praebuerunt, laqueis inplicuisse lubet.
Stat nece matura tenerum pensare pudorem.
  In necis electu parva futura mora est.
Inscribere meo causa invidiosa sepulchro.
  Aut hoc, aut simili carmine notus eris
'Phyllida Demophoon leto dedit, hospes amantem:
  Ille necis causam praebuit, ipsa manum.'

III.

BRISEIS ACHILLI.

Quam legis, a rapta Briseïde littera venit,
  Vix bene barbarica Graeca notata manu.
Quascumque aspicies, lacrimae fecere lituras.
  Sed tamen et lacrimae pondera vocis habent.
Si mihi pauca queri de te dominoque viroque
  Fas est, de domino pauca viroque querar.
Non, ego poscenti quod sum cito tradita regi,
  Culpa tua est. quamvis haec quoque culpa tua est.

133 E om. *corpus.* 134 E *quando.* 135 E *me ut fluctus ...potens.* ε *portus.* 137 E *fre ferrum.* 141—2 E om. 142 εV *juvat.* 144 E om. in margine additur. 146 E *similis.* 148 Eε *illa.* 4 Eε *hae* pro *et.* 6 E *queror.* 8 E *hoc quoque.*

Nam simul Eurybates me Talthybiusque vocarunt,
Eurybati data sum Talthybioque comes.
Alter in alterius iactantes lumina voltum
Quaerebant taciti, noster ubi esset amor.
Differri potui. poenae mora grata fuisset.
Ei mihi, discedens oscula nulla dedi.
At lacrimas sine fine dedi, rupique capillos:
Infelix iterum sum mihi visa capi.
Saepe ego decepto volui custode reverti:
Sed me qui timidam prenderet, hostis erat.
Si progressa forem, caperer ne nocte timebam,
Quamlibet ad Priami munus itura nurum.
Sed data sim, quia danda fui. Tot noctibus absum,
Nec repetor. cessas, iraque lenta tua est.
Ipse Menoetiades tum, cum tradebar, in aurem
'Quid fles? hic parvo tempore' dixit 'eris.'
Non repetisse, parum. pugnas, ne reddar, Achille.
I nunc, et cupidi nomen amantis habe.
Venerunt ad te Telamone et Amyntore nati,
Ille gradu propior sanguinis, ille comes,
Laërtaque satus, per quos comitata redirem:
Auxerunt blandae grandia dona preces,
Viginti fulvos operoso ex aere lebetas,
Et tripodas septem pondere et arte pares:
Addita sunt illis auri bis quinque talenta,
Bis sex adsueti vincere semper equi,

9 E *vocarant.* 11 ε *spectantes.* E *vultu.* 16 E *jam tum.* 18 ε *penderet.* 19 Madv. *ne* cum *progressa forem* jungit. V om. *ne.* 21 EεV *sum.* 23 ε *in aure.* 25 ε *parum est.* E om. *Achille.* 26 E *et* 2 man. 27 E *temone—amintone.* 29 E *Lacerte.* 30 E *duxerunt.* EεV *blandas.* 31 E *lebetes.* 33 E *talentas.* 34 E *bis septem.*

Quodque supervacuum est, forma praestante puellae
  Lesbides, eversa corpora capta domo:
Cumque tot his...sed non opus est tibi coniuge...coniunx
  Ex Agamemnoniis una puella tribus.
Si tibi ab Atride pretio redimenda fuissem,
  Quae dare debueras, accipere illa negas?
Qua merui culpa fieri tibi vilis, Achille?
  Quo levis a nobis tam cito fugit amor?
An miseros tristis fortuna tenaciter urget,
  Nec venit inceptis mollior hora meis?
Diruta marte tuo Lyrnesia moenia vidi,
  Et fueram patriae pars ego magna meae.
Vidi consortes pariter generisque necisque
  Tres cecidisse. tribus, quae mihi, mater erat.
Vidi, quantus erat, fusum tellure cruenta,
  Pectora iactantem sanguinolenta virum.
Tot tamen amissis te compensavimus unum:
  Tu dominus, tu vir, tu mihi frater eras.
Tu mihi, iuratus per numina matris aquosae,
  Utile dicebas ipse fuisse capi...
Scilicet ut, quamvis veniam dotata, repellas,
  Et mecum fugias quae tibi dantur, opes.
Quin etiam fama est, cum crastina fulserit eos,
  Te dare nubiferis lintea velle notis.
Quod scelus ut pavidas miserae mihi contigit aures,
  Sanguinis atque animi pectus inane fuit.

37 E *cumque tot his opus est tibi conjuge addita conjux.* 39 E *sit.* EεV *Atrida.* 44 EV *aura.* 45 E *tua.* 48 Pa *quae mea mater.* 49 E *vi.* 55 EεV *repellar.* 57 EεV *hora.* 58 Eε *linea vela.* V *lintea plena.*

Ibis, et...o miseram...cui me, violente, relinquis,
Quis mihi desertae mite levamen erit?
Devorer ante, precor, subito telluris hiatu,
Aut rutilo missi fulminis igne cremer,
Quam sine me Phthiis canescant aequora remis,
Et videam puppes ire relicta tuas.
Si tibi iam reditusque placent patriique penates,
Non ego sum classi sarcina magna tuae.
Victorem captiva sequar, non nupta maritum:
Est mihi, quae lanas molliat, apta manus.
Inter Achaeïadas longe pulcherrima matres
In thalamos coniunx ibit eatque tuos,
Digna nurus socero, Iovis Aeginaeque nepote,
Cuique senex Nereus prosocer esse velit.
Nos humiles famulaeque tuae data pensa trahemus,
Et minuent plenas stamina nostra colos.
Exagitet ne me tantum tua, deprecor, uxor,
Quae mihi nescio quo non erit aequa modo,
Neve meos coram scindi patiare capillos,
Et leviter dicas 'haec quoque nostra fuit.'
Vel patiare licet, dum ne contempta relinquar:
Hic mihi vae miserae concutit ossa metus.
Quid tamen expectas? Agamemnona paenitet irae,
Et iacet ante tuos Graecia maesta pedes.
Vince animos iramque tuam, qui cetera vincis.
Quid lacerat Danaas impiger Hector opes?

63 E *devoror.* 64 E *at*, 2 man. *aut.* 65 E *qua—ficiis.* 67 E *redditus placeant.* 68 E *sapcina magne.* 69 E *sequar captiva.* 72 E *thalamo.* 76 E *eminuent.* 79 E *nene.* 80 E *leniter.* 81 E *ut patiare.* ε *dum non.* E *contenta.*

Arma cape, Aeacide, sed me tamen ante recepta,
  Et preme turbatos Marte favente viros.
Propter me mota est, propter me desinat ira:
  Simque ego tristitiae causa modusque tuae.
Nec tibi turpe puta precibus succumbere nostris.
  Coniugis Oenides versus in arma prece est.
Res audita mihi, nota est tibi. fratribus orba
  Devovit nati spemque caputque parens.
Bellum erat. ille ferox positis secessit ab armis,
  Et patriae rigida mente negavit opem.
Sola virum coniunx flexit. Felicior illa!
  At mea pro nullo pondere verba cadunt.
Nec tamen indignor. nec me pro coniuge gessi.
  Saepius in domini serva vocata torum.
Me quaedam, memini, dominam captiva vocabat:
  'Servitio' dixi 'nominis addis onus.'
Per tamen ossa viri subito male tecta sepulchro,
  Semper iudiciis ossa verenda meis,
Perque trium fortes animas, mea numina, fratrum,
  Qui bene pro patria cum patriaque iacent,
Perque tuum nostrumque caput, quae iunximus una,
  Perque tuos enses, cognita tela meis,
Nulla Mycenaeum sociasse cubilia mecum
  Iuro. fallentem deseruisse velis.
Si tibi nunc dicam, 'fortissime, tu quoque iura
  Nulla tibi sine me gaudia facta,' neges.

87 E *arma cape Aeacide sed ne finiat tamen*...errore e v. 89 contracto. 89 E *finiat.* 92 V *Aeacides.* 95 E *bello.* 97 E *Tola.* V *flexit conjux.* 101 ε *me memini quondam.* 107 E *quod.*

At Danai maerere putant. Tibi plectra moventur,
Te tenet in tepido mollis amica sinu.
Et si quis quaerat, quare pugnare recuses;
Pugna nocet. citharae noxque Venusque iuvant.
Tutius est iacuisse toro, tenuisse puellam,
Threïciam digitis increpuisse lyram,
Quam manibus clipeos et acutae cuspidis hastam,
Et galeam pressa sustinuisse coma.
Sed tibi pro tutis insignia facta placebant,
Partaque bellando gloria dulcis erat.
An tantum, dum me caperes, fera bella probabas,
Cumque mea patria laus tua victa iacet?
Di melius! validoque, precor, vibrata lacerto
Transeat Hectoreum Pelias hasta latus!
Mittite me, Danai. dominum legata rogabo,
Multaque mandatis oscula mixta feram.
Plus ego quam Phoenix, plus quam facundus Ulixes,
Plus ego quam Teucri...credite!...frater agam.
Est aliquid, collum solitis tetigisse lacertis,
Praesentisque oculos admonuisse sinu.
Sis licet immitis, matrisque ferocior undis,
Ut taceam, lacrimis comminuere meis.
Nunc quoque...sic omnes Peleus pater impleat annos,
Sic eat auspiciis Pyrrhus ad arma tuis!...
Respice sollicitam Briseida, fortis Achille,
Nec miseram lenta ferreus ure mora.

115 εV *et si quis quaerat.* M *et quisquam quaerit.* Pa *Si quis jam.* E *et quisquis quaerit.* E *recusset.* 116 E *juvat.* 117 E *puella.* 119 E om. *clipeos*, add. 2 man. 123 ε *parabas.* 127 *dominum Danai.* 128 E *dabo.* 131 ε *tenuisse.* 132 ε *praesentes.* EεPa *sinu.* Madv. *sui.* M *sinum.* 136 V *sic erat.* Madv. *arma patris.* E *in arma.*

Aut, si versus amor tuus est in taedia nostri,
  Quam sine te cogis vivere, coge mori.
Utque facis, coges. abiit corpusque colorque:
  Sustinet hoc animae spes tamen una tui:
Qua si destituor, repetam fratresque virumque;
  Nec tibi magnificum femina iussa mori.
Cur autem iubeas? Stricto pete corpora ferro:
  Est mihi, qui fosso pectore sanguis eat.
Me petat ille tuus, qui, si dea passa fuisset,
  Ensis in Atridae pectus iturus erat.
A! potius serves nostram, tua munera, vitam.
  Quod dederas hosti victor, amica rogo.
Perdere quos melius possis, Neptunia praebent
  Pergama. materiam caedis ab hoste pete.
Me modo, sive paras impellere remige classem,
  Sive manes, domini iure venire iube.

IV.

PHAEDRA HIPPOLYTO.

Qua, nisi tu dederis, caritura est ipsa salutem
  Mittit Amazonio Cressa puella viro.
Perlege quodcumque est. Quid epistola lecta nocebit?
  Te quoque in hac aliquid quod iuvet, esse potest.
His arcana notis terra pelagoque feruntur.
  Inspicit acceptas hostis ab hoste notas.

139 Eε *at.* 142 ε *sustinet haec animi...mei.* V *hoc animi ...tibi.* In comment. V. legit *animae.* 143 V *destituar.* 144 E *uissa.* 146 ε *fuso.* 149 EV *at.* ε *aut.* E *vita.* 150 ε *quam.* E *hostis.* 153 E *implere.* 154 εV *more.* 1 EεV *salutem.* MPa *salute.* 3 E om. *est.* *leta.* 4 E *uiuet.*

Ter tecum conata loqui, ter inutilis haesit
  Lingua, ter in primo destitit ore sonus.
Qua licet et sequitur, pudor est miscendus amori.
  Dicere quae puduit, scribere iussit amor.
Quidquid Amor iussit, non est contemnere tutum:
  Regnat et in dominos ius habet ille deos.
Ille mihi primo dubitanti scribere dixit.
  'Scribe! dabit victas ferreus ille manus.'
Adsit, et ut nostras avido fovet igne medullas,
  Figat sic animos in mea vota tuos.
Non ego nequitia socialia foedera rumpam.
  Fama... velim quaeras... crimine nostra vacat.
Venit amor gravius, quo serius. urimur intus:
  Urimur, et caecum pectora vulnus habent.
Scilicet ut teneros laedunt iuga prima iuvencos,
  Frenaque vix patitur de grege captus equus,
Sic male vixque subit primos rude pectus amores,
  Sarcinaque haec animo non sedet apta meo.
Ars fit, ubi a teneris crimen condiscitur annis:
  Quae venit exacto tempore, peius amat.
Tu nova servatae carpes libamina famae:
  Et pariter nostrum fiet uterque nocens.
Est aliquid, plenis pomaria carpere ramis
  Et tenui primam delegere ungue rosam.
Si tamen ille prior, quo me sine crimine gessi,
  Candor ab insolita labe notandus erat,
At bene successit, digno quod adurimur igni.
  Peius adulterio turpis adulter obest.

17 E *federe.* 19 E *serior.* 23 E *primo.* *amorem.* 25 E *sit.* 26 M obelo notavit. 27 εPa *capies.* 30 E *diligere.* 31 EεV *sic.*

Si mihi concedat Iuno fratremque virumque,
  Hippolytum videor praepositura Iovi.
Iam quoque... vix credes... ignotas mutor in artes:
  Est mihi per saevas impetus ire feras.
Iam mihi prima dea est arcu praesignis adunco
  Delia. iudicium subsequor ipsa tuum.
In nemus ire libet, pressisque in retia cervis
  Hortari celeris per iuga summa canes,
Aut tremulum excusso iaculum vibrare lacerto,
  Aut in graminea ponere corpus humo.
Saepe iuvat versare leves in pulvere currus,
  Torquentem frenis ora fugacis equi.
Nunc feror, ut Bacchi furiis Eleleides actae,
  Quaeque sub Idaeo tympana colle movent,
Aut quas semideae Dryades Faunique bicornes
  Numine contactas attonuere suo.
Namque mihi referunt, cum se furor ille remisit,
  Omnia, me tacitam conscius urit amor.
Forsitan hunc generis fato reddamus amorem,
  Et Venus ex tota gente tributa petat.
Iupiter Europen... prima est ea gentis origo...
  Dilexit, tauro dissimulante deum.
Perfidus Aegides, ducentia fila secutus,
  Curva meae fugit tecta sororis ope.
En, ego nunc, ne forte parum Minoia credar,
  In socias leges ultima gentis eo.

37 ϵVPa *mittor*. Sed nihil est cur codices PGE deseramus.
41—2 ϵ post 38 exhibet. 41 E *pressis in*. 45 E *servare*.
47 E *eleideis*. ϵV *eleides*. 50 E *contactus*. 51 ϵ *ipse*.
53 E *fato generis sectamur*. 54 ϵV *petit*. 55 E *Europam*.
56 ϵ *virum*. 61 E *Minoida*.

Hoc quoque fatale est. placuit domus una duabus.
Me tua forma capit. capta parente soror.
Theseïdes Theseusque duas rapuere sorores.
Ponite de nostra bina tropaea domo.
Tempore quo nobis inita est Cerealis Eleusin,
Gnosia me vellem detinuisset humus.
Tunc mihi praecipue, nec non tamen ante, placebas:
Acer in extremis ossibus haesit amor.
Candida vestis erat, praecincti flore capilli,
Flava verecundus tinxerat ora rubor:
Quemque vocant aliae vultum rigidumque trucemque,
Pro rigido, Phaedra iudice, fortis erat.
Sint procul a nobis iuvenes ut femina compti:
Fine coli modico forma virilis amat.
Te tuus iste rigor, positique sine arte capilli,
Et levis egregio pulvis in ore decet.
Sive ferocis equi luctantia colla recurvas,
Exiguo flexos miror in orbe pedes:
Seu lentum valido torques hastile lacerto,
Ora ferox in se versa lacertus habet:
Sive tenes lato venabula cornea ferro,
Denique nostra iuvas lumina, quicquid agas.
Tu modo duritiam silvis depone iugosis:
Non sum materia digna perire tua.
Quid iuvat incinctae studia exercere Dianae,
Et Veneri numeros eripuisse suos?

65 E *theusque.* 66 E *nostro.* 67 EV *Eleusis.* ε *tempore quo visa est nobis Cerealis Eleusis.* 72 E *cinxerat.* ε *pudor.* 74 E *erit.* 77 E *positi sine.* 80 E *flexes.* 81 E *lacertos.* 82 E *lacertum.* 84 EεV *iuvat.* E *agis.* 85 ε *duritias.* V *duritiem.* 86 Pa *militia* conj. Am. 2, 14, 6 collato. Frustra opinor. 87 E *vetat.*

Quod caret alterna requie, durabile non est:
  Haec reparat vires fessaque membra novat.
Arcus... et arma tuae tibi sunt imitanda Dianae..
  Si numquam cesses tendere, mollis erit.
Clarus erat silvis Cephalus, multaeque per herbas
  Conciderant illo percutiente ferae;
Nec tamen Aurorae male se praebebat amandum.
  Ibat ad hunc sapiens a sene diva viro.
Saepe sub ilicibus Venerem Cinyraque creatum
  Sustinuit positos quaelibet herba duos.
Arsit et Oenides in Maenalia Atalanta:
  Illa ferae spolium pignus amoris habet.
Nos quoque iam primum turba numeremur in ista.
  Si Venerem tollas, rustica silva tua est.
Ipsa comes veniam, nec me latebrosa movebunt
  Saxa, neque obliquo dente timendus aper.
Aequora bina suis obpugnant fluctibus Isthmon,
  Et tenuis tellus audit utrumque mare.
Hic tecum Troezena colam, Pittheïa regna:
  Iam nunc est patria gratior illa mea.
Tempore abest, aberitque diu Neptunius heros:
  Illum Perithoi detinet ora sui.
Praeposuit Theseus... nisi si manifesta negemus...
  Perithoum Phaedrae, Perithoumque tibi.
Sola nec haec ad nos iniuria venit ab illo.
  In magnis laesi rebus uterque sumus.

90 ε *renovat...levat.* 91 E om. *tibi sunt.* 93 εV *Cephalus silvis.* E *herbam.* 95 E *aurerae.* 99 E *thalanta.* 103 ε *tenebrosa.* V *salebrosa.* E *movebant.* 104 E *nec.* 107 E *pbeida.* 108 E *carior.* 110 E *pirothoni.* 111 E *theseus nobis.* EεV *nisi nos...negamus.* M *nisi nos...negemus.*

Ossa mei fratris clava perfracta trinodi
Sparsit humi. soror est praeda relicta feris.
Prima securigeras inter virtute puellas
Te peperit, nati digna vigore parens.
Si quaeras, ubi sit... Theseus latus ense peregit:
Nec tanto mater pignore tuta fuit.
At ne nupta quidem, taedaque accepta iugali.
Cur, nisi ne caperes regna paterna nothus?
Addidit et fratres ex me tibi. quos tamen omnis
Non ego tollendi causa, sed ille fuit.
O utinam nocitura tibi, pulcherrime rerum,
In medio nisu viscera rupta forent!
I nunc, sic meriti lectum reverere parentis:
Quem fugit et factis abdicat ipse suis.
Nec, quia privigno videar coitura noverca,
Terruerint animos nomina vana tuos.
Ista vetus pietas, aevo moritura futuro,
Rustica Saturno regna tenente fuit.
Iuppiter esse pium statuit, quodcumque iuvaret:
Et fas omne facit fratre marita soror.
Illa coit firma generis iunctura catena,
Imposuit nodos cui Venus ipsa suos.
Nec labor est. celare licet. pete munus ab illa.
Cognato poterit nomine culpa tegi.

120 E *mater tanto.* 121 ϵV *nec nupta.* E *quid est tela.* ϵ *recepta.* 124 E *ipse.* 127 ϵV *i nunc et.* E *immitis. sic* superscr. 128 E *quae.* EϵPa M *ille*, quod paene sensu caret. *ipse* e G. reposui. 129 E *peritura* sed *co* superscript. 132 E *tenen.* *te* superscr. Post 132 ϵ exhibet duos versus *Saturnus periit, perierunt et sua iura: Sub Jove nunc mundus, iura Jovis sequere.* 135 E *cogit.* 136 E *nu Venus.* 137 Madv. *Nec labor est celare; licet; pete munus ab ipsa* (sc. a

Tolle moras tantum, properataque foedera iunge!
  Qui mihi nunc saevit, sic tibi parcat Amor.
Non ego dedignor supplex humilisque precari.
  Heu! ubi nunc fastus altaque verba iacent?
Et pugnare diu, nec me summittere culpae
  Certa fui, certi siquid haberet amor.
Victa precor, genibusque tuis regalia tendo
  Bracchia. Quid deceat, non videt ullus amans.
Depuduit, profugusque pudor sua signa reliquit.
  Da veniam fassae, duraque corda doma!
Quod mihi sit genitor, qui possidet aequora, Minos,
  Quod veniant proavi fulmina torta manu,
Quod sit avus radiis frontem vallatus acutis,
  Purpureo tepidum qui movet axe diem...
Nobilitas sub amore iacet. miserere priorum,
  Et mihi si non vis parcere, parce meis!
Est mihi dotalis tellus Iovis insula, Crete.
  Serviat Hippolyto regia tota meo.
Per Venerem, parcas, oro, quae plurima mecum est!
  Sic numquam, quae te spernere possit, ames:
Sic tibi secretis agilis dea saltibus adsit,
  Silvaque perdendas praebeat alta feras:
Sic faveant satyri, montanaque numina Panes,
  Et cadat adversa cuspide fossus aper:
Sic tibi dent nymphae... quamvis odisse puellas
  Diceris... arentem quae levet unda sitim.

Venere). Confert Rem. 409, A. A. 2, 575. E post *illa* supersc. *Venere*. 147 E *tantatum*. 150 εV *heus*. 157 ε *quid mihi quod*. 159 E *radii*. 161 E pro *miserere* repetit *sub amore*. 169 E *dam* pro *dea*. 171 E *fauni* pro *Panes*.

Addimus his precibus lacrimas quoque. Verba precantis
Perlegis. et lacrimas finge videre meas.

V.

OENONE PARIDI.

Perlegis, an coniunx prohibet nova? perlege! non est
Ista Mycenaea littera facta manu.
Pegasis Oenone, Phrygiis celeberrima silvis,
Laesa queror de te, si sinis ipse, meo.
Quis deus opposuit nostris sua numina votis?
Ne tua permaneam, quod mihi crimen obest?
Leniter, ex merito quicquid patiare, ferendum est.
Quae venit indigno poena, dolenda venit.
Nondum tantus eras, cum te contenta marito
Edita de magno flumine nympha fui.
Qui nunc Priamides,... absit reverentia vero...
Servus eras. servo nubere nympha tuli.
Saepe greges inter requievimus arbore tecti,
Mixtaque cum foliis praebuit herba torum.
Saepe super stramen fenoque iacentibus alto
Defensa est humili cana pruina casa.
Quis tibi monstrabat saltus venatibus aptos,
Et tegeret catulos qua fera rupe suos?
Retia saepe comes maculis distincta tetendi:
Saepe citos egi per iuga longa canes.

V. * Eε sic incipiunt: sed ε distinxit quasi prologum: *Nympha suo Paridi quamvis suus esse recuset Mittit ab Idaeis verba legenda jugis.* 3 Madv. *Pedasis.* E *Oenona*, ε supersc. *silves*, *i* supersc. 4 EεV *ipse*. PaM *ipsa*. 8 EεV *in digne*. 9 E *te* superscr. 11 P *pamides*. V *adsit*. 16 EV *depressa*. ε *deprensa*. 20 EV *summa*.

Incisae servant a te mea nomina fagi,
  Et legor Oenone falce notata tua:
Et quantum trunci, tantum mea nomina crescunt:
  Crescite, et in titulos surgite recta meos.
Populo, vive, precor, quae consita margine ripae
  Hoc in rugoso cortice carmen habes
'Cum Paris Oenone poterit spirare relicta,
  Ad fontem Xanthi versa recurret aqua.'
Xanthe, retro propera, versaeque recurrite lymphae!
  Sustinet Oenonen deseruisse Paris.
Illa dies fatum miserae mihi dixit, ab illa
  Pessima mutati coepit amoris hiemps,
Qua Venus et Iuno, sumptisque decentior armis
  Venit in arbitrium nuda Minerva tuum.
Attoniti micuere sinus, gelidusque cucurrit,
  Ut mihi narrasti, dura per ossa tremor.
Consului... neque enim modice terrebar... anusque
  Longaevosque senes. constitit esse nefas.
Caesa abies, sectaeque trabes. et classe parata
  Caerula ceratas accipit unda rates.
Flesti discedens... hoc saltim parce negare:
  Praeterito magis est iste pudendus amor...
Et flesti, et nostros vidisti flentis ocellos:
  Miscuimus lacrimas maestus uterque suas.
Non sic adpositis vincitur vitibus ulmus,
  Ut tua sunt collo bracchia nexa meo.

24 VPa *ritè.* Post 22 Eε addunt, *Populus est memini fluviali consita ripa* (E *rivo*) *Est in qua nostri litera scripta memor.* 28 ε *nomen.* 31 V *nymphae.* 33 EεV *duxit.* 37 E *micueres sin'.* 38 ε *timor.* 40 E *senos,* ε supersc. 41 ε *caesaeque trabes.* 42 E *certas,* a supersc. 44—5 M obelo notavit. 45 E *flentis socellos.*

A! quotiens, cum te vento quererere teneri,
Riserunt comites, ille secundus erat.
Oscula dimissae quotiens repetita dedisti,
Quam vix sustinuit dicere lingua 'vale.'
Aura levis rigido pendentia lintea malo
Suscitat, et remis eruta canet aqua.
Prosequor infelix oculis abeuntia vela,
Qua licet, et lacrimis umet arena meis.
Utque celer venias, virides Nereïdas oro:
Scilicet ut venias in mea damna celer.
Votis ergo meis alii rediture redisti?...
Ei mihi, pro dira pelice blanda fui!
Aspicit inmensum moles nativa profundum:
Mons fuit. aequoreis illa resistit aquis:
Hinc ego vela tuae cognovi prima carinae,
Et mihi per fluctus impetus ire fuit.
Dum moror, in summa fulsit mihi purpura prora.
Pertimui. cultus non erat ille tuus.
Fit propior, terrasque cita ratis attigit aura:
Femineas vidi corde tremente genas.
Non satis id fuerat... quid enim furiosa morabar?...
Haerebat gremio turpis amica tuo.
Tunc vero rupique sinus et pectora planxi,
Et secui madidas ungue rigente genas,
Implevique sacram querulis ululatibus Iden.
Illuc has lacrimas in mea saxa tuli.
Sic Helene doleat, desertaque coniuge ploret,
Quaeque prior nobis intulit, ipsa ferat.

52 *e quod vix.* 53 *e Phrygio.* 56 *e quod licet.* 57 E *Nereias.* 60 E *et tibi.* 63 *e prima...vela.* 69 E *morabor.* 73 E *Idam.* 74 E *illincas.*

Nunc tibi conveniunt quae te per aperta sequantur
  Aequora, legitimos destituantque viros.
At cum pauper eras armentaque pastor agebas,
  Nulla nisi Oenone pauperis uxor erat.
Non ego miror opes, nec me tua regia tangit,
  Nec de tot Priami dicar ut una nurus.
Non tamen, ut Priamus nymphae socer esse recuset,
  Aut Hecubae fuerim dissimulanda nurus.
Dignaque sum et cupio fieri matrona potentis:
  Sunt mihi, quas possint sceptra decere, manus.
Nec me, faginea quod tecum fronde iacebam,
  Despice. purpureo sum magis apta toro.
Denique tutus amor meus est tibi. nulla parantur
  Bella, nec ultrices advehit unda rates.
Tyndaris infestis fugitiva reposcitur armis:
  Hac venit in thalamos dote superba tuos.
Quae si sit Danais reddenda, vel Hectora fratrem,
  Vel cum Deïphobo Polydamanta roga.
Quid gravis Antenor, Priamus quid suadeat ipse,
  Consule, quis aetas longa magistra fuit.
Turpe rudimentum, patriae praeponere raptam.
  Causa pudenda tua est. iusta vir arma movet.
Nec tibi, si sapias, fidam promitte Lacaenam,
  Quae sit in amplexus tam cito versa tuos.
Ut minor Atrides temerati foedera lecti
  Clamat, et externo laesus amore dolet,

77 EεV *nunc tecum veniunt.* εV *sequuntur.* 78 Eε *destituunt.* 84 ε *haut.* 85 ε om. *et.* 86 EV *possunt.* ε *quae possunt...tenere.* 90 E *adveit.* 93 E *ut Hectora.* 94 E *ut cum deiphebo.* 99 E *cupias.* 101 E *temerata.*

Tu quoque clamabis. Nulla reparabilis arte
  Laesa pudicitia est. deperit illa semel.
Ardet amore tui? sic et Menelaon amavit.
  Nunc iacet in viduo credulus ille toro.
Felix Andromache, certo bene nupta marito,
  Uxor ad exemplum fratris habenda fui.
Tu levior foliis, tum cum sine pondere suci
  Mobilibus ventis arida facta volant.
Et minus est in te, quam summa pondus arista,
  Quae levis assiduis solibus usta riget.
Hoc tua... nam recolo... quondam germana canebat,
  Sic mihi diffusis vaticinata comis
'Quid facis, Oenone? Quid arenae semina mandas?
  Non profecturis littora bubus aras.
Graia iuvenca venit, quae te patriamque domumque
  Perdat! io prohibe! Graia iuvenca venit!
Dum licet, obscenam ponto demergite puppim!
  Heu, quantum Phrygii sanguinis illa vehit!'
Dixerat. in cursu famulae rapuere furentem.
  At mihi flaventes diriguere comae.
Ah! nimium miserae vates mihi vera fuisti.
  Possidet, en, saltus Graia iuvenca meos!
Sit facie quamvis insignis, adultera certe est.
  Deseruit socios hospite capta deos.
Illam de patria Theseus,... nisi nomine fallor...
  Nescio quis Theseus abstulit ante sua.

105 E *Menelaon ominavit.* 106 E *jacet et.* 108 E *fuit.* 109 E *tunc cum.* 110 E *cadunt.* 111 V *quam in ~~summa~~.* 112 E *riget vel jacet.* 113 e *haec tua quae refero.* 116 E *hoc.* n super. 118 e *perdet.* 119 E *di mergite.* 120 E *venit.* 123 e *vates miserae.* 124 EV *illa juvenca.* 128 eV *arte.*

A iuvene et cupido credatur reddita virgo?
  Unde hoc conpererim tam bene, quaeris? amo.
Vim licet appelles, et culpam nomine veles:
  Quae totiens rapta est, praebuit ipsa rapi.
At manet Oenone fallenti casta marito:
  Et poteras falli legibus ipse tuis.
Me satyri celeres... silvis ego tecta latebam...
  Quaesierant rapido, turba proterva, pede,
Cornigerumque caput pinu praecinctus acuta
  Faunus, in inmensis qua tumet Ida iugis.
Me fide conspicuus Troiae munitor amavit,
  Admisitque meas ad sua dona manus.
Quaecumque herba potens ad opem radixque medendi
  Utilis in toto nascitur orbe, mea est.
Me miseram, quod amor non est medicabilis herbis:
  Deficior prudens artis ab arte mea.
Ipse repertor opis vaccas pavisse Pheraeas
  Fertur, et e nostro saucius igne fuit.
Quod nec graminibus tellus fecunda creandis,
  Nec deus, auxilium tu mihi ferre potes.
Et potes, et merui. dignae miserere puellae!
  Non ego cum Danais arma cruenta fero.
Sed tua sum tecumque fui puerilibus annis,
  Et tua, quod superest temporis, esse precor.

130 E *hec.* 132 ε *illa.* 135 E *tuta.* *casta* superscr. 140—5 Sex versus obelo damnat M. quorum jactura levis est, praesertim pueris. 146 ε *admovit.* E *manus—meas.* 150 E *deficio.* ε *destituor.* 151—2 damnat M. 151 E *fareas.* ε *per herbas.* 153 Eε *quod neque.* 158 E *temporibus peto.*

VI.

HYPSIPYLE IASONI.

Littora Thessaliae reduci tetigisse carina
Diceris auratae vellere dives ovis.
Gratulor incolumi, quantum sinis. hoc tamen ipso
Debueram scripto certior esse tuo.
Nam ne pacta tibi praeter mea regna redires,
Cum cuperes, ventos non habuisse potes.
Quamlibet adverso signatur epistola vento.
Hypsipyle missa digna salute fui.
Cur mihi fama prior, quam nuntia litera venit?
Isse sacros Martis sub iuga panda boves,
Seminibus iactis segetes adolesse virorum,
Inque necem dextra non eguisse tua:
Pervigilem spolium pecudis servasse draconem,
Rapta tamen forti vellera fulva manu...
Haec ego si possem timide credentibus 'ista
Ipse mihi scripsit' dicere, quanta forem!
Quid queror officium lenti cessasse mariti?
Obsequium, maneo si tua, grande tuli.
Barbara narratur venisse venefica tecum,
In mihi promissi parte recepta tori.
Credula res amor est. utinam temeraria dicar
Criminibus falsis insimulasse virum.
Nuper ab Haemoniis hospes mihi Thessalus oris
Venerat. et tactum vix bene limen erat,

VI. E ita incipit: *E'pnias ypsiphile bachi genus esone nato Dicit. et in verbis pars quota mentis erat.* 3 Pa *ipsum.* 5 V *quidem* pro *tibi.* 7 EeV *quaelibet...signetur.* 9 Ee *litera nuntia.* 15 e *hoc.* 20 E *futura.* *recepta* superscr.

'Aesonides' dixi 'quid agit meus?' Ille pudore
  Haesit, in opposita lumina fixus humo.
Protinus exilui, tunicisque a pectore ruptis
  'Vivit, an' exclamo 'me quoque fata vocant?'
'Vivit' ait. *timidum quod amat*,—iurare coegi:
  Vix mihi teste deo credita vita tua est.
Utque animus rediit, tua facta requirere coepi.
  Narrat aënipedes Martis arasse boves,
Vipereos dentes in humum pro semine iactos,
  Et subito natos arma tulisse viros:
Terrigenas populos civili marte peremtos
  Inplesse aetatis fata diurna suae.
Devicto serpente; iterum, si vivat Iason,
  Quaerimus. alternant spesque timorque fidem.
Singula dum narrat, studio cursuque loquendi
  Detegit ingenio vulnera nostra suo.
Heus, ubi pacta fides? ubi connubialia iura,
  Faxque, sub arsuros dignior ire rogos?
Non ego sum furto tibi cognita. pronuba Iuno
  Affuit et sertis tempora vinctus Hymen.
At mihi nec Iuno, nec Hymen, sed tristis Erinys
  Praetulit infaustas sanguinolenta faces.
Quid mihi cum Minyis, quid cum Tritonide pinu?
  Quid tibi cum patria, navita Tiphy, mea?

26 E *opposi.* 27 ε om. *que.* 28 Eε *trahunt.* 29 E secutus sum. ε *timide quod ait.* MPa *timidumque mihi.* 31 ε *vixque rediit animus.* 32 EV *narrat et aeripides.* ε *aeripedes.* 34 E *natus.* 36 E *facta.* *fata* superscr. 37 E *devictus serpens.* Et M. qui tamen 31—38 damnat. E *vivit.* 38 E post 62 exhibet. 40 Eε *facta tuo.* 41 E *ubi est.* 42 E *dignion re.* 44 E *sertis* superscr. 47 E *quid tritonide.* *cum* super. 48 E *nativita.*

Non erat hic aries villo spectabilis aureo,
  Nec senis Aeetae regia Lemnos erat.
Certa fui primo... sed me mala fata trahebant...
  Hospita feminea pellere castra manu.
Lemniadesque viros, nimium quoque, vincere norunt.
  Milite tam forti vita tuenda fuit.
Urbe virum iuvi, tectoque animoque recepi.
  Hic tibi bisque aestas bisque cucurrit hiemps.
Tertia messis erat, cum tu dare vela coactus
  Implesti lacrimis talia verba tuis:
'Abstrahor, Hypsipyle. sed dent modo fata recursus,
  Vir tuus hinc abeo, vir tibi semper ero.
Quod tamen e nobis gravida celatur in alvo,
  Vivat, et eiusdem simus uterque parens.'
Hactenus. et lacrimis in falsa cadentibus ora
  Cetera te memini non potuisse loqui.
Ultimus e sociis sacram conscendis in Argon:
  Illa volat. ventus concava vela tenet.
Caerula propulsae subducitur unda carinae:
  Terra tibi, nobis aspiciuntur aquae.
In latus omne patens turris circumspicit undas:
  Huc feror, et lacrimis osque sinusque madent.
Per lacrimas specto. cupidaeque faventia menti
  Longius adsueto lumina nostra vident.
Adde preces castas, inmixtaque vota timori,
  Nunc quoque te salvo persoluenda mihi...

49 ε *fulvo...auro.* EV *villo...auro.* 50 E *oete.* 51 E *carta.* EεV *mea fata.* 53 E *norant.* 54 M *causa.* 55 *juvi* ex optima conj. Pa edidi. EεVM *vidi.* 56 ε *bis aestus.* 65 M *concedis.* EPa *Argo.* 71 EV *cupidae...amanti.* ε *nimiumque faventia menti.* 73 E *timoris.* ε *verba.* 74 E *salvos sunt agitanda*, supersc. *persoluenda.* ε *viro.*

Vota ego persolvam? votis Medea fruetur?
Cor dolet, atque ira mixtus abundat amor.
Dona feram templis, vivum quod Iasona perdo?
Hostia pro damnis concidat icta meis?
Non equidem secura fui; semperque verebar,
Ne pater Argolica sumeret urbe nurum.
Argolidas timui. nocuit mihi barbara pelex.
Non expectata vulnus ab hoste tuli.
Nec facie meritisque placet, sed carmina novit.
Diraque cantata pabula falce metit.
Illa reluctantem cursu deducere Lunam
Nititur, et tenebris abdere Solis equos.
Illa refrenat aquas, obliquaque flumina sistit:
Illa loco silvas vivaque saxa movet.
Per tumulos errat passis discincta capillis,
Certaque de tepidis colligit ossa rogis.
Devovet absentis, simulacraque cerea fingit,
Et miserum tenuis in iecur urget acus,
Et quae nescierim melius. Male quaeritur herbis
Moribus et forma conciliandus amor.
Hanc potes amplecti, thalamoque relictus in uno
Impavidus somno nocte silente frui?
Scilicet ut tauros, ita te iuga ferre coegit:
Quaque feros anguis, te quoque mulcet ope.

75 E *ergo.* *Mede, a* superscr. 77 EeV *perdum.* 78 Ee *concidet.* 81 Ee *argolicas.* 82 EeV *expectato.* E *oste.* 83 e *non meritis facieque.* V *carmine movit,* et sic superscr. in E. 84 E *papula* (cf. 7, 142). 86 e *addere.* E *adre.* 88 E *viva, que* superscr. 89 E *sparsis.* 93 EeV *mage.* 94 E *mobilis.* 98 E *quamque* sub rasura.

Adde, quod adscribi factis procerumque tuisque
  Se facit, et titulo coniugis uxor obest.
Atque aliquis Peliae de partibus acta venenis
  Imputat, et populum, qui sibi credat, habet.
'Non haec Aesonides, sed Phasias Aeetine
  Aurea Phrixeae terga revellit ovis'
Non probat Alcimede mater tua,.. consule matrem..
  Non pater, a gelido cui venit axe nurus.
Illa sibi Tanai Scythiaeque paludibus udae
  Quaerat et a patria Phasidis usque virum.
Mobilis Aesonide, vernaque incertior aura,
  Cur tua polliciti pondere verba carent?
Vir meus hinc ieras: vir non meus inde redisti.
  Sim reducis coniunx, sicut euntis eram!
Si te nobilitas generosaque nomina tangunt,
  En ego Minoo nata Thoante feror.
Bacchus avus: Bacchi coniunx redimita corona
  Praeradiat stellis signa minora suis.
Dos tibi Lemnos erit, terra ingeniosa colenti.
  Me quoque dotales inter habere potes.
Nunc etiam peperi: gratare ambobus, Iason.
  Dulce mihi gravidae fecerat auctor onus.
Felix in numero quoque sum; prolemque gemellam,
  Pignora Lucina bina favente dedi.

100 EεV *facit.* Pa *cavet.* Madv. *sese avet.* M *favet.* 101 E *atque aliquis per te...veneni.* 103 E *non echesonides sed filia phasias Oete.* εV *filia Phasis Oetae.* 106 E *orbe.* 107 EεV *Tanais...undae.* 109 ε *Aesonides.* E *unaque.* 110 E *pollicito.* Madv. *sollicito.* 114 E *Mine*, *o* superscr. 116 E *praediat.* 118 EεM *res tales.* Pa Madv. *dotales*, quod nonnulli e vet. edd. scripserant.

Si quaeris, cui sint similes? cognosceris illis.
Fallere non norunt: cetera patris habent.
Legatos quos paene dedi pro matre ferendos.
Sed tenuit coeptas saeva noverca vias.
Medeam timui: plus est Medea noverca.
Medeae faciunt ad scelus omne manus.
Spargere quae fratris potuit lacerata per agros
Corpora, pignoribus parceret illa meis?
Hanc tamen, o demens, Colchisque ablate venenis,
Diceris Hypsipyles praeposuisse toro!
Turpiter illa virum cognovit adultera virgo.
Me tibi, teque mihi taeda pudica dedit.
Prodidit illa patrem: rapui de clade Thoanta.
Deseruit Colchos: me mea Lemnos habet.
Quid refert, scelerata piam si vincet, et ipso
Crimine dotata est emeruitque virum?
Lemniadum facinus culpo, non miror, Iason.
Quaelibet iratis ipse dat arma dolor.
Dic age, si ventis... ut oportuit... actus iniquis
Intrasses portus tuque comesque meos,
Obviaque exissem fetu comitante gemello?...
Hiscere nempe tibi terra roganda fuit!
Quo vultu natos, quo me, scelerate, videres?
Perfidiae pretio qua nece dignus eras?

125 E *pro me matre proferendos.* 127 E *Mediam.* 129 ε *potuit fratris.* 131 Pa *hanc, hanc.* 132 E *hisiphile.* 135 E *cede.* 137 E *scerata.* EV *vincit.* ε *vincat.* 139 ε *nec.* 140 M *quamlibet.* εV *quaelibet.* Pa *quamlibet infirmis.* E *quodlibet ad facinus ipse.* Madv. *quodlibet ad facinus iste.* 142 E *comedesque.* 143 V *obvia exissem.* Eε *comitata.* 144 EεV *nonne...foret.* 146 Sic E. ε *perfide, quo pretio, qua nece.* Pa *quo nece* (?).

Ipse quidem per me tutus sospesque fuisses:
Non quia tu dignus, sed quia mitis ego.
Pelicis ipsa meos implessem sanguine vultus,
Quosque veneficiis abstulit illa suis.
Medeae Medea forem. Quod siquid ab alto
Iustus adest votis Iuppiter ipse meis,
Quod gemit Hypsipyle, lecti quoque subnuba nostri
Maereat, et leges sentiat ipsa suas.
Utque ego destituor coniunx materque duorum,
Cum totidem natis orba sit illa viro.
Nec male parta diu teneat, peiusque relinquat:
Exulet, et toto quaerat in orbe fugam.
Quam fratri germana fuit miseroque parenti
Filia, tam natis, tam sit acerba viro.
Cum mare, cum terras consumpserit, aera temptet:
Erret inops, exspes, caede cruenta sua.
Haec ego, coniugio fraudata Thoantias oro.
Vivite devoto nuptaque virque toro!

VII.

DIDO AENEAE.

Sic ubi fata vocant, udis abiectus in herbis
Ad vada Maeandri concinit albus olor.

148 E *non quia dignus eras.* 151 EV *si quis.* 152 V *precibus.* 154 ϵ *illa.* 156 Sic ϵPa. E *a totidem—atque.* Sed *illa* superscr. M *a totidem...aque.* Madv. *a totidem...illa.* 158 E *exultet.* 160 E *filiam.* 161 E *cum pennis.* 162 Eϵ *inops mentis*, quod ex P ortum esse videtur ubi *expers* exstat. 164 ϵ *femina.* VII. E sic incipit: *Accipe, darnida, moriture carmen helise Que legis a nobis ultima uerba legis.*

Nec quia te nostra sperem prece posse moveri,
Adloquor: adverso movimus ista deo.
Sed merita et famam corpusque animumque pudicum
Cum male perdiderim, perdere verba leve est.
Certus es ire tamen miseramque relinquere Didon,
Atque idem venti vela fidemque ferent?
Certus es, Aenea, cum foedere solvere naves,
Quaeque ubi sint nescis, Itala regna sequi,
Nec nova Carthago, nec te crescentia tangunt,
Moenia, nec sceptro tradita summa tuo?
Facta fugis, facienda petis. quaerenda per orbem
Altera, quaesita est altera terra tibi.
Ut terram invenias, quis eam tibi tradet habendam?
Quis sua non notis arva tenenda dabit?
Alter amor tibi restat habendus et altera Dido:
Quamque iterum fallas, altera danda fides.
Quando erit, ut condas instar Carthaginis urbem,
Et videas populos altus ab arce tuos?
Omnia ut eveniant, nec te tua vota morentur,
Unde tibi, quae te sic amet, uxor erit?
Uror, ut inducto ceratae sulphure taedae.
Aenean animo noxque diesque refert.
Ille quidem male gratus et ad mea munera surdus,
Et quo, si non sim stulta, carere velim.

3 ϵ *non.* 5 E *meriti fama.* ϵV *meriti famam.* 7 Pa *Dido.* E *ddon.* 8 E *verba fidemque, vala* superscr. 11 E *mea...surgentia tangant.* 15 E *terra...habenda.* 16 E *nenda.* ϵ *tenenda.* MPa *terenda* contra P. 17 E *alter amor tibi et extat.* ϵ *alter habendus amor restat tibi.* 20 Eϵ *tua.* 21 V *omnia si veniant te nec*...E *facta.* ϵ *fata.* Pa *di tua vota.* 23 Post h. v. ϵ exhibet *ut pia fumosis addita tura rogis: Aeneas oculis semper vigilantis inhaeret.* EV om. 26 EϵV *Aeneamque.*

Non tamen Aenean, quamvis male cogitat, odi:
Sed queror infidum, questaque peius amo.
Parce, Venus, nurui, durumque amplectere fratrem,
Frater Amor: castris militet ille tuis.
Aut ego quem coepi, neque enim dedignor, amare—
Materiam curae praebeat ille meae.
Fallor, et ista mihi falso iactatur imago.
Matris ab ingenio dissidet ille suae.
Te lapis et montes innataque rupibus altis
Robora, te saevae progenuere ferae,
Aut mare, quale vides agitari nunc quoque ventis:
Quo tamen adversis fluctibus ire paras.
Quo fugis? obstat hiemps! Hiemis mihi gratia prosit.
Aspice, ut eversas concitet eurus aquas.
Quod tibi malueram, sine me debere procellis:
Iustior est animo ventus et unda tuo.
Non ego sum tanti,—quid non *tu reris* inique?
Ut pereas, dum me per freta longa fugis.
Exerces pretiosa odia et constantia magno,
Si, dum me careas, est tibi vile mori.
Iam venti ponent, strataque aequaliter unda
Caeruleis Triton per mare curret equis.
Tu quoque cum ventis utinam mutabilis esses...
Et nisi duritia robora vincis, eris.

29 ε *cogitet.* 30 E *questamque.* 33 E *atque ego quae.* ε *hunc ego quem.* Madv. *quae...amorem.* VMPa *aut ego quae.* Anacoluthon defendit Pa. 42 E *adversas.* 45 *tu reris* scripsi ego, vestigia P. secutus, qui *tanti qui non -eris* (syllaba prima incerta, Heins. *terreris*) exhibet. E *quam tu dimittis inique.* ε *quamvis merearis.* V *quid non mediteris.* Pa *quid non censeris*, q. v. aestimas. M *quod non verearis*, sed obelo notat. Madv. *quid nos metiris inique.* 52 E *ni.*

Quid, si nescires, insana quid aequora possent?
  Expertae totiens quam male credis aquae!
Ut pelago suadente etiam retinacula solvas,
  Multa tamen latus tristia pontus habet.
Nec violasse fidem temptantibus aequora prodest:
  Perfidiae poenas exigit ille locus,
Praecipue cum laesus amor; quia mater Amorum
  Nuda Cytheriacis edita fertur aquis.
Perdita ne perdam, timeo, noceamve nocenti,
  Neu bibat aequoreas naufragus hostis aquas.
Vive, precor! sic te melius, quam funere perdam.
  Tu potius leti causa ferere mei.
Finge, age, te rapido... nullum sit in omine pondus!...
  Turbine deprendi: quid tibi mentis erit?
Protinus occurrent falsae periuria linguae,
  Et Phrygia Dido fraude coacta mori:
Coniugis ante oculos deceptae stabit imago
  Tristis et effusis sanguinolenta comis.
Quid tanti est ut tum 'merui, concedite!' dicas;
  Quaeque cadent, in te fulmina missa putes?
Da breve saevitiae spatium pelagique tuaeque:
  Grande morae pretium tuta futura via est.
Nec mihi tu curae. puero parcatur Iulo:
  Te satis est titulum mortis habere meae.

53 E *possint.* ϵ *possent.* MPa *possunt*, quod quo modo defendant nescio. 56 E *tristitia.* 57 ϵ *non.* 59 E *et mater.* 61 ϵ *noceo.* 65 E *finge a age rabido.* 68 E *troica.* ϵ *Tyria.* 70 E *sanguinolenta qu comis.* 71 E *quid id est tum* (*to* superscr.) *merui concedite dices*, corrupte. ϵ *quidquid id est totum...dices.* M *totum...dicas* sed obelo notat. 75 E *nec tibi sum.* ϵ *si mihi non parcas.*

Quid puer Ascanius, quid di meruere Penates?
 Ignibus ereptos obruet unda deos?
Sed neque fers tecum, nec... quae mihi, perfide, iactas...
 Presserunt umeros sacra paterque tuos.
Omnia mentiris: nec enim tua fallere lingua
 Incipit a nobis, primaque plectar ego.
Si quaeras ubi sit formosi mater Iuli,
 Occidit a duro sola relicta viro.
Haec mihi narraras; at me movere merentem:
 Illa minor culpa poena futura mea est.
Nec mihi mens dubia est, quin te tua numina damnent:
 Per mare, per terras septima iactat hiemps.
Fluctibus eiectum tuta statione recepi,
 Vixque bene audito nomine regna dedi.
His tamen officiis utinam contenta fuissem,
 Et mihi concubitus fama sepulta foret!
Illa dies nocuit, qua nos declive sub antrum
 Caeruleus subitis compulit imber aquis.
Audieram vocem; nymphas ululasse putavi;
 Eumenides fatis signa dedere meis.
Exige, laese pudor, poenas, umbraeque Sychaei,—
 Ad quas me miseram! plena pudoris eo.

80 ε *paterna.* 81 E *falle.* 82 E *fallar.* ε *plector.* 84 E *diro.* 85 E *an me novere merentem*, sc. numina, quod proxime ad P accedit. ε *narrabas at me novere.* M *at me movere merentem.* Pa *movere; merentem Ure:* Madv. *nec me movere* vel *di me monuere.* 86 ε *inde.* MPa *ure.* M obelo notat. 87 Eε *mea munera.* 90 E *nōa regna.* 91 ε *con tempta.* 93 E *me.* 94 E *impulit.* 95 E *voces nympha.* 96 Pa *fati—mei.* 97 Locus corruptus. Eε *violate Sichaeu.* V *violare Sicheu.* Pa *violate Sichaeo.* 98 V *Ad quem.* An legendum est *Exigit ecce pudor paenas, violate Sichaee, Ad quem, etc.?*

Est mihi marmorea sacratus in aede Sychaeus:
  Oppositae frondes velleraque alba tegunt.
Hinc ego me sensi noto quater ore citari:
  Ipse sono tenui dixit 'Elissa, veni!'
Nulla mora est, venio: venio tibi debita coniunx.
  Sum tamen admissi tarda pudore mei.
Da veniam culpae: decepit idoneus auctor.
  Invidiam noxae detrahit ille meae.
Diva parens seniorque pater pia sarcina nati
  Spem mihi mansuri rite dedere tori.
Si fuit errandum, causas habet error honestas.
  Adde fidem, nulla parte pigendus erit.
Durat in extremum, vitaeque novissima nostrae
  Prosequitur fati qui fuit ante, tenor.
Occidit internas coniunx mactatus ad aras,
  Et sceleris tanti praemia frater habet.
Exsul agor, cineresque viri patriamque relinquo,
  Et feror in duras hoste sequente vias:
Adplicor ignotis, fratrique elapsa fretoque
  Quod tibi donavi, perfide, litus emo.
Urbem constitui, lateque patentia fixi,
  Moenia finitimis invidiosa locis.
Bella tument: bellis peregrina et femina temptor,
  Vixque rudis portas urbis et arma paro.
Mille procis placui qui me coiere querentes.
  Nescio quem thalamis praeposuisse suis.

99 E *inde.* 101 E *quater atque ter.* 104 E *amisso... meo.* V *a misso.* 108 Eϵ V *viri.* 109 ϵ *sic.* 113 EϵV *in terras.* 116 E *duuitas.* Pa *dubias.* 118 E *etu* corrupte. ϵ *emi.* 121 ϵ *tangor.* 123 Eϵ *cupiere.*

Quid dubitas vinctam Gaetulo tradere Iarbae?
　Praebuerim sceleri bracchia nostra tuo.
Est etiam frater, cuius manus impia possit
　Respergi nostro, sparsa cruore viri.
Pone deos et quae tangendo sacra profanas:
　Non bene caelestis impia dextra colit.
Si tu cultor eras elapsis igne futurus,
　Paenitet elapsos ignibus esse deos.
Forsitan et gravidam Didon, scelerate, relinquas,
　Parsque tui lateat corpore clausa meo.
Accedet fatis matris miserabilis infans,
　Et nondum nati funeris auctor eris:
Cumque parente sua frater morietur Iuli,
　Poenaque conexos auferet una duos.
Sed iubet ire deus. Vellem, vetuisset adire,
　Punica nec Teucris pressa fuisset humus.
Hoc duce nempe deo ventis agitaris iniquis,
　Et teris in rapido tempora longa freto?
Pergama vix tanto tibi erant repetenda labore,
　Hectore si vivo quanta fuere, forent!
Non patrium Simoënta petis, sed Thybridas undas,
　Nempe ut pervenias quo cupis, hospes eris.
Utque latet vitatque tuas abstrusa carinas,
　Vix tibi continget terra petita seni.

125 Eε *victam.* 126 E *praetulerim.* 127 E *manus* superscr. 131 E om. *eras.* 133 E *Sorsitan.* Pa *Dido.* 134 V *latitat.* 136 E *et fili nondum nati.* 137 E *sua* superscr. 138 E *huc* ad finem vers. 139 EV *si.* 140 E *terra*; *humus* superscr. 142 E *rabido* (cf. 6, 81). 143 E *rependa.* 145 E *tibridis.* 147 E *utque juvent ventusque tuas remusque carinas.* Ita ε nisi quod *juvet* exhibet. V *obstrusa.*

Hos potius populos in dotem, ambage remissa,
  Accipe et advectas Pygmalionis opes.
Ilion in Tyriam transfer felicius urbem,
  *Sis*que loco regis sceptraque sacra tene.
Si tibi mens avida est belli, si quaerit Iulus,
  Unde suo partus marte triumphus eat,
Quem superet, nequid desit, praebebimus hostem.
  Hic pacis leges, hic locus arma capit.
Tu modo... per matrem fraternaque tela, sagittas,
  Perque fugae comites, Dardana sacra, deos!
Sic superent, quoscumque tua de gente reportas,
  Mars ferus et damni sit modus ille tui,
Ascaniusque suos feliciter impleat annos,
  Et senis Anchisae molliter ossa cubent!...
Parce, precor, domui, quae se tibi tradit habendam.
  Quod crimen dicis praeter amasse meum?
Non ego sum Phthia magnisque oriunda Mycenis,
  Nec steterunt in te virque paterque meus.
Si pudet uxoris, non nupta, sed hospita dicar
  Dum tua sit Dido, quodlibet esse feret.
Nota mihi freta sunt Afrum frangentia litus:
  Temporibus certis dantque negantque viam.
Cum dabit aura viam, praebebis carbasa ventis.
  Nunc levis eiectam continet alga ratem.

149 E *dote*. ε *ambage in dote remissa*. 152 E *inque loco regis regia sceptra tene*. εV *inque loco regis sceptraque sacra tene*. M *hancque*, sc. urbem. Pa *jamque locum*. In re dubia meo judicio uti ausus sum. Sed verum esse potest quod E cum G exhibet, mutatum autem a librario verbis *regiă sceptra* offenso. 153 E *Iuli*. 155 E *quod superet*. ε *superes*. 159 Ad hunc versum E explicat. ε *si*. Madv. *reportat Mars ferus*. 165 ε *phitia*. V *pithia*. 166 ε *steterant*. 172 V *sed*.

Tempus ut observem, manda mihi. serius ibis,
Nec te, si cupies, ipsa manere sinam.
Et socii requiem poscunt, laniataque classis
Postulat exiguas semirefecta moras.
Pro meritis et siqua tibi debebimus ultra,
Pro spe coniugii tempora parva peto:
Dum freta mitescunt et amor, dum tempore et usu
Fortiter edisco tristia posse pati.
Si minus, est animus nobis effundere vitam,
In me crudelis non potes esse diu.
Aspicias utinam, quae sit scribentis imago:
Scribimus, et gremio Troicus ensis adest;
Perque genas lacrimae strictum labuntur in ensem,
Qui iam pro lacrimis sanguine tinctus erit.
Quam bene conveniunt fato tua munera nostro!
Instruis impensa nostra sepulchra brevi.
Nec mea nunc primum feriuntur pectora telo:
Ille locus saevi vulnus amoris habet.
Anna soror, soror Anna, meae male conscia culpae,
Iam dabis in cineres ultima dona meos.
Nec consumpta rogis inscribar Elissa Sychaei,
Hoc tamen in tumuli marmore carmen erit
'Praebuit Aeneas et causam mortis et ensem.
Ipsa sua Dido concidit usa manu.'

174 ε *cuperes.* 179 ε *mitescant.* εV *temperat usum.* 180 εV *ediscam.* An legendum est *Dum freta mitescunt et amorem temperat usus Fortiter ediscam*, etc.? 184 ε *in gremio.* 192 ε *dabit.* 195 ε *Aeneas mihi.*

VIII.

HERMIONE ORESTAE.

Pyrrhus Achillides, animosus imagine patris,
  Inclusam contra iusque piumque tenet.
Quod potui, renui, ne non invita tenerer.
  Cetera femineae non valuere manus.
'Quid facis, Aeacide? non sum sine vindice' dixi:
  'Haec tibi sub domino est, Pyrrhe, puella suo.'
Surdior ille freto clamantem nomen Orestis
  Traxit inornatis in sua tecta comis.
Quid gravius capta Lacedaemone serva tulissem,
  Si raperet Graias barbara turba nurus?
Parcius Andromachen vexavit Achaïa victrix,
  Cum Danaus Phrygias ureret ignis opes.
At tu, cura mei si te pia tangit, Oreste,
  Inice non timidas in tua iura manus.
An siquis rapiat stabulis armenta reclusis,
  Arma feras, rapta coniuge lentus eris?
Si socer exemplo nuptae repetitor ademptae,
  Nupta foret Paridi mater, ut ante fuit.
Nec tu mille rates sinuosaque vela pararis;
  Nec numeros Danai militis. ipse veni!
Sic quoque eram repetenda tamen: nec turpe marito,
  Aspera pro caro bella tulisse toro.
Quid, quod avus nobis idem Pelopeïus Atreus,
  Et, si non esses vir mihi, frater eras?

3 ε *quae potui feci.* 8 ε *suo est.* 19 εV *sit.* 24 εV *numerum.*

Vir, precor, uxori, frater succurre sorori:
Instant officio nomina bina tuo.
Me tibi Tyndareus, vita gravis auctor et annis,
Tradidit: arbitrium neptis habebat avus.
At pater Aeacidae promiserat, inscius acti.
Plus quoque, qui prior est ordine, possit avus.
Cum tibi nubebam, nulli mea taeda nocebat:
Si iungar Pyrrho, tu mihi laesus eris.
Et pater ignoscet nostro Menelaus amori:
Succubuit telis praepetis ipse dei.
Quem sibi permisit, genero concedit amorem.
Proderit exemplo mater amata suo.
Tu mihi, quod matri pater est; quas egerat olim
Dardanius partis advena, Pyrrhus agit.
Ille licet patriis sine fine superbiat actis.
Et tu quae referas facta parentis, habes.
Tantalides omnis ipsumque regebat Achillem:
Hic pars militiae, dux erat ille ducum.
Tu quoque habes proavum Pelopem Pelopisque parentem.
Si melius numeres, a Iove quintus eris.
Nec virtute cares. Arma invidiosa tulisti:
Sed tu quid faceres? induit illa pater.
Materia vellem fortis meliore fuisses.
Non lecta est operi, sed data causa tuo.
Hanc tamen implesti; iuguloque Aegisthus aperto
Tecta cruentavit, quae pater ante tuus.
Increpat Aeacides, laudemque in crimina vertit:
Et tamen aspectus sustinet ille meos.

34 V *posset.* 43 *ε patris.* 44 *ε quae tu.* 48 *ε si numeres omnes.* Pa *si medios numeres.* 50 V *patrem.* 52 *ε Nec.*

Rumpor, et ora mihi pariter cum mente tumescunt,
  Pectoraque inclusis ignibus usta dolent.
Hermione coram quisquamne obiecit Oresti,
  Nec mihi sunt vires, nec ferus ensis adest?
Flere licet certe. flendo diffundimus iram,
  Perque sinum lacrimae fluminis instar eunt.
Has solas habeo semper, semperque profundo:
  Ument incultae fonte perenne genae.
Num generis fato, quod nostros errat in annos,
  Tantalides matres apta rapina sumus?
Non ego fluminei referam mendacia cygni,
  Nec querar in plumis delituisse Iovem.
Qua duo porrectus longe freta distinet Isthmos,
  Vecta peregrinis Hippodamia rotis.
Castori Amyclaeo et Amyclaeo Polluci
  Reddita Mopsopia Taenaris urbe soror:
Taenaris Idaeo trans aequora ab hospite rapta
  Argolicas pro se vertit in arma manus.
Vix equidem memini, memini tamen. omnia luctus,
  Omnia solliciti plena timoris erant.
Flebat avus Phoebeque soror fratresque gemelli,
  Orabat superos Leda suumque Iovem.
Ipsa ego, non longos etiam tum scissa capillos,
  Clamabam 'sine me, me sine, mater, abis?'
Nam coniunx aberat. Ne non Pelopeïa credar,
  Ecce Neoptolemo praeda parata fui.
Pelides utinam vitasset Apollinis arcus!
  Damnaret nati facta proterva pater.

61 Pa *defundimus.* εVM *diff-.* 65 εV *hoc...fatum.* 66 ε *omnes.* 69 ε *detinet.* 72 εV *Messopia Tyndaris.* 73 εV *Tyndaris.* 77 ε *Phoebi.* V *flebatque soror.*

Nec quondam placuit, nec nunc placuisset Achilli,
Abducta viduum coniuge flere virum.
Quae mea caelestis iniuria fecit iniquos?
Quodve mihi miserae sidus obesse querar?
Parva mea sine matre fui; pater arma ferebat:
Et duo cum vivant, orba duobus eram.
Non tibi blanditias primis, mea mater, in annis
Incerto dictas ore puella tuli:
Non ego captavi brevibus tua colla lacertis,
Nec gremio sedi sarcina grata tuo:
Non cultus tibi cura mei; nec pacta marito
Intravi thalamos matre parante novos.
Obvia prodieram reduci tibi,... vera fatebor...
Nec facies nobis nota parentis erat.
Te tamen esse Helenam, quod eras pulcherrima, sensi
Ipsa requirebas, quae tua nata foret.
Pars haec una mihi, coniunx bene cessit Orestes:
Is quoque, ni pro se pugnet, ademptus erit.
Pyrrhus habet captam reduce et victore parente:
Hoc munus nobis diruta Troia tulit.
Cum tamen altus equis Titan radiantibus instat,
Perfruor infelix liberiore malo.
Nox ubi me thalamis ululantem et acerba gementem
Condidit, in maesto procubuique toro,
Pro somno lacrimis oculi funguntur obortis,
Quaque licet fugio sicut ab hoste viro.
Saepe malis stupeo, rerumque oblita locique
Ignara tetigi Scyria membra manu:

88 ε *quod mihi vae.* 104 V *munus et hoc...dedit.*

Utque nefas sensi, male corpora tacta relinquo
Et mihi pollutas credor habere manus.
Saepe Neoptolemi pro nomine nomen Orestis
Exit; et errorem vocis ut omen amo.
Per genus infelix iuro generisque parentem,
Qui freta, qui terras et sua regna quatit:
Per patris ossa tui, patrui mihi, quae tibi debent,
Quod sic sub tumulo fortiter ulta iacent:
Aut ego praemoriar, primoque exstinguar in aevo,
Aut ego Tantalidae Tantalis uxor ero.

IX.

DEIANIRA HERCULI.

Gratulor Oechaliam titulis accedere nostris:
Victorem victae subcubuisse queror.
Fama Pelasgiadas subito pervenit in urbes
Decolor et factis infitianda tuis,
Quem numquam Iuno seriesque inmensa laborum
Fregerit, huic Iolen inposuisse iugum.
Hoc velit Eurystheus, velit hoc germana Tonantis,
Laetaque sit vitae labe noverca tuae.
At non ille velit, cui nox... sic creditur... una
Non tanti, ut tantus conciperere, fuit.
Plus tibi quam Iuno, nocuit Venus: illa premendo
Sustulit, haec humili sub pede colla tenet.

120 εV *quae* Pa *quod se.* 3 ε *Pelasgiades.* 9 ε *At nunc ille venis cui nox si.* V *at non ille venis cui nox* (*si creditur*) *una.* 12 ε *humilis.*

Respice vindicibus pacatum viribus orbem,
Qua latam Nereus caerulus ambit humum.
Se tibi pax terrae, tibi se tota aequora debent:
Implesti meritis solis utramque domum.
Quod te laturum est, caelum prius ipse tulisti:
Hercule subposito sidera fulsit Atlans.
Quid nisi notitia est misero quaesita pudori,
Si cumulas stupri facta priora nota?
Tene ferunt geminos pressisse tenaciter angues,
Cum tener in cunis iam Iove dignus eras?
Coepisti melius, quam desinis. ultima primis
Cedunt. dissimiles hic vir et ille puer.
Quem non mille ferae, quem non Stheneleïus hostis,
Non potuit Iuno vincere, vincit amor.
At bene nupta feror, quia nominer Herculis uxor,
Sitque socer rapidis qui tonat altus equis.
Quam male inaequales veniunt ad aratra iuvenci,
Tam premitur magno coniuge nupta minor.
Non honor est, sed onus species laesura ferentis.
Siqua voles apte nubere, nube pari.
Vir mihi semper abest, et coniuge notior hospes,
Monstraque terribiles persequiturque feras.
Ipsa domo vidua, votis operata pudicis,
Torqueor, infesto ne vir ab hoste cadat.
Inter serpentes aprosque avidosque leones
Iactor, et haesuros terna per ora canes.
Me pecudum fibrae simulacraque inania somni
Ominaque arcana nocte petita movent.

15 εV *tota*. 20 ε *si macula stupri...notas*. Pa *turpi*. 27 εVM *nominor*. 32 ε *apto*. 38 εV *cemo*. 40 εV *omniaque*.

Aucupor infelix incertae murmura famae,
  Speque timor dubia, spesque timore cadit.
Mater abest, queriturque deo placuisse potenti:
  Nec pater Amphitryon, nec puer Hyllus adest.
Arbiter Eurystheus irae Iunonis iniquae
  Sentitur nobis, iraque longa deae.
Haec mihi ferre parum? Peregrinos addis amores,
  Et mater de te quaelibet esse potest.
Non ego Partheniis temeratam vallibus Augen,
  Nec referam partus, Ormeni nympha, tuos:
Non tibi crimen erunt, Theutrantia turba, sorores,
  Quarum de populo nulla relicta tibi est.
Una, recens crimen, referetur adultera nobis,
  Unde ego sum Lydo facta noverca Lamo.
Maeandros, terris totiens errator in isdem,
  Qui lassas in se saepe retorquet aquas,
Vidit in Herculeo suspensa monilia collo
  Illo, cui caelum sarcina parva fuit.
Non puduit fortis auro cohibere lacertos,
  Et solidis gemmas opposuisse toris.
Nempe sub his animam pestis Nemeaea lacertis
  Edidit, unde umerus tegmina laevus habet.
Ausus es hirsutos mitra redimire capillos.
  Aptior Herculeae populus alba comae.
Nec te Maeonia lascivae more puellae
  Incingi zona dedecuisse putes?

46 ϵV *deae est.* 47 ϵV *parum est.* 49 ϵ *Auguē.* V *Agnen.* 53 ϵ *praefertur.* V *refertur.* 55 ϵ *qui totiens terris errat mainder in hiisdem.* V *Maeander totiens qui terris errat in isdem.* 56 ϵV *lapsas.* 60 ϵ *imposuisse.* V *apposuisse.* 62 V *tegmina leonis.* (?) *terga leonis.* 66 ϵV *pudet.*

Non tibi succurrit crudi Diomedis imago,
Efferus humana qui dape pavit equas?
Si te vidisset cultu Busiris in isto,
Huic victor victo nempe pudendus eras.
Detrahat Antaeus duro redimicula collo,
Ne pigeat molli subcubuisse viro.
Inter Ioniacas calathum tenuisse puellas
Diceris, et dominae pertimuisse minas.
Non fugis, Alcide, victricem mille laborum
Rasilibus calathis inposuisse manum,
Crassaque robusto deducis pollice fila,
Aequaque formosae pensa rependis erae?
A! quotiens, digitis dum torques stamina duris,
Praevalidae fusos comminuere manus.
Crederis infelix scuticae tremefactus habenis
Ante pedes dominae pertimuisse minas.
Eximiis pompis praeconia summa triumphi
Factaque narrabas dissimulanda tibi:
Scilicet inmanes elisos faucibus hydros
Infantem caudis involuisse manum:
Ut Tegeaeus aper cupressifero Erymantho
Incubet et vasto pondere laedat humum.
Non tibi Threïciis adfixa penatibus ora,
Non hominum pingues caede tacentur equae:
Prodigiumque triplex, armenti dives Hiberi
Geryones, quamvis in tribus unus erat:
Inque canes totidem trunco digestus ab uno
Cerberos implicitis angue minante comis:

73 ε *pudeat.* 81 V *diceris.* 81, 83 M obelo notat. 86 ε *nuda delacerasse manu.* 87 ε *utque tegeus aper.* 88 ε *incubat...laedit.* V *incubuit vasto et...laesit.*

Quaeque redundabat fecundo vulnere serpens
Fertilis et damnis dives ab ipsa suis,
Quique inter laevumque latus laevumque lacertum
Praegrave conpressa fauce pependit onus:
Et male confisum pedibus formaque bimembri
Pulsum Thessalicis agmen equestre iugis.
Haec tu Sidonio potes insignitus amictu
Dicere? non cultu lingua retenta silet?
Se quoque nympha tuis ornavit Iardanis armis,
Et tulit e capto nota tropaea viro.
I nunc, tolle animos et fortia gesta recense.
Quum tu non esses, iure vir illa fuit.
Qua tanto minor es, quanto te, maxime rerum,
Quam quos vicisti, vincere maius erat.
Illi procedit rerum mensura tuarum:
Cede bonis. heres laudis amica tuae.
O pudor! hirsuti costis exuta leonis
Aspera texerunt vellera molle latus.
Falleris et nescis. non sunt spolia illa leonis,
Sed tua. tuque feri victor es, illa tui.
Femina tela tulit Lernaeis atra venenis,
Ferre gravem lana vix satis apta colum,
Instruxitque manum clava domitrice ferarum,
Vidit et in speculo coniugis arma sui.
Haec tamen audieram: licuit non credere famae,
Et venit ad sensus mollis ab aure dolor.

96 ε *ditior ipsa.* 103 ε *tuis ingentibus instruit armis.* Pa *oneravit.* V *Iamdanis.* 106 Sic Madv. Heins. conj. *quom.* PaM *quod.* Sed subjunctivus *esses* 'quum' desiderat. 110 ε *tuae est.* 111 εV Madv. *costis.* PaM *costas.* 113 ε *ista.* 114 εV *ferae.*

Ante meos oculos adducitur advena pelex,
Nec mihi, quae patior, dissimulare licet.
Non sinis averti: mediam captiva per urbem
Invitis oculis aspicienda venit.
Nec venit incultis captarum more capillis,
Fortunam vultu fassa tegente suam.
Ingreditur late lato spectabilis auro,
Qualiter in Phrygia tu quoque cultus eras.
Dat vultum populo sublimis ut Hercule victo.
Oechaliam vivo stare parente putes.
Forsitan et pulsa Aetolide Deianira
Nomine deposito pelicis uxor erit:
Eurytidosque Ioles et insani Alcidae
Turpia famosus corpora iunget Hymen.
Mens fugit admonitu, frigusque perambulat artus,
Et iacet in gremio languida facta manus.
Me quoque cum multis, sed me sine crimine amasti.
Ne pigeat, pugnae bis tibi causa fui.
Cornua flens legit ripis Achelous in udis,
Truncaque limosa tempora mersit aqua.
Semivir occubuit in letifero Eueno
Nessus, et infecit sanguis equinus aquas.
Sed quid ego haec refero? scribenti nuntia venit
Fama, virum tunicae tabe perire meae.

123 ε *sinit.* 125 ε *non.* 126 ε *tegente suam.* V *tegente suo.* Pa *decente.* M *tegendo.* Optimum Cod. P *subsequor.* 129 εV *sublime sub Hercule.* 131 ε *expulsa.* 133 M *insanii.* Pa *Aonii* contra omnes Cod. et Edd. 135 ε *attonitu.* 139 ε *condit rapidis...undis.* V *legit rapidis...undis.* Pa errore typog. *ripis...in undis.* 141 ε *lernei tabe veneni.* V *occubuit vi: lemiferoque veneno.* Madv. *lentifero eveno.* 143 ε *refero haec.* 144 ε *perisse.*

Ei mihi, quid feci? quo me furor egit amantem?
  Impia quid dubitas Deianira mori?
An tuus in media coniunx lacerabitur Oeta,
  Tu sceleris tanti causa superstes eris?
Siquid adhuc habeo facti, cur Herculis uxor
  Credar, coniugii mors mihi pignus erit.
Tu quoque cognosces in me, Meleagre, sororem.
  Impia quid dubitas Deianira mori?
Heu devota domus! solio sedet Agrios alto:
  Oenea desertum nuda senecta premit:
Exulat ignotis Tydeus germanus in oris:
  Alter fatali vivus in igne fuit:
Exegit ferrum sua per praecordia mater.
  Impia quid dubitas Deianira mori?
Deprecor hoc unum per iura sacerrima lecti,
  Ne videar fatis insidiata tuis.
Nessus ut est avidum percussus arundine pectus,
  'Hic' dixit 'vires sanguis amoris habet.'
Inlita Nesseo misi tibi texta veneno.
  Impia quid dubitas Deianira mori?
Iamque vale, seniorque pater germanaque Gorge,
  Et patria et patriae frater adempte tuae,
Et tu lux oculis hodierna novissima nostris,
  Virque,... sed o possit!... et puer Hylle, vale!

145 ε *heu.* 147 ε *ethna.* 149 εV *et quid.* 150 ε *dicar.* 153 εV *acrior.* 166 ε *et patria patriae.* 168 ε *virque si hoc.* V *ille* pro *Hylle.*

X.

ARIADNE THESEO.

Mitius inveni quam te genus omne ferarum.
  Credita non ulli quam tibi peius eram.
Quae legis, ex illo, Theseu, tibi litore mitto,
  Unde tuam sine me vela tulere ratem:
In quo me somnusque meus male prodidit et tu,
  Per facinus somnis insidiate meis.
Tempus erat, vitrea quo primum terra pruina
  Spargitur et tectae fronde queruntur aves:
Incertum vigilans, a somno languida, movi
  Thesea prensuras semisupina manus:
Nullus erat: referoque manus, iterumque retempto,
  Perque torum moveo bracchia, nullus erat.
Excussere metus somnum. conterrita surgo,
  Membraque sunt viduo praecipitata toro.
Protinus adductis sonuerunt pectora palmis,
  Utque erat e somno turbida, rapta coma est.
Luna fuit: specto, siquid nisi litora cernam.
  Quod videant oculi, nil nisi litus habent.
Nunc huc, nunc illuc, et utroque sine ordine curro.
  Alta puellares tardat arena pedes.
Interea toto clamanti litore 'Theseu!'
  Reddebant nomen concava saxa tuum,
Et quotiens ego te, totiens locus ipse vocabat.
  Ipse locus miserae ferre volebat opem.

3 ε *quam*, cf. I. 1. 6 ε *pro*. 10 εV *semisopita*.

Mons fuit: apparent frutices in vertice rari:
Hinc scopulus raucis pendet adesus aquis:
Ascendo: vires animus dabat: atque ita late
Aequora prospectu metior alta meo.
Inde ego... nam ventis quoque sum crudelibus usa...
Vidi praecipiti carbasa tenta noto.
Aut vidi, aut certe cum me vidisse putarem,
Frigidior glacie semianimisque fui.
Nec languere diu patitur dolor. excitor illo,
Excitor et summa Thesea voce voco.
'Quo fugis?' exclamo 'scelerate revertere Theseu,
Flecte ratem! numerum non habet illa suum.'
Haec ego: quod voci deerat, plangore replebam:
Verbera cum verbis mixta fuere meis.
Si non audires, ut saltem cernere posses,
Iactatae late signa dedere manus.
Candidaque inposui longae velamina virgae,
Scilicet oblitos admonitura mei.
Iamque oculis ereptus eras. Tum denique flevi.
Torpuerant molles ante dolore genae.
Quid potius facerent, quam me moa lumina flerent,
Postquam desierant vela videre tua?
Aut ego diffusis erravi sola capillis,
Qualis ab Ogygio concita Baccha deo:
Aut mare prospiciens in saxo frigida sedi,
Quamque lapis sedes, tam lapis ipsa fui.

26 ε *hic.* VM *nunc.* 30 εV *tensa.* 31 ε *aut etiam cum me.* V *aut certi cum me.* MPa *aut tamquam quae me* quod nihili esse mihi videtur. Malim *ut vidi.* 37 εV *hoc.* 43 ε *tunc.* 44 V *torpebant.* 45 ε *facerent potius.*

Saepe torum repeto, qui nos acceperat ambos,
Sed non acceptos exhibiturus erat,
Et tua, quae possum pro te, vestigia tango,
Strataque quae membris intepuere tuis.
Incumbo, lacrimisque toro manante profusis
'Pressimus' exclamo 'te duo: redde duos.
Venimus huc ambo, cur non discedimus ambo?
Perfide, pars nostri, lectule, maior ubi est?'
Quid faciam? quo sola ferar? vacat insula cultu:
Non hominum video, non ego facta boum.
Omne latus terrae cingit mare: navita nusquam,
Nulla per ambiguas puppis itura vias.
Finge dari comitesque mihi ventosque ratemque,
Quid sequar? Accessus terra paterna negat.
Ut rate felici pacata per aequora labar,
Temperet ut ventos Aeolus, exul ero.
Non ego te, Crete centum digesta per urbes,
Aspiciam, puero cognita terra Iovi.
At pater et tellus iusto regnata parenti
Prodita sunt facto, nomina cara, meo,
Cum tibi, ne victor tecto morerere recurvo,
Quae regerent passus, pro duce fila dedi:
Cum mihi dicebas 'per ego ipsa pericula iuro,
Te fore, dum nostrum vivet uterque, meam.'
Vivimus, et non sum, Theseu, tua... Si modo vivis,
Femina periuri fraude sepulta viri.
Me quoque qua fratrem, mactasses, improbe, clava.
Esset quam dederas, morte soluta fides.

55 ε *incumboque toro lacrymis.* 61 εV *nusquam est.* 69 V *parente.* 73 ε *tu mihi.*

Nunc ego non tantum quae sum passura, recordor,
Sed quaecumque potest ulla relicta pati.
Occurrunt animo pereundi mille figurae:
Morsque minus poenae quam mora mortis habet.
Iam iam venturos aut hac aut suspicor illac
Qui lanient avido viscera dente, lupos.
Forsitan et fulvos tellus alat ista leones.
Quis scit an et saevam tigrida Dia ferat?
Et freta dicuntur magnas expellere phocas.
Quis vetat et gladios per latus ire meum?
Tantum ne religer dura captiva catena,
Neve traham serva grandia pensa manu:
Cui pater est Minos, cui mater filia Phoebi,
Quodque magis memini, quae tibi pacta fui.
Si mare, si terras porrectaque litora vidi,
Multa mihi terrae, multa minantur aquae.
Caelum restabat, timeo simulacra deorum.
Destituor rapidis praeda cibusque feris.
Sive colunt habitantque viri, diffidimus illis:
Externos didici laesa timere viros.
Viveret Androgeos utinam, nec facta luisses
Impia funeribus, Cecropi terra, tuis:
Nec tua mactasset nodoso stipite, Theseu,
Ardua parte virum dextera, parte bovem:
Nec tibi quae reditus monstrarent, fila dedissem.
Fila per adductas saepe recepta manus.

85 ϵV *alit.* 86 ϵV *Quis scit an haec saevas insula tigres habet.* M *tigridas insula habet.* 87 ϵ *magnos.* 93 ϵ *tango.* 99 ϵ *androgeus.* V *fata tulisses.* 100 V *impensa.*

Non equidem miror, si stat victoria tecum,
Strataque Cretaeam belua tinxit humum.
Non poterant figi praecordia ferrea cornu:
Ut te non tegeres, pectore tutus eras.
Illic tu silices, illic adamanta tulisti,
Illic qui silices, Thesea, vincat, habes.
Crudeles somni, quid me tenuistis inertem?
Aut semel aeterna nocte premenda fui.
Vos quoque crudeles, venti, nimiumque parati,
Flaminaque in lacrimas officiosa meas.
Dextera crudelis, quae me fratremque necavit,
Et data poscenti, nomen inane, fides.
In me iurarunt somnus ventusque fidesque.
Prodita sum causis una puella tribus.
Ergo ego nec lacrimas matris moritura videbo,
Nec mea qui digitis lumina condat, erit?
Spiritus infelix peregrinas ibit in auras,
Nec positos artus unguet amica manus?
Ossa superstabunt volucres inhumata marinae?
Haec sunt officiis digna sepulchra meis?
Ibis Cecropios portus, patriaque receptus
Cum steteris turbae celsus honore tuae,
Et bene narraris letum taurique virique
Sectaque per dubias saxea tecta vias,
Me quoque narrato sola tellure relictam:
Non ego sum titulis subripienda tuis.

106 ε *tinxit.* V *stravit.* MPa *texit.* 108 ε *durus.* 112 εV *at*, cf. xii. 13. 120 V *digitus.* ε *claudat.* 122 ε *non.* 126 ε *turbae...in arce.* M *turbae...in ore.* Pa *urbis ..in arce.* V *honore*, vulgo, quod praetuli: 'a triumphantibus translatio.' 129 εV *solam.*

Nec pater est Aegeus, nec tu Pittheïdos Aethrae
Filius: auctores saxa fretumque tui.
Di facerent, ut me summa de puppe videres:
Movisset vultus maesta figura tuos.
Nunc quoque non oculis, sed qua potes, aspice mente
Haerentem scopulo, quem vaga pulsat aqua:
Aspice demissos lugentis more capillos
Et tunicas lacrimis sicut ab imbre gravis.
Corpus ut inpulsae segetes aquilonibus horret,
Litteraque articulo pressa tremente labat.
Non te per meritum...quoniam male cessit...adoro:
Debita sit facto gratia nulla meo:
Sed nec poena quidem. Si non ego causa salutis,
Non tamen est, cur sis tu mihi causa necis.
Has tibi plangendo lugubria pectora lassas
Infelix tendo trans freta longa manus:
Hos tibi, qui superant, ostendo maesta capillos:
Per lacrimas oro, quas tua facta movent:
Flecte ratem, Theseu, versoque relabere velo!
Si prius occidero, tu tamen ossa feres.

XII.

MEDEA IASONI.

AT tibi Colchorum...memini...regina vacavi,
Ars mea, cum peteres, ut tibi ferret opem.

133 ε *de summa rupe.* 144 ε *tu sis.* 145 ε *lugendo.*
149 ε *ventoque relabere verso.* VM *versoque relabere vento.*
1 ε *Ut.*

Tunc quae dispensant mortalia fata sorores
Debuerant fusos evoluisse meos.
Tum potui Medea mori bene. quidquid ab illo
Produxi vitam tempore, poena fuit.
Ei mihi! cur umquam iuvenalibus acta lacertis
Phrixeam petiit Pelias arbor ovem?
Cur umquam Colchi Magnetida vidimus Argon,
Turbaque Phasiacam Graia bibistis aquam?
Cur mihi plus aequo flavi placuere capilli
Et decor et linguae gratia ficta tuae?
Aut semel in nostras quoniam nova puppis arenas
Venerat, audacis attuleratque viros,
Isset anhelatos non praemedicatus in ignes
Immemor Aesonides oraque adunca boum,
Semina iecisset, totidem sevisset et hostes,
Et caderet cultu cultor ab ipse suo.
Quantum perfidiae tecum, scelerate, perisset,
Dempta forent capiti quam mala multa meo!
Est aliqua ingrato meritum exprobrare voluptas:
Hac fruar, haec de te gaudia sola feram.
Iussus inexpertam Colchos advertere puppim,
Intrasti patriae regna beata meae.
Hoc illic Medea fui, nova nupta quod hic est.
Quam pater est illi, tam mihi dives erat.
Hic Ephyren bimarem, Scythia tenus ille nivosa
Omne tenet, Ponti qua plaga laeva iacet.

3 εPa *fila.* 6 ε *Heu.* 13 εV *at.* 17 ε *jecisset totidemque resumeret hostes.* Pa conj. *semina sevisset totidem quot semina et hostes.* M secutus sum nisi quod *jecisset* pro *sevisset* edidi secundum G et vett. Edd. 18 εV *ut.* 25 V *fui.*

Accipit hospitio iuvenes Aeeta Pelasgos,
  Et premitis pictos corpora Graia toros.
Tunc ego te vidi, tunc coepi scire, quis esses.
  Illa fuit mentis prima ruina meae.
Et vidi et perii. nec notis ignibus arsi,
  Ardet ut ad magnos pinea taeda deos.
Et formosus eras, et me mea fata trahebant.
  Abstulerant oculi lumina nostra tui.
Perfide, sensisti: quis enim bene celat amorem?
  Eminet indicio prodita flamma suo.
Dicitur interea tibi lex, ut dura ferorum
  Insolito premeres vomere colla boum.
Martis erant tauri plus quam per cornua saevi,
  Quorum terribilis spiritus ignis erat:
Aere pedes solidi, praetentaque naribus aera,
  Nigra per adflatus haec quoque facta suos.
Semina praeterea populos genitura iuberis
  Spargere devota lata per arva manu,
Qui peterent natis secum tua corpora telis:
  Illa est agricolae messis iniqua suo.
Lumina custodis, succumbere nescia somno,
  Ultimus est aliqua decipere arte labor.
Dixerat Aeetes. maesti consurgitis omnes,
  Mensaque purpureos deserit alta toros.
Quam tibi tunc longe regnum dotale Creusae
  Et socer et magni nata Creontis erant?
Tristis abis: oculis abeuntem prosequor udis,
  Et dixit tenui murmure lingua 'vale!'

29 V *excipit.* ε *juvenes pater oeta.* 31 Pa *quid.* 39 εV *dixerat interea tibi rex.* 48 V *erat.* 54 εV *erat.*

Ut positum tetigi thalamo male saucia lectum,
Acta est per lacrimas nox mihi, quanta fuit.
Ante oculos taurique meos segetesque nefandae,
Ante meos oculos pervigil anguis erat.
Hinc amor, hinc timor est: ipsum timor auget amorem.
Mane erat, et thalamo cara recepta soror
Disiectamque comas adversaque in ora iacentem
Invenit, et lacrimis omnia plena meis.
Orat opem Minyis. petit altera, et altera habebat:
Aesonio iuveni quod rogat illa, damus.
Est nemus et piceis et frondibus ilicis atrum,
Vix illuc radiis solis adire licet.
Sunt in eo... fuerant certe... delubra Dianae:
Aurea barbarica stat dea facta manu.
Noscis, an exciderunt mecum loca? Venimus illuc,
Orsus es infido sic prior ore loqui
'Ius tibi et arbitrium nostrae fortuna salutis
Tradidit, inque tua est vitaque morsque manu.
Perdere posse sat est, siquem iuvet ipsa potestas:
Sed tibi servatus gloria maior ero.
Per mala nostra precor, quorum potes esse levamen,
Per genus et numen cuncta videntis avi,
Per triplicis vultus arcanaque sacra Dianae,
Et si forte aliquos gens habet ista deos:
O virgo, miserere mei, miserere meorum:
Effice me meritis tempus in omne tuum!

58 V *tibi.* 62 Pa *est.* 65 V *habebit.* 68 ε *illud.* 69 ε *fuerantque diu.* V *sunt in eo et fuerant certe.* 71 ε *noscis an exciderant.* V *Nescio an exciderint.* 75 εV *juvat.*

Quod si forte virum non dedignare Pelasgum,...
Sed mihi tam faciles unde meosque deos?...
Spiritus ante meus tenues vanescat in auras,
Quam thalamo, nisi tu, nupta sit ulla meo:
Conscia sit Iuno, sacris praefecta maritis,
Et dea, marmorea cuius in aede sumus!'
Haec animum... et quota pars haec sunt?... movere puellae
Simplicis, et dextrae dextera iuncta meae.
Vidi etiam lacrimas. an pars est fraudis in illis?
Sic cito sum verbis capta puella tuis.
Iungis et aeripedes inadusto corpore tauros
Et solidam iusso vomere findis humum.
Arva venenatis pro semine dentibus imples:
Nascitur et gladios scutaque miles habet.
Ipsa ego, quae dederam medicamina, pallida sedi,
Cum vidi subitos arma tenere viros:
Donec terrigenae... facinus mirabile!... fratres
Inter se strictas conseruere manus.
Insopor ecce vigil squamis crepitantibus horrens
Sibilat, et torto pectore verrit humum.
Dotis opes ubi erant? ubi erat tibi regia coniunx,
Quique maris gemini distinet Isthmos aquas?
Illa ego, quae tibi sum nunc denique barbara facta,
Nunc tibi sum pauper, nunc tibi visa nocens,
Flammea subduxi medicato lumina somno,
Et tibi, quae raperes, vellera tuta dedi.

84 *e unde parabo deos.* V *deosque meos.* 85 *e vanescet.* 89 *e et quota pars horum.* V *et quota pars posset movisse.* 96 *e*V *habens.* 99 *e*V *miserabile.* 100 *e*V *in se constrictas.* 101 *e*V *Pervigil ecce draco.* Pa *Insopor ecce draco.*

Proditus est genitor, regnum patriamque reliqui,
Munus in exilio quodlibet esse tuli.
Virginitas facta est peregrini praeda latronis.
Optima cum cara matre relicta soror.
At non te fugiens sine me, germane, reliqui.
Deficit hoc uno littera nostra loco.
Quod facere ausa mea est, non audet scribere dextra,
Sic ego, sed tecum, dilaceranda fui.
Nec tamen extimui... quid enim post illa timerem?...
Credere me pelago femina, iamque nocens.
Numen ubi est? ubi di? meritas subeamus in alto,
Tu fraudis poenas, credulitatis ego.
Compressos utinam Symplegades elisissent,
Nostraque adhaererent ossibus ossa tuis,
Aut nos Scylla rapax canibus misisset edendos!
Debuit ingratis Scylla nocere viris.
Quaeque vomit totidem fluctus totidemque resorbet,
Nos quoque Trinacriae subposuisset aquae!
Sospes ad Haemonias victorque reverteris urbes:
Ponitur ad patrios aurea lana deos.
Quid referam Peliae natas pietate nocentes
Caesaque virginea membra paterna manu?
Ut culpent alii, tibi me laudare necesse est,
Pro quo sum totiens esse coacta nocens.
Ausus es... o! iusto desunt sua verba dolori...
Ausus es 'Aesonia' dicere 'cede domo!'

113 V *te non.* 118 PaM *tamque*, quod frigidum mihi videtur. εV *jamque.* 123 Pa conj. *mersisset:* sed quod e v. 126 contra MSS. affert nihili est: *quoque* enim cum *nos* non cum *supposuisset* conjungendum est. 127 ε *revertit urbes.* 128 ε *aurea preda.* V *lata.*

Iussa domo cessi, natis comitata duobus
  Et, qui me sequitur semper, amore tui.
Ut subito nostras Hymen cantatus ad aures
  Venit, et accenso lampades igne micant,
Tibiaque effundit socialia carmina vobis,
  At mihi funerea flebiliora tuba,
Pertimui, nec adhuc tantum scelus esse putabam;
  Sed tamen in toto pectore frigus erat.
Turba ruunt, et 'Hymen' clamant, 'Hymenaee' frequentant.
  Quo propior vox haec, hoc mihi peius erat.
Diversi flebant servi, lacrimasque tegebant.
  Quis vellet tanti nuntius esse mali?
Me quoque, quidquid erat, potius nescire iuvabat:
  Sed tamquam scirem, mens mea tristis erat.
Cum minor e pueris... lusus studioque videndi
  Constitit ad geminae limina prima foris...
'Hinc mihi, mater, abi! pompam pater' inquit 'Iason
  Ducit, et adiunctos aureus urguet equos.'
Protinus abscissa planxi mea pectora veste,
  Tuta nec a digitis ora fuere meis.
Ire animus mediae suadebat in agmina turbae,
  Sertaque compositis demere rapta comis.

139 ε *effudit.* 143 εV om. *et.* εV *hymenaea.* 149 Pa *cum clamore Pheres jussus.* Piget me a docto viro et de Ovidio optime merito dissidere: nihil autem video cur versus mutari debeat. Minor e pueris ('our younger child') a matre jussus qui sit tumultus speculatur et puerili studio ad ipsa limina procedit. Bene Ovidius has partes minori e pueris dedit, major enim cum rem melius intellexisset non tam subito matri nuntiaturus erat. 151 ε *hic.*

Vix me continui, quin sic laniata capillos
  Clamarem 'meus est' iniceremque manus.
Laese pater gaude. Colchi gaudete relicti.
  Inferias umbrae fratris habete mei.
Deseror, amissis regno patriaque domoque,
  Coniuge, qui nobis omnia solus erat.
Serpentes igitur potui taurosque furentes,
  Unum non potui perdomuisse virum.
Quaeque feros pepuli doctis medicatibus ignes,
  Non valeo flammas effugere ipsa meas.
Ipsi me cantus herbaeque artesque relincunt.
  Nil dea, nil Hecates sacra potentis agunt.
Non mihi grata dies. noctes vigilantur amarae,
  Et tener a misero pectore somnus abit.
Quae me non possum, potui sopire draconem.
  Utilior cuivis quam mihi cura mea est.
Quos ego servavi, pelex amplectitur artus,
  Et nostri fructus illa laboris habet.
Forsitan et, stultae dum te iactare maritae
  Quaeris et iniustis auribus apta loqui,
In faciem moresque meos nova crimina fingas.
  Rideat et vitiis laeta sit illa meis.
Rideat, et Tyrio iaceat sublimis in ostro:
  Flebit, et ardores vincet adusta meos!
Dum ferrum flammaeque aderunt sucusque veneni,
  Hostis Medeae nullus inultus erit.
Quod si forte preces praecordia ferrea tangunt,
  Nunc animis audi verba minora meis.

165 ε *rapui.* V *repuli.* 170 ε *Non...erat.* V *nec teneram misero...habet.* Pa conj. *et tener a misero...abit,* quod edidi. M *nec tener in...habet.* 177 εV *fingis.* 180 ε *vincat.*

Tam tibi sum supplex, quam tu mihi saepe fuisti:
  Nec moror ante tuos procubuisse pedes.
Si tibi sum vilis, communis respice natos:
  Saeviet in partus dira noverca meos.
Et nimium similes tibi sunt, et imagine tangor,
  Et quotiens video, lumina nostra madent.
Per superos oro, per avitae lumina flammae,
  Per meritum et natos, pignora nostra, duos:
Redde torum, pro quo tot res insana reliqui:
  Adde fidem dictis, auxiliumque refer.
Non ego te imploro contra taurosque virosque,
  Utque tua serpens victa quiescat ope.
Te peto, quem merui, quem nobis ipse dedisti,
  Cum quo sum pariter facta parente parens.
Dos ubi sit, quaeris? campo numeravimus illo,
  Qui tibi laturo vellus arandus erat.
Aureus ille aries villo spectabilis aureo,
  Dos mea: quam dicam si tibi 'redde,' neges.
Dos mea tu sospes. dos est mea Graia iuventus:
  I nunc, Sisyphias, improbe, confer opes.
Quod vivis, quod habes nuptam socerumque potentis,
  Hoc ipsum, ingratus quod potes esse, meum est.
Quos equidem actutum... Sed quid praedicere poenam
  Attinet? ingentis parturit ira minas.
Quo feret ira, sequar. facti fortasse pigebit.
  Et piget infido consuluisse viro.
Viderit ista deus, qui nunc mea pectora versat.
  Nescio quid certe mens mea maius agit.

185 εV *nam...quod.* ε om. *sum.* 197 ε *qui nobis.* 205 ε *potentē.* 207 ε *quos equidem perdam.* 208 ε *continet.*

XIII.

LAODAMIA PROTESILAO.

Mittit, et optat amans quo mittitur ire, salutem,
Haemonis Haemonio Laodamia viro.
Aulide te fama est vento retinente morari:
Ah! me cum fugeres, hic ubi ventus erat?
Tum freta debuerant vestris obsistere remis.
Illud erat saevis utile tempus aquis.
Oscula plura viro mandataque plura dedissem:
Et sunt quae volui dicere multa tibi.
Raptus es hinc praeceps, et qui tua vela vocaret,
Quem cuperent nautae, non ego, ventus erat.
Ventus erat nautis aptus, non aptus amanti:
Solvor ab amplexu, Protesilae, tuo,
Linguaque mandantis verba imperfecta reliquit:
Vix illud potui dicere triste vale.
Incubuit boreas, abreptaque vela tetendit:
Iamque meus longe Protesilaus erat.
Dum potui spectare virum spectare iuvabat:
Sumque tuos oculos usque secuta meis.
Ut te non poteram, poteram tua vela videre,
Vela diu vultus detinuere meos.
At postquam nec te, nec vela fugacia vidi,
Et quod spectarem, nil nisi pontus erat,
Lux quoque tecum abiit, tenebrisque exanguis obortis
Succiduo dicor procubuisse genu.

4 ϵ *ha!* 5 ϵ *tunc.* 8 ϵV *plura.* 13 ϵV *mandatis.*

Vix socer Iphiclus, vix me grandaevus Acastus,
Vix mater gelida maesta refecit aqua.
Officium fecere pium, sed inutile nobis.
Indignor miserae non licuisse mori.
Ut rediit animus, pariter rediere dolores.
Pectora legitimus casta momordit amor.
Nec mihi pectendos cura est praebere capillos,
Nec libet aurata corpora veste tegi.
Ut quas pampinea tetigisse Bicorniger hasta
Creditur, huc illuc, qua furor egit, eo.
Conveniunt matres Phylaceïdes, et mihi clamant
'Indue regales, Laodamia, sinus!'
Scilicet ipsa geram saturatas murice lanas,
Bella sub Iliacis moenibus ille gerat?
Ipsa comas pectar, galea caput ille prematur:
Ipsa novas vestes, dura vir arma ferat?
Qua possum, squalore tuos imitata labores
Dicar, et haec belli tempora tristis agam.
Dyspari Priamide, damno formose tuorum,
Tam sis hostis iners, quam malus hospes eras.
Aut te Taenariae faciem culpasse maritae,
Aut illi vellem displicuisse tuam.
Tu, qui pro rapta nimium, Menelae, laboras,
Ei mihi quam multis flebilis ultor eris!
Di, precor, a nobis omen removete sinistrum,
Et sua det reduci vir meus arma Iovi.

29 εV *utque animus rediit.* 34 V *quo.* 35 ε *phylacidis.* 37 εV *vestes.* 38 ε *ipse.* εV *geret.* 39 εV *premetur.* 40 εV *feret.* 41 εV *quo.* 43 εV *dux Pari.* 45 ε *at.* 48 ε *heu.*

Sed timeo, quotiens subiit miserabile bellum;
More nivis lacrimae sole madentis eunt.
Ilion et Tenedos Simoisque et Xanthus et Ide
Nomina sunt ipso paene timenda sono.
Nec rapere ausurus, nisi se defendere posset,
Hospes erat. vires noverat ille suas.
Venerat, ut fama est, multo spectabilis auro,
Quique suo Phrygias corpore ferret opes,
Classe virisque potens, per quae fera bella geruntur,
Et sequitur regni pars quota quemque sui?
His ego te victam, consors Ledaea gemellis,
Suspicor. haec Danais posse nocere puto.
Hectora nescio quem timeo: Paris Hectora dixit
Ferrea sanguinea bella movere manu.
Hectora, quisquis is est, si sum tibi cara, caveto:
Signatum memori pectore nomen habe.
Hunc ubi vitaris, alios vitare memento,
Et multos illic Hectoras esse puta:
Et facito ut dicas, quotiens pugnare parabis,
'Parcere me iussit Laodamia sibi.'
Si cadere Argolico fas est sub milite Troiam,
Te quoque non ullum vulnus habente cadat.
Pugnet et adversos tendat Menelaus in hostis:
Hostibus e mediis nupta petenda viro est.
Causa tua est dispar. tu tantum vivere pugna,
Inque pios dominae posse redire sinus.
Parcite, Dardanidae, de tot, precor, hostibus uni,
Ne meus ex illo corpore sanguis eat.

51 ε *quotiens que subit.* 53 V *ida.* 72 Madv. *cadet.* 73 in εV sequuntur *Ut rapiat Paridi quam Paris ante sibi. Irruat et causa qui vincit vincat et armis.*

Non est, quem deceat nudo concurrere ferro,
Saevaque in obpositos pectora ferre viros.
Fortius ille potest multo, quam pugnat, amare.
Bella gerant alii: Protesilaus amet.
Nunc fateor; volui revocare, animusque ferebat:
Substitit auspicii lingua timore mali.
Cum foribus velles ad Troiam exire paternis,
Pes tuus offenso limine signa dedit.
Ut vidi, ingemui tacitoque in pectore dixi
'Signa reversuri sint, precor, ista viri!'
Haec tibi nunc refero, ne sis animosus in armis.
Fac meus in ventos hic timor omnis eat.
Sors quoque nescio quem fato designat iniquo,
Qui primus Danaum Troada tangat humum.
Infelix, quae prima virum lugebit ademptum!
Di faciant, ne tu strenuus esse velis!
Inter mille rates tua sit millensima puppis,
Iamque fatigatas ultima verset aquas.
Hoc quoque praemoneo. de nave novissimus exi:
Non est, quo properas, terra paterna tibi.
Cum venies, remoque move veloque carinam,
Inque tuo celerem litore siste gradum!
Sive latet Phoebus, seu terris altior exstat,
Tu mihi luce dolor, tu mihi nocte venis.
Aucupor in lecto mendaces caelibe somnos.
Dum careo veris, gaudia falsa iuvant.
Sed tua cur nobis pallens occurrit imago?
Cur venit ah! verbis multa querella tuis?

83 εV *qui pugnat amore.* 88 V *limite.* 94 εV *tanget.* 100 VM *properes.* Madv. *properas.* 110 Sic Madv. εVM. *cur venit a verbis.* Pa *cur venit a verbis muta querella latens* quem sequi non ausus sum.

Excutior somno, simulacraque noctis adoro:
Nulla caret fumo Thessalis ara meo:
Tura damus, lacrimamque super, qua sparsa relucet,
Ut solet adfuso surgere flamma mero.
Quando ego, te reducem cupidis amplexa lacertis,
Languida laetitia solvar ab ipsa mea?
Quando erit, ut lecto mecum bene iunctus in uno
Militiae referas splendida facta tuae?
Quae mihi dum referes, quamvis audire iuvabit,
Multa tamen rapies oscula, multa dabis.
Semper in his apte narrantia verba resistunt:
Promptior est dulci lingua refecta mora.
Sed cum Troia subit, subeunt ventique fretumque,
Spes bona sollicito victa timore cadit.
Hoc quoque, quod venti prohibent exire carinas,
Me movet: invitis ire paratis aquis.
Quis velit in patriam vento prohibente reverti?
A patria pelago vela vetante datis!
Ipse suam non praebet iter Neptunus ad urbem.
Quo ruitis? Vestras quisque redite domos!
Quo ruitis, Danai? Ventos audite vetantis!
Non subiti casus, numinis ista mora est.
Quid petitur tanto nisi turpis adultera bello?
Dum licet, Inachiae vertite vela rates!
Sed quid ago revocans? omen revocantis abesto,
Blandaque compositas aura secundet aquas.

113 ε *quae.* 114 V *a fuso.* 116 ε *tristitia.* 122 εVM *referre.* Pa Madv. *refecta.* 135 ε *Sed quid ego revoco? levum procul omen abesto.* V *sed quid ego revoco haec? omen revocantis abesto.* MPa *sed quid ago? revoco? revocaminis omen abesto!* Cur G deseratur equidem non video.

Troasin invideo, quae sic lacrimosa suorum
Funera conspicient, nec procul hostis erit.
Ipsa suis manibus forti nova nupta marito
Imponet galeam barbaraque arma dabit.
Arma dabit, dumque arma dabit, simul oscula sumet:
Hoc genus officii dulce duobus erit...
Producetque virum, dabit et mandata reverti,
Et dicet 'referas ista fac arma Iovi!'
Ille, ferens dominae mandata recentia secum
Pugnabit caute, respicietque domum.
Exuet haec reduci clipeum, galeamque resolvet,
Excipietque suo corpora lassa sinu.
Nos sumus incertae. nos anxius omnia cogit,
Quae possunt fieri, facta putare timor.
Dum tamen arma geres diverso miles in orbe,
Quae referat vultus est mihi cera tuos.
Illi blanditias, illi tibi debita verba
Dicimus, amplexus accipit illa meos.
Crede mihi, plus est quam quod videatur imago:
Adde sonum cerae, Protesilaus erit.
Hanc specto, teneoque sinu pro coniuge vero,
Et, tamquam possit verba referre, queror.
Per reditus corpusque tuum, mea numina, iuro,
Perque pares animi coniugiique faces,
Perque, quod ut videam canis albere capillis,
Quod tecum possis ipse referre, caput,
Me tibi venturam comitem, quocumque vocaris,
Sive... quod heu timeo, sive superstes eris.
Ultima mandato claudetur epistula parvo:
Si tibi cura mei, sit tibi cura tui!

137 εV *Troadas*. 147 εV *exeret et*. 166 εM *sit tibi...sit mihi*. Pa *si tibi* e nonnull. codd. cui assentior.

XIV.

HYPERMNESTRA LYNCEO.

Mittit Hypermnestra de tot modo fratribus uni.
Cetera nuptarum crimine turba iacet.
Clausa domo teneor gravibusque coercita vinclis:
Est mihi supplicii causa, fuisse piam.
Quod manus extimuit iugulo demittere ferrum,
Sum rea: laudarer, si scelus ausa forem.
Esse ream praestat, quam sic placuisse parenti.
Non piget inmunes caedis habere manus.
Me pater igne licet, quem non violavimus, urat,
Quaeque aderant sacris, tendat in ora faces:
Aut illo iugulet, quem non bene tradidit ensem,
Ut qua non cecidit vir nece, nupta cadam:
Non tamen, ut dicant morientia 'paenitet' ora,
Efficiet. non est, quam piget esse piam.
Paeniteat sceleris Danaum saevasque sorores.
Hic solet eventus facta nefanda sequi.
Cor pavet admonitu temeratae sanguine noctis,
Et subitus dextrae praepedit orsa tremor.
Quam tu caede putes fungi potuisse mariti,
Scribere de facta non sibi caede timet.
Sed tamen experiar. Modo facta crepuscula terris,
Ultima pars lucis, primaque noctis erat:
Ducimur Inachides magni sub tecta Pelasgi,
Et socer armatas accipit ipse nurus.

1 εV *hypermestra.* Sic ubique. 3 ε *durisque.* 5 εV *dimittere.* 12 ε *cadat.* 14 Madv. *pia.* 15 ε *danaum sceleris.* 17 ε *attonitu.* 18 ε *timor.* 22 εV *noctis...lucis.* 24 ε *ille.*

Undique conlucent praecinctae lampades auro:
  Dantur in invitos impia tura focos:
Vulgus 'Hymen, Hymenaee' vocant. fugit ille vocantis,
  Ipsa Iovis coniunx cessit ab urbe sua.
Ecce mero dubii, comitum clamore frequentes,
  Flore novo madidas impediente comas,
In thalamos laeti... thalamos, sua busta!... feruntur,
  Strataque corporibus, funere digna, premunt.
Iamque cibo vinoque graves somnoque iacebant,
  Securumque quies alta per Argos erat:
Circum me gemitus morientum audire videbar...
  Et tamen audieram, quodque verebar, erat.
Sanguis abit, mentemque calor corpusque relinquit,
  Inque novo iacui frigida facta toro.
Ut leni zephyro graciles vibrantur aristae,
  Frigida populeas ut quatit aura comas,
Aut sic, aut etiam tremui magis. Ipse iacebas,
  Quaeque tibi dederam vina, soporis erant.
Excussere metum violenti iussa parentis:
  Erigor, et capio tela tremente manu.
Non ego falsa loquar. ter acutum sustulit ensem,
  Ter male sublato reccidit ense manus.
Admovi iugulo... sine me tibi vera fateri...
  Admovi iugulo tela paterna tuo:
Sed timor et pietas crudelibus obstitit ausis,
  Castaque mandatum dextra refugit opus.

27 εV *hymenea.* 31 ε *in thalamos laeti juvenes.* 42 Pa *plena.* Vide quod explicavit ille. Mihi quidem falsum esse eo videtur, quod Hypermnestra non dormit sed trepida vigilat. 46 ε *Concidit.* V *decidit.* Pa *recidit.* *Reccidit=rececidit;* ut *rettulit* pro *retetulit.*

Purpureos laniata sinus, laniata capillos
Exiguo dixi talia verba sono
'Saevus, Hypermnestra, pater est tibi. iussa parentis
Effice. germanis sit comes iste suis.
Femina sum et virgo, natura mitis et annis:
Non faciunt molles ad fera tela manus.
Quin age, dumque iacet, fortis imitare sorores:
Credibile est caesos omnibus esse viros.
Si manus haec aliquam posset committere caedem,
Morte foret dominae sanguinolenta suae.
Aut meruere necem patruelia regna tenendo
Quae tamen externis danda forent generis?
Finge viros meruisse mori. quid fecimus ipsae?
Quo mihi commisso non licet esse piae?
Quid mihi cum ferro? quid bellica tela puellae?
Aptior est digitis lana colusque meis.'
Haec ego. dumque queror, lacrimae sua verba sequuntur
Deque meis oculis in tua membra cadunt.
Dum petis amplexus sopitaque bracchia iactas,
Paene manus telo saucia facta tua est.
Iamque patrem famulosque patris lucemque timebam.
Expulerunt somnos haec mea dicta tuos,
'Surge age, Belide, de tot modo fratribus unus!
Nox tibi; ni properas: ista perennis erit.'
Territus exsurgis; fugit omnis inertia somni:
Aspicis in timida fortia tela manu.

61 ε *haut.* V *quid.* 62 Pa *regna tenenda forent.* Locus ut videtur corruptus: nihil autem muto quum nihil exploratum habeo. 63 ε *necem.* 64 εV *piam.* 67 ε *mea.* 72 εV *expulerant.*

Quaerenti causam 'dum nox sinit, effuge' dixi:
'Dum nox atra sinit, tu fugis, ipsa moror.'
Mane erat, et Danaus generos ex caede iacentis
Dinumerat. summae criminis unus abes.
Fert male cognatae iacturam mortis in uno,
Et queritur facti sanguinis esse parum.
Abstrahor a patriis pedibus, raptamque capillis...
Haec meruit pietas praemia... carcer habet.
Scilicet ex illo Iunonia permanet ira,
Quo bos ex homine est, ex bove facta dea.
At satis est poenae teneram mugisse puellam,
Nec, modo formosam, posse placere Iovi.
Adstitit in ripa liquidi nova vacca parentis,
Cornuaque in patriis non sua vidit aquis:
Conatoque queri mugitus edidit ore,
Territaque est forma, territa voce sua.
Quid furis, infelix? quid te miraris in umbra?
Quid numeras factos ad nova membra pedes?
Illa Iovis magni pelex metuenda sorori,
Fronde levas nimiam caespitibusque famem:
Fonte bibis, spectasque tuam stupefacta figuram,
Et, te ne feriant quae geris arma, times.
Quaeque modo, ut posses etiam Iove digna videri,
Dives eras, nuda nuda recumbis humo.
Per mare, per terras cognataque flumina curris:
Dat mare, dant amnes, dat tibi terra viam.
Quae tibi causa fugae? Quid, Io, freta longa pererras?
Non poteris vultus effugere ipsa tuos.

82 V *factum.* 86 Madv. *quom.* 87 ε *An.* V *ah!*
91 εV *et conata.* 100 ε *uda.*

Inachi, quo properas? eadem sequerisque fugisque:
Tu tibi dux comiti, tu comes ipsa duci.
Per septem Nilus portus emissus in aequor
Exuit insanae pelicis ora bovis.
Ultima quid referam, quorum mihi cana senectus
Auctor? Dant anni, quod querar, ecce mei.
Bella pater patruusque gerunt: regnoque domoque
Pellimur: eiectos ultimus orbis habet.
Ille ferox solio solus sceptroque potitur:
Cum sene nos inopi turba vagamur inops.
De fratrum populo pars exiguissima restat.
Quique dati leto, quaeque dedere, fleo.
Nam mihi quot fratres, totidem periere sorores:
Accipiat lacrimas utraque turba meas.
En ego, quod vivis, poenae crucianda reservor:
Quid fiet sonti, cum rea laudis agar,
Et consanguinéae quondam centensima turbae
Infelix uno fratre manente cadam.
At tu, siqua piae, Lynceu, tibi cura sororis,
Quaeque tibi tribui munera, dignus habes,
Vel fer opem, vel dede neci; defunctaque vita
Corpora furtivis insuper adde rogis,
Et sepeli lacrimis perfusa fidelibus ossa,
Sculptaque sint titulo nostra sepulchra brevi
'Exul Hypermnestra... pretium pietatis iniquum...
Quam mortem fratri depulit, ipsa tulit.'
Scribere plura libet, sed pondere lassa catenae
Est manus, et vires subtrahit ipse timor.

112 εV *ejectas.* 113 εV *solus solio.* 131 M *lupsa.*

NOTES

I.

PENELOPE ULYSSI.

Troy has fallen after a ten years' siege. The surviving Greek warriors have returned to their various cities. Penelope has been told of all that happened at Troy; of her husband's deeds and of his safety; but still he does not return. Nearly ten years have passed since the fall of Troy, and no news can be obtained of him. She has sent to Sparta and to Pylos for information in vain. Every captain whose ship has touched at Ithaca has been questioned, and entrusted with a letter for the absent king on the chance of meeting with him. But still the terrible uncertainty remains, still Penelope is a mourning widow, beset by greedy suitors who devour her substance, and with no protection but her young son and the aged Laertes. Her father too is pressing her to reckon her husband as dead, and marry one of the suitors. Still she is faithful to her absent lord, and writes once more in words of longing and love. The Epistle must be supposed to be written just at the end of the ten years' wandering, and on the eve of Ulysses' return, if v. 99, 100 is to be pressed.

[The materials for this Epistle are to be found in the Odyssey: but Ovid uses them freely and without caring much for consistency. For instance, Telemachus who at the opening of the Odyssey has evidently arrived at man's estate, holding his own against the suitors, and taking part in the agora, is spoken of as a *puer* v. 98. And in v. 15 Penelope speaks of him as *sent* in quest of his father, whereas he is said in the Odyssey to have gone without her knowledge.]

1. **hanc**, sc. *epistolam*, cf. 10, 3. **lento** 'loitering.' *Lentus* (lenitus) means first 'flexible' as leather or a twig. Then by an easy transition metaphorically 'inactive,' 'otiose,' 'wanting in vigour.' Cf. 66.

2. 'Send me no answer in words, but let your answer be your own presence.' This arrangement of the words is the only one with any authority, though it must be confessed to be somewhat awkward and wanting in point. Palmer's reading *ut tamen* is however open to much objection on the score of the order of words.

4. **vix tanti fuit** 'was scarcely worth such a price,' *i.e.* your absence. The subject is here *Priamus Trojaque*. Sometimes it is a sentence, as in Cic. *Cat.* 2, 7 *Est mihi tanti, Quirites, hujus invidiae tempestatem subire* and 7, 45. Vid. Roby, § 1192.

5. Ovid is fond of the combination **tum cum**, which being purely temporal is always followed by the indicative. Vid. 3, 23. 5, 109.

6. **insanis** as applied to the sea is metaphorical, 'raging.' 7. 53 *insana quid aequora possent. Ep.* 18, 28 *insani freti.* Bentley according to Jahn wished to write *incanis*, because the waves would have been far from 'insane' to drown an adulterer! A warning to conjectural emendators.

7. **frigida** 'cold with grief and solitude,' cf. 10, 49.

8. **non quererer** 'I had not now been complaining.' The tense implies that the complaint is still of daily occurrence, and is even then as she writes being uttered. In verse 10, by using the pluperf. **lassasset** she speaks of the task as over, at any rate for the time. This has from very old times been changed to *lassaret*, from the idea of representing the spinning as still going on.

9. **spatiosam fallere noctem** 'to beguile the long long night.' Ovid uses *spatiosus* of *senectus*, *Met.* 12, 186. *vetustas*, *Met.* 15, 623. *aevum*, *Met.* 8, 529. *bellum*, *Met.* 13, 206. *tempus*, *Am.* 1, 8, 81. All referring to time: a use which seems almost peculiar to him.

10. **pendula tela**: *tela* is the 'warp,' the upright threads into which the 'weft' is woven. *pendula* refers to this upright position: elsewhere Ovid calls it *stans*, *recta*, *Met.* 4, 275. *Fast.* 3, 819. See Rich. The mode of weaving and the difference between *tela* and *subtemen* may be learnt by studying Ov. *Met.* 6, 55, sq. *Tela jugo vincta est; stamen secernit arundo: Inseritur medium radiis subtemen acutis, &c.*

The story of Penelope's ruse to put off the suitors until she had woven a shroud for Laertes, and of which she undid by night as much as she had woven by day, is told in the Odyssey, 11, 85—109. But Ovid does not seem to refer directly to this. He only takes the general fact, often alluded to in Homer, of

Penelope being engaged with the loom, and represents her as working at night to beguile the long hours of sleeplessness.

I have however sometimes thought that Ovid may really be referring to this midnight unravelling of the work. I have thought so for two reasons. (1) It seems strange that Ovid should pass over such an incident in Penelope's life. (2) The epithet *pendula* very ill describes the warp as fastened on the loom. *Pendulus* means 'hanging loose down'. So Ovid *F.* 4, 386 has *pendula Libra. Met.* 7, 117 *palearia p.* This would exactly represent the position of the cloth when *unfastened at one end* to allow of unravelling the work. *Tela* would then represent the woven cloth, and *pendula* cease to be a merely ornamental epithet.

11. **quando** 'when?' is properly interrogative, and when used of time can only be employed in interrogative sentences, direct or indirect.

14. 'At the mention of Hector's name I was ever pale.' **in nomine**, lit. 'in the case of his name:' so *in pelice saevae Met.* 4, 547.

15. Another instance of the carelessness with which Ovid uses his authority: for in Homer *Odyss.* 4, 187 Antilochus is said to be killed by Memnon, τόν ῥ' Ἠοῦς ἔκτεινε φαεινῆς ἀγλαὸς υἱός, nor is there any trace of a variation in the story in other writers.

17. **Menoetiaden**: Patroclus son of Menoetius. **falsis sub armis**: 'in armour not his own,' alluding to the wearing the armour of Achilles by Patroclus on the day on which he was killed. *Il.* 16, 64, sq.

18. 'I wept to think that stratagem (in which you excel all men) could lack success.'

19. Tlepolemus was killed by Sarpedon king of Lycia. *Il.* 5, 628—665.

23. **deus aequus** 'the friendly god.' *F.* 6, 766 *per volucres aequos multa monere deos. Tr.* 1, 1, 45 *judex mirabitur aequus.*

27. **nymphae** 'the nymphs receive gifts in gratitude for the safety of their husbands.' This is Palmer's interpretation [*Hermathene* xx. p. 104], and is much better than the old way of explaining *nymphae* as 'brides,' a sense in which it does not occur elsewhere. He quotes Propert. 4, 4, 25; we may add *Odyss.* xiv. 435, where the swineherd offers to the Nymphs and Hermes for the safe return of Odysseus.

grata dona 'thank-offerings.'

28. **illi**: the warriors. 'They joyfully proclaim that the fates of Troy have yielded to their own.' The notion of one person's luck being stronger than another's is illustrated by Loers from *Aen.* 7, 293 *fatis contraria nostris Fata Phrygum.* And Valer. Fl. 7, 446 *fatis sum victa suis.* So a man may conquer his own unkindly star, *Aen.* 11, 16 *vivendo vici mea fata.*

29. **iusti senes**: from the notion of the elders of the city acting as senators, magistrates, &c. It is the natural epithet for *senex*, cf. *F.* 4, 524. *Met.* 8, 704.

30. **pendet ab ore** 'hangs upon the lips,' so Virg. *Aen.* 4, 79 *pendetque iterum narrantis ab ore*, where Conington quotes the Greek phrase κρέμασθαι ἔκ τινος.

31—32. **mensa...posita**: 'when the dessert is on the table,' *i.e.* when the *secunda mensa* is put before the guests. The table or a tray was brought in ready set out, and removed afterwards, so *Met.* 13, 676 *somnum mensa petiere remota.* The habit of drawing plans of battles, &c., with the finger dipped in wine is referred to again in *Amor.* 2, 5, 17 *mensa conscripta mero. Tr.* 2, 454 *tacitam mensae duxit in orbe notam.* So Tibull. 1, 10, 31 *Ut mihi potanti possit sua dicere facta Miles et in mensa pingere castra mero.*

33. **Sigeia tellus**: the town and promontory of Sigeum, near which most of the Homeric battles were fought, and where Achilles was buried. Cf. *M.* 12, 71 *jam Sigaea rubebant litora.*

35. **Aeacides**: Achilles, grandson of Aeacus. **tendebat** 'used to pitch his tent.' Virg. *Aen.* 2, 29 *hic saevus tendebat Achilles*, ib. 8, 605 *legio latis tendebat in arvis.*

36. **admissos** 'galloping at full speed:' used in 2, 114, metaphorically of a rapid stream. Cf. *Am.* 3, 2, 78 *evolat admissis discolor agmen equis.*

37—8. Ovid again uses his authority loosely, for Telemachus went of his own accord, or at the instigation of Pallas, without his mother's knowledge. Nestor's narrative to Telemachus is in *Odyss.* 4, 101—200.

quaerere misso 'sent to seek.' The infin. of the purpose is not uncommon in Ovid. Cf. *Met.* 5, 660 *misit Mopsopium juvenem sacros agitare jugales.*

39—40. The story of the slaughter of Rhesus and Dolon by Ulysses and Diomede in their night expedition is told in *Il.* 10, 331—502. Rhesus king of the Thracians is killed by Diomede as he sleeps (v. 495—6); Dolon is met by the heroes on the way, and perhaps may be said to have perished *dolo*, because they lie hid to let him pass before attacking him (349—351), and afterwards Ulysses seems to promise him his life (383). But it is not without reason that the reading *dolo* has been doubted.

40. **hic...ille** 'the former,' 'the latter.' Sometimes reversed, cf. 9, 24; sometimes expressed by *ille—ille*, 3, 27.

41. **nimium nimiumque**: repetition implying impassioned earnestness. We may compare *A. A.* 2, 127 *iterumque iterumque*. Tib. 3, 6, 21 *Convenit iratus nimium nimiumque severos*. *Tr.* 5, 6, 35 *Elige nostrorum minimum minimumque laborum*. Cf. 2, 129.

42. **Thracia tangere castra** 'to enter the Thracian camp:' referring still to the above-mentioned expedition of Ulysses and Diomede. **tangere** 'to enter' is rather a favourite expression of Ovid's. Cf. 6, 24. 12, 57. 13, 94. *A. A.* 3, 748 *ut tangat portus fessa carina suos*. *Met.* 6, 601 *ut sensit tetigisse domum Philomela nefandam*. *Trist.* 3, 1, 71 *nec me... Atria libertas tangere passa sua est*.

43. **tot.** According to Homer, Diomede kills twelve men, whom Ulysses draws out of the way as fast as they are killed, and while Diomede is killing the thirteenth, Rhesus, Ulysses is securing his horses. *Il.* 10, 483—489.

uno. Diomede.

45. **micuere sinus** 'my breast palpitated with fear.' *sinus* for *pectora* is rare; cf. 2, 37, and 3, 132, if *sinu* is there right. *Micare* is properly 'to move quickly,' 'to twinkle,' hence 'to shine.' Ovid often uses it of the palpitation of fear, *F.* 3, 36 *terreor admonitu corque timore micat*. Ib. 331 *corda micant regis*. So of the throbbing of the uncovered veins of Marsyas, *Met.* 6, 389 *trepidae sine ulla pelle micant venae*. And of the pricking up of the ears of a horse, *micat auribus*, Virg. *G.* 3, 84.

amicum agmen: *i.e.* the Greek host.

46. **Ismariis**: *i.e.* the horses of the Thracian Rhesus. Ismarus is a mountain and town of Thrace. Notice that it is the constant habit of Roman poets to use a name which properly belongs to some mountain, river, or town for the whole country in which they lie. Thus in the next Epistle *Rhodopeia* means Thracian, from Mt Rhodope. In Virg. *G.* 2, 30 *Niphates* a river in Armenia stands for Armenia, or rather the Armenians. Illustrations may be gathered from almost every Latin poem.

47. **vestris** 'of you Greeks,' not 'of you, Ulysses;' which would require *tuis*. Cf. 75.

48. 'And that all is level ground which once was a city wall.' *Atque solum quo Troja fuit, Aen.* 10, 60. (Loers.)

50. **virque carendus abest** 'and I must for ever submit to my husband's absence.' The ordinary construction is the impersonal one, *Tr.* 1, 5, 83 *mihi patria tellure carendum est.* Ter. *Haut.* 400 *mihi tui carendum erat.* Cic. *Tusc.* 1, 12, 26 *sensu carendum esse.* Cp. Ov. *A. A.* 3, 65 *utendum est aetate tua.* But the passive use of the gerend of a verb governing the ablative is not uncommon. See Plaut. Trin. 1159. Cic. de Sen. § 57 *ad quem fruendum*, and Att. 13, 39 *ad patrem domo sibi carendum.* Plautus and Terence construct *fruor* and *fungor* indifferently with ablative and accusative, and *utendus* is used by Ovid (*A. A.* 1, 433) and Plautus (*Pers.* 1, 3, 38) as a passive. So *fruendus* in the spurious (?) Epist. 20, 118 *servetur facies ista fruenda mihi.* But *id quod amo careo* (Plaut. *Curc.* 1, 2, 46) is probably a case of attraction. Roby, *L. G.* vol. 2. p. lxxvii.

dempto fine 'for ever,' cf. *Tr.* 3, 11, 2 *meque reum dempto fine cruentus agas.*

52. 'Which the conqueror, turned settler, ploughs with the oxen he has taken from the conquered foe.' We do not hear of any of the Greeks colonising the Troad; but it was the frequent habit of the Romans to do so in the case of conquered countries.

53—4. **seges** 'a cornfield.' **resecandaque** &c.: 'and the soil fattened with Trojan blood and calling for the sickle overflows with its harvest.' **luxuriat** may be applied either to the soil, as here, or to the crop, as in *A. A.* 1, 360 *ut seges in pingui luxuriabit humo.*

57. **victor abes.** 'Though a conqueror you return not.'

58. **quo orbe** 'in what part of the world.' So in *Trist.* 3, 1, 26 *longinquo referam lassus ab orbe pedem.* Infr. 13, 151 *diverso miles in orbe.*

63—4. **Pylon...misimus** 'I have sent to Pylos and to old Nestor's land, the land of Neleus.' Neleus was father to Nestor. This refers again to Telemachus' expedition, as do the next two lines; which we have already said (vid. v. 37) was not made under Penelope's direction.

antiqui Nestoris: *antiquus* for *vetus* can only be justified on the ground that Nestor having outlived three generations of men (*Il.* 1, 250) might be regarded not only as old, but as a man of a past age. (Loers.)

65. **Sparte** is the Greek form. Ovid seems to use it invariably and not *Sparta.* Virg. *Aen.* 2, 577 has *Spartam.*

66. **lentus**, see on 1.

67. **moenia Phoebi**: *i.e.* the walls of Troy built by Apollo and Neptune for Laomedon; cf. 5, 139.

69—70. 'If my prayers had not been answered, and Troy had not fallen, I at least should have known where you were fighting, and should have had nothing worse than war to fear, and my complaint would have been uttered in common with many others.'

For the tenses cf. 7—10.

71. **demens** 'distraught with grief.'

72. **in** 'for.' Cf. 2, 44. 5, 58. **area** 'field,' a word which Ovid is fond of using both in simple and metaphorical sense; *Tr.* 4, 3, 84 *et patet in laudes area lata tuas.* *Am.* 3, 1, 26 *Haec animo, dices, area facta meo est.* It seems to be derived from the idea of an open space suited for a battle: *Am.* 3, 15 *Corniger increpuit thyrso graviore Lyaeus: pulsanda est magnis area major equis.* Cf. *F.* 5, 707 *Liber ab arboribus locus est, apta area pugnae.* It is properly any open space in a town. Vid. Rich.

75. **quae vestra libido est** 'such is the incontinence of you men.' The plural *vestra* is used because she is speaking not only of Ulysses but of men generally, vid. 47.

quae—est 'such is, &c.' Cf. *ex P.* 1, 7, 59 *quaeque tua est pietas...jus aliquod tecum fratris amicus habet.* *Ex P.* 2, 2, 21 *quaeque tua est pietas...te laedi, cum quis laeditur inde, putas.*

77—8. **forsitan**: generally with subjunctive. See index.

rustica 'homely,' with none of the accomplishments of a town-bred woman. It is opposed to *procax* in *Am.* 2, 4, 13. Ovid seems to use it elsewhere to mean 'prudish,' *Rem.* 329 *Et poterit dici petulans quae rustica non est; et poterit dici rustica si qua proba est.*

quae tantum,...sinat 'whose only accomplishment is to dress her rough wools.' *Rudes lanae* seems to mean wool in its rough state before it is spun. *A. A.* 2, 219 *Inter Ioniacas calathum tenuisse puellas Creditur, et lanas excoluisse rudes.* But there is also perhaps allusion to the meaning of *rustica*.

80. 'And may it not be the case that though free to return, you choose to remain away!' **revertendi liber** 'free in regard to returning.' Cf. 5, 147 *utilis medendi*, ib. 150 *prudens artis.* *F.* 3, 383 *Mamurius morum fabraene exactior artis?* *Tr.* 1, 3, 7 *mens apta parandi.* See my note on Ter. *Haut.* 727. Munro on Lucr. 1, 137. Roby § 1321.

81. **Icarius**, father of Penelope, is mentioned in *Odyss.* 1, 329 and elsewhere. Her mother Periboea is only mentioned in later writers; while according to other traditions she was not Periboea but Polycaste.

82. **cogit** 'tries to compel me.'

83. **licet** admits the infin. or subj. with or without *ut*. Cf. 3, 81. **oportet** admits the infinitive, or subjunctive *without ut*.

86. **vires temperat ipse suas** 'and refrains—even he—from putting all the pressure on me that he might,' *i.e.* if he used his parental authority. She is referring to *cogit* in 82, and *ipse* is emphatic and has almost the sense of *ultro*, 'not only I resist, but *he* too sees himself the necessity of refraining.'

87—9. Ovid follows the Odyssey in these names and in the substance of the complaint.

ὅσσοι γὰρ νήσοισιν ἐπικρατέουσιν ἄριστοι
Δουλιχίῳ τε Σάμῃ τε καὶ ὑλήεντι Ζακύνθῳ,
τόσσοι μητέρ' ἐμὴν μνῶνται, τρύχουσι δὲ οἶκον.
τοὶ δὲ φθινύθουσιν ἔδοντες
οἶκον ἐμόν· τάχα δή με διαρραίσουσι καὶ αὐτόν.

Odyss. 16, 121.

90. **viscera nostra &c.** 'your goods, our very vitals, are torn to pieces and devoured as by beasts of prey.' The word *dilacerantur* is used as suiting *viscera* in apposition to *opes.* Cf. *Tr.* 1, 7, 20 *libellos Imposui rapidis viscera nostra rogis.* The fact that Ovid never elsewhere uses *viscera* for 'heart,' is a strong if not conclusive argument against Palmer's translation, 'My heart is rent, your wealth is squandered.' I do not think that any instance is to be found in other writers either of *viscera* used for heart; whereas there is an exactly parallel use of it, for 'means,' 'substance,' in Cic. *Q. Fr.* 1, 3, 7 *de visceribus tuis.*

91—2. **Pisander** and **Polybus** are named in *Odyss.* 22, 243.

Medonta is a mistake for Ἀμφιμέδοντα, *Od.* 22, 242.

The name Μέδων occurs elsewhere in the Odyssey, but not as one of the suitors: another instance of the laxity with which Ovid uses his authority.

Eurymachus, one of the suitors slain by Ulysses, *Odyss.* 22, 81.

Antinous, the first of the suitors slain, *Od.* 22, 15, sq.

93. **turpiter** 'to your dishonour,' to be joined with *absens.* It does not imply anything criminal on the part of Ulysses, but indicates the result of his absence, whether voluntary or not, as

bringing shame to him. It may be compared with such uses of *male* as that in 7, 54 *quam male credis* 'with what ill results do you trust.'

94. **partis tuo s.** 'obtained by your blood,' *i.e.* in war and danger. Cf. *Tr.* 4, 4, 59 *sunt circa gentes quae praedam sanguine quaerunt.* (Loers.)

95. **Irus egens,** Ἶρος ἀλήτης *Od.* 18, 25. The description of him at the beginning of the 18th Odyss. will best illustrate what Ovid is thinking of.

ἦλθε δ' ἐπὶ πτωχὸς πανδήμιος, ὃς κατὰ ἄστυ
πτωχεύεσκ' Ἰθάκης, μετὰ δ' ἔπρεπε γαστέρι μάργῃ
ἀζηχὲς φαγέμεν καὶ πιέμεν.

Melanthius, the goatherd of Ulysses. *Od.* 17, 247.

96. **ultimus pudor** 'add the finishing stroke of dishonour to your losses.' *Pudor* is in apposition to *Irus* and *Melanthius.*

accedere in occurs in *Fast.* 3, 164 *in lustrum accedere debet una dies.* But **in tua damna** also indicates the end arrived at, cf. 4, 16. 5, 58. For the sense of **ultimus** cf. 12, 50 *ultimus labor.*

99—100. The plot of the suitors to kill Telemachus is described in *Odyss.* 15 and 16. It takes place on his return, when he has already been recognised by his father, who has also returned. This, if Ovid cared to be consistent, dates the letter on the very eve of Ulysses' restoration; in which case Telemachus ought certainly not to be called *puer.* But the poet is not much concerned as to consistency.

per insidias 'by treachery,' cf. *per facinus* 12, 6; *per jurgia Tr.* 5, 11, 1; *places raras dotata per artes Am.* 2, 4, 17.

invitis omnibus seems to refer to the dislike of the suitors to Telemachus' expedition, *Odyss.* 2, 303 sq.

101. **ordine** 'in their due order,' *i.e.* the elder dying before the younger. Loers aptly quotes Tacitus *Ann.* 16, 11 *servavitque ordinem fortuna, ac seniores prius, tum cui prima aetas exstinguuntur.*

103—4. **hinc faciunt** 'the neatherd (Philaetius) and the old nurse (Euryclea) and thirdly the faithful keeper of the stye (Eumaeus) all act on this side,' *i.e.* they all faithfully protect your son and preserve your estate against the suitors. For *faciunt* cf. 2, 39. Palmer gives a similar explanation, in preference to the old reading *hoc faciunt* which was interpreted as = *hoc precantur.*

cura for *curator*; cf. *mora*=id quod moratur *Am.* 2, 11, 15; *consilium*=adviser *F.* 3, 274; *Cui deus, 'en adsum tibi cura fidelior,' inquit, A. A.* 1, 555, though *cura* may there mean 'lover.'

tertius is only equivalent to another conjunction, cf. *Tr.* 2, 1, 53 *Per mare per terras per tertia numina juro*, and is masculine because *cura* stands for Emmaeus.

108. **erat** for *esset*. Cf. 112. 11, 56. 'His is now just the age that should have had a father's protection,' Liv. 37, 36 *Ad Hellespontum obsistendum erat...si pacem petituri eratis*, and other examples in Roby § 1533. It is more particularly frequent with the gerundive [16, 152 *tam bona constanter preda tenenda fuit*] and the future participle, *Tr.* 1, 6, 14 *in mea venturus, si paterere, fuit*, 1, 7, 40 *emendaturus, si licuisset, eram.*

109. **vires pellere** 'strength to repel.' *Pellere* is equivalent to *pellendi* or *ad pellendum*. Cf. *vires currendi, Am.* 4, 6, 70; *vires dictandi, Tr.* 3, 3, 86.

110. **ara** 'an altar of refuge;' *Tr.* 4, 5, 2 *Unica fortunis ara reperta meis*, an intelligible metaphor, which *aura*, the reading of many MSS., is not; although rather naturally suggested by the close neighbourhood of *portus*.

112. 'Who ought to have been trained when young to imitate his father's character.' Elsewhere Ovid uses *erudio* differently. *M.* 8, 215 *damnosas erudit artes. F.* 3, 294 *Atque ita qua possint erudit arte capi.* Ib. 820 *erudit percurrere.* **artes** are *qualities aequired*, hence, taken together, they represent what we call 'character.' *F.* 2, 508 *et patrias artes militiamque colant.* Virg. *G.* 3, 101 speaks of the *artes* of a horse.

114. **extremum fati sustinet diem** 'prolongs his last hours and will not end them,' cf. 3, 142. One of those pregnant expressions in which Ovid delights. The notion seems to be that Laertes has reached his destined day of death, and yet prolongs it in order to live long enough to let Ulysses close his eyes. The various passages quoted in illustration seem not parallel; for in each *sustinet* governs some word such as *animam, spiritus*, &c., which does not require any pregnant sense to be attached to *sustinere*. The nearest is Livy 2, 65, *rem sustinendo* 'by keeping the business going.'

116. **ut** 'even though,' cf. 2, 137. 3, 134. 6, 108. 7, 15, 21, 55, 147. 10, 65. From which instances it will be seen that this use of *ut*, not uncommon in other writers, is a peculiarly favourite one with Ovid.

II.

PHYLLIS DEMOPHOONTI.

PHYLLIS queen of Thrace, daughter of Sithon, received Demophoon son of Theseus on his way home from the Trojan war. They became enamoured and Demophoon promised her marriage. After some time Demophoon set sail to Athens, promising to return in a month; but three months had passed and the fourth was drawing to a close, and yet he had not returned. Phyllis writes this letter, reproaching him with his ingratitude and his perfidy, reminding him of his vows of affection, her own services and favours, and expressing her despair and determination to die.

[The story is completed by Servius. Phyllis hanged herself, and over her tomb a tree grew which at a particular season of the year grew wet as with tears. Another tradition was that Phyllis was changed by the Gods into an almond tree, and that Demophoon landing in Thrace soon afterwards, and embracing the tree then bare of leaves, it suddenly shot forth its blossoms. A pretty fable founded on the fact of the almond tree blossoming before its leaves come on.]

'Phyllida Demophoon praesens moderatius ussit:
Exarsit velis acrius illa datis.'

A. A. 2, 352.

1. **Rhodopeia**: *i.e.* Thracian, see on 1, 45.

3. **cornua...coissent** 'had met to form the full moon,' cf. *M.* 2, 344 *Luna quater junctis implerat cornibus orbem*, ib. 7, 79 *Tres aberant noctes ut cornua tota coirent efficerentque orbem*, ib. 529 *junctis implevit cornibus orbem Luna.*

4. 'Your anchor was due by promise to my shores.' **pacta** is from *pango*, vid. index. According to one account which Ovid follows in *Rem.* 591—607 Phyllis hangs herself on the day appointed for Demophoon's return after waiting in vain for him. But he has chosen to vary the story here, to give more vraisemblance to the Epistle.

6. **Actaeas**: *i.e.* Athenian. Attica is called *Actaea* from ἀκτή a shore. *M.* 1, 313 *Separat Aonios Actaeis Phocis ab arvis*, and often elsewhere in Ovid.

Sithonis 'Thracian.' From Sithon father of Phyllis. So in *Ep.* 11, 13 *Sithonius Aquilo.* Sithonia is properly a district in Thrace, the middle one of the three Chalcidian peninsulas.

9—10. Hope too was long-enduring. Slowly do we believe what pains us when believed. But now even in spite of lover's incredulity they reach her heart.

lentus passes from the sense of 'flaccid,' 'immoveable' to a better one of 'enduring,' 'persistent.' Vid. on 1, 1.

invita et amante 'though as a lover she is unwilling to believe these things, yet they pain her,' *i.e.* because she believes in spite of herself. The sense is not very clear, and the reading doubtful. But I cannot think that either Palmer or Merkel has improved it.

12. 'I often thought when the south wind blew up for a storm that it was wafting back your white sails.' The south wind would set shoreward, and be peculiarly the harbinger of storms, as in the Adriatic. Cf. *Arbiter Hadriae* Hor. *O.* 1, 3, 15. She was *mendax* to herself, even so far as to think he would come in a storm.

13. **Thesea devovi** 'I cursed Theseus.' Lit. 'devoted to the infernal gods.' There does not seem any allusion to magical arts here,—though the word is used in that sense also. Vid. 6, 91. For the sense of 'curse,' cf. *ex P.* 2, 9, 41 *Quis non Antiphaten Lestrygona devovet? A. A.* 3, 241 *devovet ut tangit dominae caput.* **quia nollet** 'because (as I thought) he would not.'

14. **nec** 'and yet after all perhaps he did not detain you.' Cf. 8, 60.

10—14. When it is stormy she at one time curses Theseus for detaining him; at another, fears that he has set out but has been shipwrecked. 15—20. When the weather is favourable she thinks that only ill-health could be detaining him, and beseeches the gods in his favour.

15. **dum vada tendis ad Hebri** 'while on your way to Thrace.' The Hebrus rises in Mt Haemus, and flows into the Aegean, and is here put poetically for Thrace generally. Vid. 1, 46.

16. **cana**: *i.e.* 'stormy,' cf. 3, 65. 5, 54 (Loers).

17—20. 'Often in suppliant terms I earnestly besought the gods with prayer at their altars of incense, that you, oh base one, might be well;—often when I saw the sky and sea unruffled by the winds, I said to my own heart, "If he is well he will come."'

18. **devenerata** for *devenerata sum:* as 7, 59 *laesus* for *laesus fuerit.* 9, 160 *insidiata* for *insidiata esse. De-* is intensive as in *deperire*, *demereor*, see index. Roby § 1918.

turicremis: *A. A.* 3, 393 *Visite turicremas vaccae Memphitidos aras.*

19. **caelo pelagoque** I regard as datives after *faventes.* 'The winds favouring the sky and sea' seems to mean that they leave the sky and sea in their natural and unruffled state.

20. **venit** 'he will come.' The present is used idiomatically to represent a future that is certain, a use particularly common in colloquial Latin, see Terence *Haut.* 804 *ecfero*, 'I will bring it out directly,' cf. ib. 872, 931. And our own idiom, *e.g.* in N. T. 'The first said, *I go, Sir*, and went not.'

22. 'And I was ingenious at finding reasons for your absence,' *ingeniosa ad causas reperiendas.* Cf. *F.* 4, 684 *ad segetes ingeniosus ager.* *M.* 11, 313 *Nascitur Autolycus furtum ingeniosus ad omne*, cf. 6, 117. *Ibis* 186 *Aeacus in poenas ingeniosus erat.*

23. **lentus**, cf. 1, 1. **iurata numina** 'all your oaths by the gods,' cf. *A.* 3, 11, 22 *quid referam......et perjuratos in mea damna deos.* *Met.* 2, 46 *Dis juranda palus.* Elsewhere *juratus* is applied to the person bound by the oath, 'sworn.'

25. 'Oh Demophoon, you gave your promises to the winds to which you spread your sails.' Cf. 7, 8 *Atque idem venti vela fidemque ferent?* *R.* 286 *Irrita cum velis verba tulere noti.* *M.* 8, 134 *an inania venti Verba ferunt idemque tuas, ingrate, carinas?* The idea of scattering words and promises to the winds is common to the Poets, *e.g.* Prop. 3, 24, 8 *quidquid jurarunt ventus et unda rapit.* Tib. 1, 4, 21 *Veneris perjuria venti irrita per terras et freta summa ferunt.*

28. **crimine**=*amore*, cf. 4, 25. **demeruisse** 'to have thoroughly deserved you,' cf. on 18.

30. 'But this wrong-doing has (or ought to have with *you*) all the weight and semblance of a virtue.'

instar as a substantive, cf. *Art. A.* 3, 490 *Sed tamen Aetnaei fulminis instar habet.*

31. **iura**, *i.e. jura lecti*, cf. 9, 159.

32. **plurimus in ore** 'ever on your lips.' Cf. *M.* 11, 562 *sed plurima nautis in ore Halcyone conjux.* *Tr.* 4, 10, 128 *in toto plurimus orbe legor.* Am. 1, 15, 18 *multus legar.* In a different sense, vid. 4, 167.

33. **socios in annos** 'to last for years of wedlock.' *In* with words expressing time expresses extension up to a limit. For socios, cf. *sociae leges*, 4, 62; *socios deos*, 5, 126. *Hymenaeus* (1) the god of marriage, (2) the marriage hymn. Here used for 'marriage.'

34. 'Which was my only surety, my only pledge of marriage.' Referring to the *sponsalia*, or betrothal, in which a woman's father or legal guardian would contract her to the man. If for any cause the marriage then arranged did not take place, there might be a legal investigation, and damages assessed against the intending bridegroom or the guardian according as the *judex* decided that the fault lay with the one or the other (vid. Aul. Gell. 4, 4). Accordingly no doubt some security was given by both parties. Phyllis seems to mean that the only security given in her case was Demophoon's promise. One of the many legal allusions in this book. Cf. on 8, 16.

35—44. 'You swore by every god, by everything most sacred. So many oaths have been broken by you that your single punishment could hardly make satisfaction for them all.'

37—8. **tuum...avum**, *i.e.* Neptune. Theseus was the son of Aegeus, but was reputed to be the son of Neptune. Phyllis therefore is made to express the common doubt as to the pedigree of Demophoon. **mulcet**: cf. *M.* 1, 331 *positoque tricuspide telo Mulcet aquas rector pelagi.*

39. 'By Venus' and by Cupid's weapons which are too powerful with me.' *facere* 'to do anything to a person' may be followed by the dative, by the ablative with *de*, by the simple ablative. Cf. Ter. *Haut.* 317 *quid facias illo?* Ov. *Am.* 1, 10, 8 *et quidquid magno de Jove fecit amor.* For *facere* used with dative, Heinsius quotes Prop. 3, 1, 20 *non faciet capiti dura corona meo.* Cp. Hor. *Ep.* 1, 11, 17.

40. **altera tela, &c.**: Cupid is represented with bow and arrows and a torch. For the repetition of the word, characteristic of Ovid, cf. 2, 62. 3, 8—10, 140. 4, 144. 5, 8, 120. 8, 80. 9, 146—152, 158, 164. 13, 166.

41. 'And by Juno, who is the kindly guardian of the marriage couch,' cf. 12, 87 *Conscia sit Juno sacris praefecta maritis*; *ex P.* 3, 1, 73 *exigit hoc socialis amor foedusque maritum.*

42. **et per taediferae, &c.**: *i.e.* by *Ceres*, referring to the torch-light processions in the Eleusinian mysteries. Cf. *F.* 3, 786 *taedifera dea.* The custom is fabled to have originated in Ceres' search for Proserpine, *F.* 4, 494 *Illic accendit geminas pro lampade pinus; Hinc Cereris sacris nunc quoque taeda datur.*

44. **in poenas** 'to pay the penalties,' cf. 1, 72. *Ibis* 160 *et brevior poena vita futura tua est.*

45. **at** 'nay more, in my mad folly I also repaired your shattered ships.' *Ex P.* 2, 3, 28 *in mediis lacera nave relinquor aquis.* *Tr.* 5, 7, 35 *Euboicis lacerata est fluctibus...puppis.*

47. **remigium** 'oars.' Virg. *Aen.* 8. 80 *remigioque aptat.* Though in *Aen.* 3, 470, *remigium supplet,* he seems to mean 'rowers.' And this meaning Heinsius would give here.

48. Cf. *Am.* 2, 19, 34 *ei mihi, ne monitis torquear ipse meis.*

49. **copia,** sc. *est,* cf. 3, 48.

50. 'I believed in your profession of a divine pedigree,' cf. 37. **generi numinibusque**: an hendiadys for *generis numinibus.* Palmer reads *nominibus,* which would make very good sense, but I prefer to abide by the MSS.

53. **dis quoque** 'I believed too in your oaths,' lit. in the gods by whom you swore, cf. 35—42.

quo iam tot pignora nobis 'what use, pray, were all those pledges?' *pignora* is accusative. Cf. *A.* 2, 19, 7 *Quo mihi fortunam, quae nunquam fallere curet?* ib. 3, 4, 41 *quo tibi formosam, si non nisi casta placebat?* Hor. *Epist.* 1, 5, 12 *Quo mihi fortunam, si non conceditur uti?*.

54. **parte qualibet inde** 'by any fraction of them you pleased.' *inde=pignorum* or *e pignoribus.* Cf. Mart. 1, 43, 9 *Nudus aper...et nihil inde datur.* ib. 9, 59, 7 *inde satur.* Ter. *Ad.* 1, 1, 21 *nati filii duo, inde majorem adoptavi.*

55. 'I am not distressed at having assisted you with harbourage and lodging,' cf. 6, 55. **locus,** 'a place to remain in,' *Tr.* 4, 2, 58 *erepti nobis jus habet illa loci.*

56. **meriti** 'of my services,' cf. 30.

57. **cumulasse hospitium** 'it repents me that to my shame I completed my hospitality by wedding you.' For *cumulasse,* cf. 9, 20. It gives an idea of something supererogatory.

58. Cf. Tib. 1, 8, 20 *sed femori conseruisse femur.*

62. **aequa** 'justifiable,' 'just.' *Met.* 7, 174 *nec tu petis aequa.* For repetition of *venit,* cf. 5, 8 *quae venit indigne poena dolenda venit,* and note on sup. 40. The adjective is nearly equivalent to an adverb, cf. *A.* 2, 10, 4 *duas uno tempore turpis amo.*

63—4. **non est operosa gloria** ''tis a cheaply earned reputation.' *Operosus*=(1) 'industrious' (of persons), *A.* 2, 10, 5 *operosae cultibus ambae,* (2) the cause or material of industry, *A. A.* 1, 695 *Reice succinctos operoso stamine fusos,* hence, 'made with much labour,' *Met.* 1, 258 *mundi moles operosa,* (3) 'difficult,' 'troublesome,' *ex P.* 4, 10, 81 *res non operosa volenti.*

favore 'respect,' 'consideration.' *Tr.* 5, 3, 53 *vestrum merui candore favorem.*

65—66. 'I was deceived by your words, as was natural both in a woman and a lover; God grant that you may earn no better fame than this;' *i.e.* of having deceived a trusting woman, which after all is a disgrace. For *summa* 'utmost extent' cf. sup. 56. 14, 80. And for another meaning of it 7, 12.

67—74. 'At Athens you should have a statue put up with an inscription detailing all the mighty deeds of your father Theseus, and concluding with a verse describing your own famous achievement, "This is he by whose treachery a woman who entertained and loved him was betrayed."'

inter Aegidas: among the statues of others of your family, the descendants of Aegeus, father of Theseus, who is called *Aegides* in 4, 59.

68. **titulis** in its proper sense of 'inscription.'

69. **Sciron lectus** 'when the destruction of Sciron has been read of in the inscription.' A pregnant use of *legor*, see on 3, 13. **Sciron**, a robber infesting Megara, slain by Theseus.

Procrustes, son of Neptune, who put all his captives on his bed, stretching out those who were too short, and cutting off the legs of those too long for it; he was killed by Theseus.

70. **Sinis**, called πιτυοκάμπτης 'the pine-bender.' He lived on the Isthmus of Corinth, and used to bend down two pines and fasten a leg of a captive to each tree; the pines springing up rent the body in twain. Killed by Theseus.

tauri—viri, *i.e.* the Minotaur slain by Theseus.

71. **domitae Thebae** 'the conquest of Thebes,' in a war against Creon king of Thebes for refusing burial to the Argives. The subject of Euripides' ἱκετίδες.

bimembres 'the Centaurs,' conquered by Theseus at the marriage of Pirithous.

72. **pulsata nigri regia dei** 'knocked at:' referring to Theseus' descent to Hades to carry off Proserpine for Pirithous (*amatorem Pirithoum* Hor. *Od.* 3, 4, 80).

The same feats of Theseus are detailed in *Met.* 7, 436,

tellus Epidauria per te
Clavigeram vidit Vulcani occumbere prolem:
Vidit et immitem Cephesias ora Procrusten:
Cercyonis letum vidit Cerealis Eleusin.

Occidit ille Sinis, magnis male viribus usus;
Qui poterat curvare trabes, et agebat ab alto
Ad terram late sparsuras corpora pinus.
Tutus ad Alcathoën Lelegeïa moenia limes
Composito Scirone patet...
...scopulis nomen Scironis inhaeret.

72. 'And the dark palace of the gloomy god at whose doors he knocked.' Cf. *M.* 5, 448 *parvas fores pulsavit.*

75—6. 'Although your father performed so many heroic actions, the only one you have taken to heart and imitated is his abandonment of Ariadne.' **sedit** 'deeply impressed itself,' cf. *Rem.* 108, 268 *pectore sedit amor.* **Cressa,** *i.e.* Ariadne, abandoned by Theseus in Naxos.

77. **excusat** 'has reason to find excuses for,' 'is ashamed of.' Statius (*Silv.* 4, 6, 70) seems to have imitated this use, *Magnoque ex agmine laudum Fertur Thebanos tantum excusasse triumphos.*

78. 'Oh false one, you act the part of heir to your father's treachery.'

agere heredem: *agere partes* occurs several times in Ovid, *e.g.* infr. 8, 41. But the accusative of the person played is not so common, *A. A.* 1, 611 *est tibi agendus amans imitandaque vulnera verbis;* it belongs to the Comic writers, *e.g.* Ter. *Haut.* 39—40 *Ne sycophanta impudens avarus leno assidue sint agendi mihi.*

79. **illa:** sc. Ariadne, who wedded Bacchus after her desertion by Theseus.

80. 'And sits aloft on the chariot drawn by harnessed tigers.' **tigribus** is put for chariot and tigers, as *equi* stands for chariot and horses, Virg. *G.* 3, 358 *invectus equis.*

capistratis: the *capistrum* is a halter or head-stall. Vid. Rich. *M.* 10, 125 *frenabas ora capistris.* In Virg. *G.* 3, 399 *capistra* are nose-pieces with spikes put on young animals to prevent their sucking their dams. In the Vàtican bas-relief of Ariadne and Bacchus they appear to be collars of vine-branches.

82. **quod ferar:** the subj. because the rumour is alleged by the Thraces as their reason. Cf. 9, 27.

83—5. 'Let her follow her husband to Athens, that land of learning, we can get another to be king of Thrace.. The result will show the wisdom of her choice.' Spoken in bitter irony.

The speaker means she will find that it would have been wiser to have wedded one of her own country. Ovid in making the Thracian speak ironically of Athens as *doctae* is thinking of Athens as it came to be in historical times. Prop. 4, 21, 1 *ad doctus proficisci cogor Athenas.* **jam nunc** is used in impatient irony, like *i nunc.* See on 3, 26.

84. **armigeram...erit** 'someone else will be found to be king of warlike Thrace.' **regat** the subj. after the limiting or defining relative.

exitus acta probat seems a kind of proverb like *eventus stultorum magister* Livy 22, 39.

86. **notanda** 'to be branded.' **ab eventu** 'in accordance with their result.'

87—8. 'Why, if you were to appear in our waters again, the very men who cry out upon my folly would say I had acted wisely for myself and my people.'

The argument is: 'I know I ran a risk in trusting to your honour, but these people are not entitled to charge me with folly, for if you proved true and all turned out well they would declare that I had shown a prudent boldness.'

89. **nec te mea regia tanget** 'nor will my palace attract you again.' Cp. 5, 81, and see Index.

The connection of the couplet with the preceding is this. These men have no right to charge me with folly, for if you *did* return they would say I had been wise; but in point of fact I have not been wise, for you will not return.

90. **Bistonia**: Thracian. The Thracians are called *Bistones* from a town and district said to have been founded by Biston, son of Mars. There was also a lake *Bistonis* near Abdera.

fessa 'tired with your voyage from Athens.' **fessaque** 'nor will you wash your tired limbs': for *que* following negative, cf. 7, 82.

91—98. 'Ever before my eyes is the scene of our parting: your embraces, your tears, your lamentations that the winds were favourable for your voyage, your entreaties that I should await with confidence your return.'

99—100. 'But how can I feel any confidence in your return?

You meant when you went never to come back. You lied to me when you said the weather was favourable for your departure.'

91. **oculis inhaeret**: *Tr.* 4, 3, 19 *Vultibus illa tuis tanquam praesentibus haeret.* 1, 6, 3 *pectoribus tu nostris, uxor, inhaeres.*

92. **premeret portus** 'when your fleet on the point of starting was riding in my harbour.' *Premerent portus* seems to be a condensed expression for *in portu premerent terram vel litus* 'in harbour and close to shore.' Cf. *Met.* 14, 416 *presserat occiduus Tartesia litora Phoebus* 'was close upon.'

94. **per longas moras**: cf. on 1, 99. 'And to join your lips to mine with lingering pressure.'

98. **face** for *fac* is the more usual form in Plautus, but is rare in later Latin. For the construction of *facere* with subj. without *ut* cf. supr. 66. 13, 92, 144.

100. **expectem**: subj. used in rhetorical questions, or, questions implying a negation. Zumpt, § 530. See index.

101—2. 'Yet in spite of its futility I do expect you. Return however late. Let your pledged word be only forfeited so far as the date of your coming is concerned,' *i.e.* you promised to come within a month, that pledge is broken, but you can still keep your promise of return, though not at the time named.

modo is to be taken with *redeas.* **lapsa sit** is used as a word suitable to the gliding by of time, for *fides* really means the promise to return at a certain *time.* *F.* 6, 771 *tempora labuntur.*

105. **utque...excidimus** 'and since I have fallen from your remembrance,' 'been forgotten.' Loers quotes Hom. *Il.* 23, 595 ἐκ θυμοῦ πεσεῖν. Cf. also infr. 12, 71. *Tr.* 4, 5, 10 *excidit heu nomen quam mihi paene tuum.* Tib. 3, 1, 20 *an toto pectore deciderim.*

nullam...Phyllida 'no such person as Phyllis.'

107. 'I am she, Demophoon, who when you had been drifting in long wandering ways gave you a Thracian harbour and entertainment.'

109—110. 'You—whose scanty means mine augmented, you to whom in your poverty I in my wealth gave many a boon and would have given many more.'

The relative passes irregularly to refer to Demophoon: a transition caused by the impassioned nature of the address as Palmer says. In the next line it goes back again to Phyllis.

111. **Lycurgus**, son of Dryas, a king of Thrace and persecutor of the followers of Bacchus, and slain by that god, *Thracis et exitium Lycurgi* Hor. *O.* 2, 19, 16.

112. 'A kingdom scarcely fit to be ruled by a woman.' **apta regi** : cf. *ferre apta* 9, 116. **nomine femineo**=*a feminâ.* So *nomen Romanum, Latinum, Aeolium* for *Romani, Latini, Aeolii.* For the ablat. of agent without preposition, see index.

113—114. *i. e.* all Thrace. Thrace corresponds nearly to the modern Roumelia. **Haemus** is the Balkan range on the North separating Thracia from Scythia. **Rhodope** is a branch of the same range, hence fabled to be daughter of Haemus, and extending to the S.E. (mod. Despoto Dagh). The **Hebrus** (mod. Maritza) rises in the Haemus range and falls into the Aegean Sea, near Aenus (Enos). It is called **sacer** from the Bacchic orgies celebrated near it. In *F.* 3, 737 he calls it *arenosus.* It is a swift river, *volucer Hebrus* Virg. *Aen.* 1, 317.

admissas 'at full speed,' a metaphor from driving horses, cf. 1, 36.

115. **cui** 'You, Demophoon, for whom my maiden state was first resigned.' From its sense of 'offering firstfruits' *libata* here signifies the first marriage of a maiden. Cf. 4, 27.

avibus sinistris: the omens were taken at a marriage, the *auspex* attending for the purpose. Juv. 10, 336 *veniet cum signatoribus auspex.* *M.* 6, 433 *Hac ave conjuncti Progne Tereusque.* Birds on the left hand were an evil omen, but lightning on the left a good omen, *tonitrus sinistri, Tr.* 1, 9, 49. There seem however to have been wide differences among experts on the subject. Cic. *de Div.* 2, 39.

116. **recincta** 'unfastened.' A bride's dress was fastened round the waist by a woollen girdle *cingulum*, the untying of which was a part of the solemn ceremony. Loers quotes *Odyss.* 11, 244 λῦσε δὲ παρθενίην ζώνην. Cp. Eur. Alc. 117.

117. **pronuba** 'Tisiphone the Fury presided at our marriage,' *i.e.* instead of Juno; cf. 6, 43. *Pronuba* also means the matron who conducted the bride to the *thalamus.* Ramsay p. 424.

118. **devia avis** the screech-owl, a bird of ill-omen. *M.* 10, 453 *ter omen Funereus bubo letali carmine fecit.* *Devia* 'lonely,'

shunning the haunts of men in the daytime. *Ex P.* 3, 1, 27 *regio ab omni devia cursu.*

119. **Allecto** 'the Fury with her collar of short adders.' Hor. *Epod.* 5, 15 *Canidia brevibus implicata viperis crines.* Cf. 6, 45.

120. 'And our marriage-torches waved, but the brand was snatched from a funeral pile.' **mota** refers to waving of the torches to keep them alight, *A.* 1, 2, 11 *vidi ego jactatas mota face crescere flammas, et vidi nullo concutiente mori.* The marriage procession to the bridegroom's house was at night, and therefore torches formed part of the necessary accompaniments. Cf. 12, 137. 6, 46. Anything connected with funeral ceremonies would be of bad omen at a marriage, especially that the torches should have been taken from or lighted at a funeral pile. Cf. *M.* 6, 430 *Eumenides tenuere faces de funere raptas.* Ovid is fond of contrasting the ceremonies of marriage and death: for instances in these Epistles see 12, 140. 14, 10, 32 and *Rem.* 38 *non tua fax avidos digna subire rogos.*

sepulchrali face: the ablative expresses the material, 'torches consisting of brands from the funeral pyre.' Such an ablative may often conveniently be translated as though in apposition to the word it describes.

121—2. 'I tread wearily over rocks and bushy shores, and wherever the broad seas lie open to my eyes.' 10, 25 *mons fuit, apparent frutices in vertice rari,* would seem to confirm Merkel's reading *culmina,* if it were not that *culmina* is not properly used of a mountain. Phyllis is climbing to all points of vantage, where she may take a wide view, cf. 10, 29 *late Aequora prospectu metior alta meo:* sometimes she comes down to the shore, sometimes climbs to the cliff. **calco** is not a usual word for 'walking:' it seems to refer to the heavy step of a weary person.

124. *i.e.* to see whether the wind was favourable for your return voyage.

126. 'I at once conjecture them to be the answers of the gods to my wishes,' lit. 'the gods propitious to me.' This is a difficult phrase, but I cannot think with Palmer that *meos deos* = 'my ship,' the images of the gods on the stern being put for the whole vessel. It is rather to be explained by 12, 84 *Sed mihi tam faciles unde meosque deos.*

128. **mobile**: referring to the constant ebb and flow of the billows on the beach.

129—130. **minus et minus**: cf. 1, 42. **utilis** 'mistress of my limbs.' **linquor** 'I faint.' Cf. Tac. *A.* 3, 46 *quasi exanimes linquebantur.*

131. **modice** 'with a gradual curve.' Cf. *M.* 11, 229 *Est sinus Haemoniae curvos falcatus in arcus: Brachia procurrunt.*

132. **rigent** 'stand sheer up,' *M.* 11, 150 *riget arduus alto Tmolus in ascensu.*

137. **ut** 'though,' see on 1, 116. 'Though in hardness you surpass iron and adamant and even yourself.' Cf. 10, 110. *Am.* 3, 7, 57 *illa graves potuit quercus adamantaque durum Surdaque blanditiis saxa movere suis.*

adamas (*ἀδάμας*) is properly the hardest steel, and then used poetically for the hardest conceivable substance.

141—2. 'My neck too, because it yielded itself to the embraces of your faithless arms, I long to tie close with a halter.'

praebuĕrunt: Heinsius at 7, 166 collects a great number of instances of this license in Ovid: *steterunt, quaesierunt, exciderunt, absciderunt, horruerunt, expulerunt, fuerunt, mollierunt, profuerunt, contigerunt, annuerunt, audierunt, finierunt, polluerunt.*

For the construction **praebere nectenda** cf. 13, 31.

143. **stat** 'I am resolved to atone for my frailty by an early death.' For *stat* cf. *F.* 4, 602 *statque semel juncti rumpere vincla tori.* For *pensare* *M.* 13, 192 *laudem cum sanguine penset.* **tenerum pudorem** 'frail modesty' stands for 'the frailty of my modesty.' *tener* is here that which is easily dissolved, as he speaks of snow *ad Liv.* 102 *Solvuntur tenerae vere tepente nives.*

144. 'There shall be but small delay in choosing.'

futura est=*erit*, cf. 7, 86.

145. **invidiosa** 'calculated to draw hatred upon you,' cf. 7, 120. 8, 49

147—8. For a similar inscription cf. 7, 195.

III.

BRISEIS ACHILLI.

When Agamemnon had been forced in obedience to Calchas to send Chryseis back to her father, he consoled himself by taking Briseis from Achilles. And she was accordingly taken from the tent of Achilles by the heralds Talthybius and Eurybates (*Il.* 1, 217—350). When Achilles in wrath abstained from the battle, and the Greeks accordingly suffered defeats, Agamemnon sends Ajax, Ulysses, and Phoenix to offer him reparation, and the restoration of Briseis, if he will fight. But Achilles refuses (*Il.* 9, 162—429).

Ovid acting on the statement (*Il.* 1, 348) that Briseis went from Achilles 'unwillingly' imagines her to be writing this loving and reproachful letter immediately after the failure of the deputation, when Achilles might have recovered her.

ἡ δ' ἀέκουσ' ἅμα τοῖσι γυνὴ κίεν.

1—2. **rapta** alludes to Briseis being taken by force from Achilles, **barbarica** to her having been originally a captive and not a Greek. She was daughter of Briseus of Lyrnesus (*Il.* 2, 690) in Cilicia, which was plundered by Achilles, *Met.* 12, 108 *cum Lyrnesia primus Moenia disjeci.*

3—4. 'The blots you see are tear-stains, but my tears speak for me.' *Tr.* 1, 1, 12 *Neve liturarum pudeat: qui viderit illas de lacrimis factas sentiet ille meis.* Ib. 3, 1, 15 *littera suffusas quod habet maculosa lituras, laesit opus lacrimis ipse poeta suum.*

pondera 'force.' Cf. 2, 30.

5—6. 'About you my master and husband.' Ovid is fond of thus repeating his words. Instances will be found in vv. 8, 9, 140 of this Epist. and in 2, 99. 4, 44. 5, 120. 8, 80. 13, 166. Cf. *Am.* 2, 5, 59 *non oscula tantum Juncta queror: quamvis haec quoque juncta queror.*

7. **regi**: sc. Agamemnon.

8. **quamvis...tua est**: 'In Lucretius and post-Ciceronian writers (rarely in Livy) *quamvis* is found with the indicative.' Roby § 1627. Ovid uses it with both subjunctive and indicative, but with the former it means 'even if' (as a supposition); with the latter 'however much' 'although' (as a fact). Consider the distinction of meaning in these two lines:

'quid enim servare laboret
Unde nihil, *quamvis non tueare*, perit?'
(*Am.* 2, 2, 11.)
'*quamvis ingenio non valet*, arte valet.'
(*Am.* 1, 15, 14.)

9—10. The heralds sent by Agamemnon to fetch Briseis. *Il.* 1, 320.

11—12. 'Turning their eyes the one upon the other's countenance they seemed silently to ask, where was now our love.'

quaerebant: the imperf. used in graphic description, as of a picture &c. **ubi**: cf. 2, 31.

13. **differri potui** 'my surrender might have been put off.' Another instance of Ovid's fondness for using words in a pregnant sense, cf. 1, 114, and *Met.* 12, 76 *decimum dilatus in annum Hector erat*, 'Hector's death had been put off to the tenth year.'

16. 'In my misery I thought I was once more being made a captive,' *i.e.* as when you originally captured me.

17—20. Briseis says, I often thought of giving my conductor the slip and going back to you: but in the eyes of a frightened girl there was always some enemy at hand to catch her. If (instead of returning to you) I had gone forward I feared that I should during the night be picked up by some roving Trojans and carried as a present to one of Priam's daughters-in-law.

v. 18 has been misunderstood from not noticing the emphasis on *timidam*: the *hostis* is quite general and may refer to either Greek or Trojan, whichever impeded her return to Achilles. 'There was an enemy to catch poor frightened me (I thought).'

21. 'But granted that I was given because it was necessary that I should be given; still I have been away many nights, and yet you make no effort to recover me.'

noctibus not *noctes*. The *noctes* are regarded as separate points of time.

22. **lenta** 'slow to be roused,' cf. 2, 9.

23—4. **in aurem dixit** 'whispered to me,' cf. Hor. *S.* 1, 9, 9 *in aurem dicere nescio quid puero.*

Menoetiades: Patroclus, son of Menoetius. He is commissioned by Achilles to bring out and deliver up Briseis, *Il.* 1, 345.

25. **parum** 'not enough,' cf. 9, 47.

pugnas, ne reddar 'you even make efforts to prevent my restoration.' Cf. *Rem.* 122 *pugnat in adversas ire natator aquas.* She refers to Achilles' rejection of the proposals of the ambassadors sent by Agamemnon.

26. **i nunc**: a formula introducing a forcible expression of irony or contempt, summing up previous arguments, expressed or implied. Cf. 4, 127. 12, 204. *A. A.* 2, 636 *i nunc claude fores, custos odiose puellae.* Mart. 2, 6, 1 *i nunc edere me jube libellos.* Juv. 10, 310 *i nunc et juvenis specie laetare tui.* Sometimes without *nunc.* *Am.* 3, 3, 1 *Esse deos, i, crede! fidem jurata fefellit et facies illi quae fuit ante manet.* Juv. 10, 166 *i demens et saevas curre per Alpes.*

27—8. **Telamone et A. n.** Ajax and Phoenix. *Il.* 9, 168.

ille—ille for *hic—ille*, cf. *Tr.* 1, 10, 50 *illa suos habeat nec minus illa suos* (ventos). 'The former connected with you in blood, the latter your friend.' Ajax was first cousin to Achilles, both being grandsons of Aeacus. Phoenix had accompanied Achilles to Troy as his friend and guardian at his father's desire (*Il.* 9, 438—443). For **gradus** used in regard to relationship cf. *Fast.* 4, 27 *Venus gradibus multis in gente reperta.*

29. **per quos...redirem** 'who were to conduct me back to you.'

30. Referring to the long pleading of Ulysses to induce Achilles to accept the presents, and the restoration of Briseis, and to return to the war. *Il.* 9, 225—306.

31—6. The gifts are taken from the Iliad (9, 264—272).

ἕπτ' ἀπύρους τρίποδας δέκα δὲ χρυσοῖο τάλαντα
αἴθωνας δὲ λέβητας ἐείκοσι, δώδεκα δ' ἵππους
πηγοὺς, ἀθλοφόρους, οἳ ἀέθλια ποσσὶν ἄροντο.
δώσει δ' ἑπτὰ γυναῖκας, ἀμύμονα ἔργ' εἰδυίας
Λεσβίδας, ἃς ὅτε Λέσβον ἐϋκτιμένην ἕλες αὐτὸς
ἐξέλεθ', αἳ τότε κάλλει ἐνίκων φῦλα γυναικῶν.

32. **arte** 'workmanship.'

35. **quodque supervacuum est** 'and, a thing quite superfluous, some Lesbian girls.' Superfluous, she says, partly on the ground that she herself was to be given back, partly with a touch of feminine jealousy.

37. One of the three daughters of Agamemnon. *Il.* 9, 286
τρεῖς δέ οἱ εἰσι θύγατρες ἐνὶ μεγάρῳ εὐπήκτῳ,
Χρυσόθεμις καὶ Λαοδίκη καὶ Ἰφιάνασσα·
τάων ἥν κ' ἐθέλῃσθα φίλην ἀνάεδνον ἄγεσθαι
πρὸς οἶκον Πηλῆος.

It should be observed how much more closely Ovid follows Homer in this Epistle than in the first. The probability is that in common with readers of his own and subsequent times he was more accurately acquainted with the Iliad than with the Odyssey.

39—40. 'What you would have had to pay (*i.e.* if you had been obliged to purchase me back from Atrides), do you refuse to accept as a present?'

41. **vilis** 'worthless,' *i.e.* that you won't take even as a gift.

42. **a nobis** 'from me.'

43—44. 'Can it be that a sad destiny relentlessly pursues the unhappy, and that no kindlier hour arrives for aught that I undertake?'

By **miseros** Briseis means herself, but the masculine plural in Latin is used by a speaker (1) when she or he refers to a class of people, (2) when she or he wishes from courtesy or a shrinking from naming a particular person to make the reference appear to be general though it is really particular. Thus in Ter. *Haut.* 151 *ingenio te esse in liberos leni puto* 'to your children,' though the person addressed had but one son. ib. 966 *abii ad proximos* though the speaker is referring to his daughter. Briseis speaks of her destiny with a melancholy fatalism, a belief in which may often be traced in Ovid's writings, *e.g. Tr.* 2, 148 *Spes mihi magna subit, cum te, mitissime princeps, Spes mihi, respicio cum mea fata, cadit.*

44. **mollior hora** 'a time of relenting,' cf. *ex P.* 3, 3, 83—4 *Pone metus igitur: mitescet Caesaris ira, et veniet votis mollior hora tuis.*

45. **Lyrnesia moenia**: vid. ad 1.

46. **patriae pars magna** 'a person of great consequence in my country,' cf. Virg. *Aen.* 2, 6 *quorum pars magna fui.*

47—8. 'I saw three fall, partners in death as in birth,—three whose mother was mine too,' *i.e.* her three brothers. The passage is taken from Briseis' lament over Patroclus, *Il.* 19, 292 εἶδον πρὸ πτόλιος δεδαϊγμένον ὀξέϊ χαλκῷ τρεῖς τε κασιγνήτους, τούς μοι μία γείνατο μήτηρ κηδείους. The Greek suggests the correctness of *mihi* instead of Palmer's *mea.*

49. **quantus erat** 'at full length,' cf. 12, 58 *nox mihi quanta fuit.* *A. A.* 3, 264 *inque tuo jaceas quantulacunque toro,* 'all your little length,' and *Am.* 2, 4, 34 *multa jacere toro,* 'at great length.'

50. 'My husband writhing convulsively with bloody breast.' Cf. *M.* 10, 721 *utque aethere vidit ab alto Exanimem inque suo jactantem sanguine corpus.* Achilles slew her husband, *Il.* 19, 295.

51—2. 'Though I had lost so many I had you to make up for them all; you were master, husband, brother to me.'

compensare follows the law of verbs of exchange, *i.e.* it may be to take or give in exchange. Here it means to take in exchange, the thing given or relinquished being in the ablative. The thought in 52 is suggested by Homer *Il.* 6, 429, Ἕκτορ ἀτὰρ σύ μοί ἐσσι πατὴρ καὶ πότνια μήτηρ ἠδὲ κασίγνητος, σὺ δέ μοι θαλερὸς παρακοίτης says Andromache to Hector: Zingerle also compares Prop. 1, 11, 23 *Tu mihi sola domus, tu Cynthia sola parentes.* Cf. inf. 12, 162. And the thought is the same in Soph. *Aj.* 518 τίς δῆτ' ἐμοὶ γένοιτ' ἂν ἀντὶ σοῦ πατρίς; τίς πλοῦτος;

53—6. 'You were wont yourself to say to me, swearing by the divinity of your sea-nymph mother, that I had gained by your capture of me. A gain indeed! What, that you might reject me even though I come to you with a rich dower, and might fly from the wealth offered you because accompanied by me!'

53. **iuratus**: applied to the person bound by the oath. In 2, 23 it was applied to the divinities by whom the oath was sworn.

matris aquosae: *i.e.* Thetis.

55. **quamvis**: cf. on 8.

dotata refers to the rich presents offered by Agamemnon, with the restoration of Briseis, to Achilles if he would only fight once more. Cf. sup. 30—38.

57. 'Nay there is even a report, &c.' *Il.* 9, 682 αὐτὸς δ' ἠπείλησεν ἅμ' ἠοῖ φαινομένηφι νῆας ἐυσσέλμους ἅλαδ' ἑλκέμεν ἀμφιελίσσας οἴκαδ' ἀποπλείειν.

60. **animi** 'sense,' cf. 13, 29 *ut rediit animus pariter rediere dolores.* For the various meanings of *animus* in Ovid, see index.

65. **Phthiis** 'of Phthia' a city of Phthiotis in Thessaly, the country of Achilles.

67—82. 'If you must go, it would not be much trouble to take me too. I will go as a captive not a wife; some Grecian beauty shall be your wife; I will serve as a handmaid at the loom. Only let not your wife treat me harshly: but if she must do so, that will be better than to be left by you.'

70. 'I have a hand well fitted to soften wools.' **mollire** seems to refer to the skilful manipulation of the wool as it comes off the *colus* so that it should be soft and fleecy and not like thread. *F.* 3, 817—8 *Pallade placata lanam mollite, puellae; Discite jam plenas exonerare colos.* *M.* 2, 411 *non erat hujus opus lanam mollire trahendo.* Ib. 6, 20 *seu digitis subigebat opus, repetitaque longo Vellera mollibat nebulas aequantia tractu.*

73. **digna nurus socero** 'some wife worthy of a father-in-law who is a grandson of Jove and Aegina, and whom Nereus would not disdain as the wife of his grandson.'

The father-in-law, *i.e.* Achilles' father, is Peleus son of Aeacus, who was son of Aegina and Jupiter. Nereus was father of Thetis, mother of Achilles.

74. **prosocer**: the father of a father- (or mother)-in-law. It does not seem to be used elsewhere until we come to legal writers.

75. **data pensa**: the tasks of wool weighed out for the girls to spin (*pendere*).

76. 'And the threads which I draw shall thin the full distaffs,' *i.e.* I will spin. The rough wool is wound on the *colus* and drawn off into threads by the *fusus*.

77. **exagitet** 'bully,' properly a word from hunting. *A. A.* 3, 662 *lepus exagitatus erit.*

78. 'Whom I cannot help thinking will be unkind to me.'

aequa: cf. on 1, 23.

nescio quo modo 'somehow or other;' a way of avoiding definite statement. Cf. *Tr.* 3, 3, 8 *terraque nescio quo non placet ipsa modo.*

79. 'And do not allow my hair to be torn in your presence,' *i.e.* by your wife my mistress in a rage. The cruelties of mistresses to their slave girls are often mentioned in the Latin Poets. Cf. *A. A.* 3, 238 *Tuta sit ornatrix. Odi quae sauciat ora unguibus, et rapta brachia figit acu.* Cf. *Am.* 1, 14,

16 *Ornatrix tuto corpore semper erat. Ante meos saepe est oculos ornata, nec unquam Brachia derepta saucia fecit acu.* Juv. 6, 491 *Disponit crinem laceratis ipsa capillis Nuda humero Psecas infelix.* Mart. 2, 66 *Unus de toto peccaverat orbe comarum Anulus, incertâ non bene fixus acu. Hoc facinus Lalage, speculo quod viderat, ulta est, Et cecidit saevis icta Plecusa comis.*

81. 'Or, if you must, let me be thus illtreated, so long as I am not despised by you and left behind.'

dum ne, or *dummodo ne*, is the regular combination in negative sentences introduced by *dum.* It seems a mixture of two phrases, *dum pateris, ne relinquar.* Cf. Liv. 3, 21 *imitamini, patres, turbam inconsultam, dum ego ne imiter tribunos*, Cic. *Fam.* 10, 25 *Celeriter tibi veniendum censeo, dummodo ne quid haec festinatio imminuat ejus gloriae quam consecuti sumus.* Roby § 1668.

83. **quid tamen expectas** 'What more do you want?' *i.e.* by way of reparation from Agamemnon.

85. **animos** 'anger.'

86. **opes** 'forces.' Referring to the victories of the Trojans during Achilles' absence, and Hector's attack on the ships.

90. 'And let me be the cause of your gloomy wrath ending as I was the occasion of its beginning.'

modus 'limit.' Cf. *F.* 3, 165 *hic anni modus est.* It is also constructed with dative. *A. A.* 2, 25 *sit modus exilio.*

92—7. Ovid here reproduces one of the arguments addressed to Achilles by Phoenix. *Il.* 9, 529—599.

Oenides : Meleager son of Oeneus.

95—97. **bellum erat**: in a war between the Aetolians of Calydon and the Curetes for the skin of the boar which Meleager had killed, Meleager slew his mother's brother. His mother Althaea, enraged at this, prayed to the gods to destroy her son; on hearing which Meleager was angry and would no longer fight for the Aetolians, who were consequently daily vanquished by the Curetes, who even scaled the walls of Calydon. Meleager withstood all entreaties from his father, mother, sisters and friends to come to the rescue; but finally did so at the prayer of his wife Cleopatra.

98. **cadunt** 'fall idly,' 'are disregarded.' Loers quotes Prop. 1, 10, 24 *neu tibi pro vano verba benigna cadant.* **pro nullo pondere**, cf. 6, 110.

99. **pro coniuge gessi** 'gave myself the airs of a wife. Cf. 4, 31 *me sine crimine gessi.*

101—2. 'Some captive maiden I remember once called me mistress. "You add," said I, "a burden to my servitude by that title,"' *i.e.* by calling me 'mistress,' you only remind me more bitterly that I am a slave. **nominis onus** = 'a title which is a burden.' *nominis* is a genitive of definition or, as sometimes it is called, in apposition; like *vox libertatis* 'the word liberty.' Roby § 1302.

103—4. **viri**: of her first husband slain by Achilles. **iudiciis meis** 'in my opinion.' Ovid often uses this plural. *Am.* 2, 2, 22 *judiciis aegra sit illa tuis.* *A. A.* 2, 416 *judiciis ista venena meis.*

105—6. Her brothers, cf. 46—7. **mea numina** 'whom I look to as my guardian divinities.' Cf. 13, 159. So Brutus says to the dead Lucretia, *F.* 2, 842, *perque tuos manes qui mihi numen erunt.*

qui bene, &c. 'who fell gloriously for their country and with its fall.' Palmer well quotes Gray, 'Ye died amid your dying country's cries.'

107—108. **cognita tela meis** 'your weapons which my race have had too good cause to know,' *i.e.* because her family and countrymen had fallen by them. **caput**, cf. *Tr.* 5, 4, 45 *per caput ipse suum solitus jurare tuumque.*

109. **Mycenaeum**: sc. Agamemnon. Ulysses says that Agamemnon will give the same assurance. *Il.* 9, 274—6, cf. *Il.* 19, 258.

110. **deseruisse velis** 'by all means abandon me.'

The use of *velis* with infinitive for an imperative is singular, though the negative *noli* is the common construction. Cf. *A.* 1, 4, 38 *oscula praecipue nulla dedisse velis.*

113—126. 'But, I am told, the Greeks imagine you to be in sorrow. The truth is, you are enjoying the pleasures of music and love. Your real reason for declining to fight is that you prefer the safer delights of sensuality. It was different once. Once you used to delight in deeds of valour and warlike fame. Can it be that all your love of war was ended when you conquered my country? Heaven forbid! and grant that Hector may still fall by your spear!'

113. **tibi plectra moventur** 'you are playing on your lyre.' Homer (*Il.* 9, 186) describes Achilles as thus occupied

when the ambassadors come to him. The **plectrum** (πλῆκτρον, πλήσσω) is the quill or short stick used to strike the chords of a stringed instrument. Vid. Rich.

116. **citharae**: the same word as *guitar* through the Italian *chitarra*, a stringed instrument presenting the shape of the human chest and neck (*guttur*). Vid. Rich.

118. The **lyra** differs from the *cithara* in that its strings are set in an open frame without a sounding-board. It is called 'Thracian' from the Thracian Orpheus who was said to have first received it from Apollo. Ovid has the same line again, *Am.* 2, 11, 32 *Tutius est fovisse torum legisse libellos Threiciam digitis increpuisse lyram.* **increpare** 'to strike.' Cf. *M.* 14, 820 *equos ictu verberis increpuit.*

123. **dum me caperes** 'up to the time of your capture of me.'

dum 'until' takes the present and imperfect subjunctive only. Roby § 1664. *Donec* and *quoad* are rarely found in this construction.

125. **Di melius** 'Heaven forbid!' a common formula of deprecation. *Am.* 2, 7, 19 *Di melius quam me...sordida amica juvet.* *A. A.* 2, 388. Cf. Virg. *G.* 3, 513 *Di meliora piis erroremque hostibus illum.* *Met.* 7, 37 *Di meliora velint.*

126. **Pelias hasta**: *i.e.* the spear of Achilles. Cf. *Met.* 13, 109. On mount Pelion Achilles was educated by the Centaur Chiron. Cf. *Pelias arbor* 'the Argo' 12, 8. In *Met.* 12, 74 it is called *Peliaca cuspis.*

127. **legata** 'if sent as an ambassador,' instead of the three warriors sent in the Iliad.

129—30. Vid. Introd. **Teucri frater**: Ajax.

131. **est aliquid** ''tis something,' 'it has some influence.' Cf. 4, 29. *Am.* 1, 12, 3 *Omina sunt aliquid.* *F.* 6, 27 *est aliquid nupsisse Jovi.*

132. 'And to have reminded the eyes of a lover on the spot with (the well-known) bosom.'

[I have left this line as it stands because I could not feel certain of any alteration, which however I feel sure that it requires. *Sinu* should perhaps be changed with Madvig to *sui*, or to the varions reading of the best MS. *suis*, sc. *oculis*.]

133. **sis licet**: vid. on 1, 83.

matrisque ferocior undis 'more cruel than your mother's (Thetis) waves.' Cf. 7, 44 *justior est animo ventus et unda tuo.* Cf. 8, 9 *surdior ille freto. Met.* 14, 711 *Saevior illa freto surgente, cadentibus Haedis.* Cf. Shakespeare, 'You may as well go stand upon the beach and bid the main flood bate his usual height.'

134. **ut** 'even though.' Cf. 1, 116. **comminuere** 'your stern resolution will be shaken by my tears.' *comminuo*, lit. break up. Cf. 9, 80, in a metaphorical sense, 'to weaken.' *Ex P.* 3, 3, 34 *Forsitan exiguas, aliquas tamen, arcus et ignis Ingenii vires comminuere mei.*

135—138. **nunc quoque** 'Even now, late as it is, bestow a thought, oh valiant Achilles, on your fluttering Briseis (so may your father live out all his days, and your son Pyrrhus go to the wars with auspices like your own!) and torture her not in your own cruelty with lingering delay.'

sic: a common way of introducing a conditional prayer. Cf. 4, 148, 168, 171. 7, 159. Cp. Hor. Od. 1, 3, 1 *Sic te Diva, potens Cypri* etc.

136. **auspiciis tuis** 'with as good fortune as you did yourself.' *A. A.* 1, 191 *Auspiciis animisque patris, puer, arma movebis, Et vinces animis auspiciisque patris.* **Pyrrhus**, son of Achilles by Deidamia; he was also called Neoptolemus.

138. **ferreus** 'hardhearted.' Cf. 1, 68. 4, 14.

ure 'torture.' Cf. 7, 24.

140. **cogis...coge**: cf. on 2, 40.

142. 'Yet a hope in you is the one thing which induces me to live as I do.' **hoc animae** 'this amount of life.' For the phrase compare *id aetatis, eo miseriarum, hoc laboris*, and in interrogations *quid hominis es?* Roby § 1296.

sustinet 'keeps going.' Cf. 1, 114.

145—8. 'But if you are going thus practically to bid me die, why merely *bid* me? Why not kill me with your own hand? I have blood that will flow if you stab me. Use the sword against me which you were going to use against Agamemnon.'

147—8. **si dea passa fuisset**: *i.e.* Pallas. Referring to the account of the quarrel between Achilles and Agamemnon (*Il.* 1, 194—5), when Achilles half drew his sword but was restrained by Pallas.

149—150. **tua munera**: the life you granted me when you sacked my native city and slew my kinsmen.

quod dederas: *i.e.* my life.

151. **Neptunia Pergama**: because built by Apollo and Neptune for Laomedon. Cf. 1, 67.

152. **materiam caedis** 'something for you to slay.' Cf. 7, 34. 8, 51.

153—4. 'Whatever you do, whether you go or stay, use your right as my master and bid me come to you.'

IV.

PHAEDRA HIPPOLYTO.

Theseus king of Athens by the Amazon Hippolyte (or Antiopa, see on verse 117) had a son called Hippolytus, who was a sworn follower of Artemis, both as to chastity and the love of hunting. Theseus afterwards married Phaedra, daughter of Minos king of Crete, who lived with him at Athens. Hippolytus lived at Troezen in Argolis: but on the occasion of his initiation at Eleusis Phaedra had seen him. She became desperately enamoured of him, of which he was or affected to be entirely unconscious. After some time Theseus himself retired to Troezen, the home of his grandfather Pittheus, to escape the consequences of blood-pollution which he had incurred; thither Phaedra accompanied him, and her love for Hippolytus was renewed by his proximity. During their stay at Troezen, Theseus went away for a time to consult the oracle at Delphi and Ovid supposes Phaedra to take that opportunity of writing this letter to Hippolytus.

[The main conception is taken from Euripides' play. Ovid especially follows him in this,—that Phaedra's love is not a mere guilty passion, but is a heaven-sent plague, over which she has no control, and against which she struggles vainly. The story of Euripides goes on to relate that Phaedra hanged herself in despair, leaving a letter falsely accusing Hippolytus of offering violence to her; whereupon Theseus prayed Poseidon to slay his son, and only found out his innocence when this rash prayer had been answered, *Fast.* 6, 737 sq.]

Φαίδρην τε Πρόκριν τε ἴδον καλήν τ' Ἀριάδνην.
Odyss. 11, 321.

1. **salutem** 'The Cretan girl sends to the son of the Amazon her good wishes for his health, which she will never enjoy herself unless you give it her.' **salutem** is used in a double sense (1) as the ordinary form of polite greeting (2) literally 'health and happiness.' The same double meaning of *vale* occurs in 9, 168, and elsewhere, as the Greek *χαίρειν*. Cf. Eur. *Bacch.* 1380 *χαῖρ' ὦ μελέα θύγατερ· χαλεπῶς δ' εἰς τόδ' ἂν ἥκοις.*

2. **Amazonio**: Hippolytus was son of the Amazon Hippolyte; or, as others say, of her sister Antiopa.

Cressa puella: Phaedra daughter of Minos, king of Crete.

5—6. 'These written words contain a secret; yet look at them. An enemy will at least look at a billet from his foe.'

For the repetition **notis...notas** cf. on 2, 40.

8. **in primo ore** 'on my very lips.' So *limina prima*, 12, 150. We might translate 'The sound halted on the very threshold of my mouth.'

9—10. 'Even where love is lawful and freely offered, some feeling of bashfulness must be mingled with it, (much more in this case); so, what I was ashamed to *say* love bade me *write*.'

qua licet et sequitur. Many ways of construing these words have been proposed:

(1) Where love is lawful and easy (*sequitur*).

(2) When love is lawful and proper (*utile, conveniens*).

(3) Palmer makes *pudor* the subject of *sequitur*, and construes 'Shame should be joined to love as far as possible and wherever it will accompany it.'

Of these ways the last appears to me most to lack point. Phaedra is not enunciating a moral axiom but stating a fact. 'There is a certain bashfulness that must accompany love in a woman even when it is a lawful love and one that pursues her (is not pursued by her as mine is).' The subject of *sequitur* is *amor*, almost equivalent to *amator*. With *licet* understand *amare*. Cf. *Am.* 1, 9, 9 *Militis officium longa est via. Mitte puellam, Strenuus exempto fine sequetur amans. Met.* 1, 692 *non semel et Satyros eluserat illa sequentes.*

12. 'Love reigns and has jurisdiction over the gods, the lords of all.' Cf. *ex P.* 2, 2, 12 *In rerum dominos movimus arma deos. Am.* 3, 10, 48 *haec decet ad dominos munera ferre deos.* So Horace, *terrarum dominos evehit ad deos.*

For *jus habere in* cf. *Met.* 13, 918 *in aequora Proteus jus habet.*

14. 'That steely heart will surrender.

dare manus a well-known phrase for *vinci* arising from the custom of holding up the hands as an acknowledgment of defeat. *Tr.* 1, 3, 88 *vixque dedit victas utilitate manus.* Virg. *Aen.* 11, 568 *neque ipse manus feritate dedisset.*

ferreus: cf. 1, 58. 3, 138. It is a favourite metaphor with Tibullus also, vid. 1, 2, 65 *ferreus ille fuit* and 1, 10, 2 *Quam ferus et vere ferreus ille fuit.*

15—16. 'Let love be nigh, and just as he heats my marrow with his overmastering fire, so may he transfix your heart to gratify my desires.'

The two weapons of love are referred to, the torch and the bow (cf. 2, 40): Phaedra is suffering from the slow fire of a concealed love (*vulnus alit venis et caeco carpitur igni* Virg. *Aen.* 2, 2). She prays that Hippolytus may experience the sudden shaft of passion and so yield to her wishes. Loers quotes *A. A.* 1, 21

Et mihi cedet Amor, quamvis mea vulneret arcu
Pectora, jactatas excutiatque faces:
Quo me fixit Amor, quo me violentius ussit
Hoc melius facti vulneris ultor ero.

For **in mea vota** cf. on 1, 72. 2, 44. 5, 58, and *Am.* 1, 13, 46 *commisit noctes in sua vota duas.*

[The change of *figat* to *fingat* is at first sight tempting; but it will be seen on further consideration to be alien to the metaphor. According to Ovid here the use of the fire of love is not plastic but torturing.]

17—18. 'I shall not (if you consent to my wishes) be breaking the marriage-tie from mere wantonness. My reputation is spotless,'—and guards me from such a charge.

She is speaking, in the spirit of the Phaedra of Euripides, of her love as no mere outburst of animal passion but a divine visitation. ἐμάνην ἔπεσον δαίμονος ἄτᾳ.

nequitia: for the special sense of *nequitia* cf. *F.* 1, 414 *Nequitia est quae te non sinit esse senem. Nequitia* is the ablative of 'the efficient cause in the agent herself by which a thing is done.' See Con. on Virg. *Aen.* 11, 568.

velim quaeras: cf. 8, 51.

19. 'Love has come with all the greater force because it has come late in life to me. I have a consuming fire within; a consuming fire, and a hidden wound is there in my heart.' Cf. *F.* 2, 762 *Interea juvenis funestos regius ignes Concipit et caeco raptus amore furit.*

The argument is continued from the verses preceding—'I have always been chaste, I cannot be suspected on that head: all the worse are my sufferings now, aggravated moreover as they are by concealment.'

The Phaedra of Euripides hangs herself because her nurse divulges the secret of the unlawful love which she had always kept concealed.

21. **scilicet** (*scire licet*) is used here to introduce an illustration as in 6, 97. In 9, 85 it introduces an expansion or detail of what had just been said; in 10, 42 it suggests that the statement is either mistaken or ironical; in 13, 37. 14, 85 it expresses indignant irony.

iuga prima 'the yoke the first time it is worn,' cf. *Am.* 1, 2, 14 *detractant pressi dum juga prima boves.*

22. **de grege captus** 'caught from the herd of wild unbroken horses.'

grex is used of horses running loose *Met.* 2, 690, cf. *Rem.* 235 *aspicis ut prensos urant juga prima juvencos Et nova velocem cingula laedat equum.*

23. **rude** 'inexperienced,' 'raw,' so *ex P.* 3, 4, 32 *rudis miles ad arma. Met.* 13, 290 *rudis et sine pectore miles.* And this comparison of love to war is constantly expressed or implied by Ovid.

subit used because love is spoken of as a *jugum* or *sarcina;* Hor. *S.* 1, 9, 21 *asellus tergo subiit onus.* **male vixque**: *μόλις.*

24. **sarcina** from root of *sarcio* is anything 'patched together,' then 'bundle' 'baggage,' then any 'weight' or 'burden.' It is used of sorrow in *ex Pont.* 3, 7, 14 *etenim pejora tulisti: Jam tibi sentiri sarcina nulla potest.*

25—26. 'Love becomes a matter of business, when that frailty is thoroughly learnt from girlhood; she who comes to it late in life loves more deeply.'

The whole sentence is founded on the idea of the contrast between one who serves a regular apprenticeship to a trade and one who takes it up late in life as an *ὀψιμαθής.* **crimen** ≑ *amor.*

exacto tempore 'when the time of life for it is over,' to be explained by its opposition to *a teneris annis*, and is equivalent to *serius* in v. 19. Cf. *exacta aetate mori* Cic. *Tusc.* 1, 39, *exactis aestatibus* Virg. *G.* 2, 190.

peius like our 'worse' is little more than *magis*, cf. infr. 34. 7, 30.

27. **nova**: *i.e.* 'fresh,' which no one has touched before.

For **libamina** see on 2, 115, 'firstfruits.'

28. **pariter** 'on equal terms,' *i.e.* because it will be the first frailty in the case of us both.

29. **est aliquid.** Cf. 3, 131. *Met.* 13, 241 *est aliquid de tot Graecorum millibus unum A Diomede legi.*

plenis ramis: abl. of quality, 'orchards with well-laden boughs.'

31—2. 'If however that previous unsullied purity, with which I innocently lived, *was* destined to be smirched by an unwonted stain.'

candor 'whiteness,' not used in this particular sense elsewhere that I can find: Ovid frequently uses it (1) lit. for 'whiteness,' or 'brightness,' (2) mentally 'candour.' Here it seems a metaphor from some metal, such as a polished shield.

ab insolita labe: *ab* with instrumental ablatives is often found in Ovid, cf. 6, 150; 10, 9, 138, see also *Tr.* 2, 462 *fallere ab arte viros.* *Am.* 2, 15, 14 *laxus ab arte.* Ib. 2, 4, 31 *causa tangor ab omni.* Ib. 1, 13, 41 *vir marcet ab annis.* *A. A.* 1, 510 *a nulla acu comptus.* Ib. 724 *debet a radiis esse niger.* Ib. 3, 91 *silices tenuantur ab usu.* Ib. 545 *placida mollimur ab arte.* *Rem.* 159 *Venus est a cuspide laesa.* *Ex Pont.* 1, 2, 54 *ab admonitu pejor fit status.*

33—34. 'Yet it is one point in my favour that my passion is for a worthy object, the baseness of a paramour is more against our credit than the intrigue itself.'

at introduces contrast between the dark and bright side of the story.

igni is abl., cf. Virg. *Aen.* 4, 2 *carpitur igni.* *Met.* 3, 490 *caeco paulatim carpitur igni.* **igni**: the oldest form of the ablative of **i**-stems and consonantal stems was in -īd, e.g. *marid, conventionid*: next ē long appears: from circ. 150 B.C. we find *-ei*, e.g. *virtutei*, and in *i*-stems *fontei, omnei*; or ī, e.g. *luci, vesperī, deditionī.* After this period the form in ĕ became by far the most common; but the ī survived in many words, especially in original *i*-stems, e.g. *igni, turri.* These forms are most common in Lucretius, see Munro on 1, 978 where among others he quotes *colli, igni, imbri, navi, tussi.*

The general tendency however was to weaken the termination to ĕ. Accordingly Ovid has even *de mare Tr.* 5, 2, 20 and infr. 8, 64 *fonte perenne,* cf. Lucr. 1, 161 *e mare;* so in Val. Flacc. 1, 14 *turre* occurs. [Wordsworth, *Fragments of Early Lat.* p. 69 sq.] **adurimur** 'burnt into,' 'destroyed,' cf. 12, 180: *ad* has much the same sense as it has in *adedo* 10, 26. **bene successit** seems a phrase taken from some game.

For **peius** see on 26. For the sentiment cf. 7, 105.

35—36. **fratremque virumque** 'him who is at once her brother and husband.'

videor praepositura 'doubtless I should prefer': no doubt of the fact is expressed by this phrase, cf. 129.

37. 'Now too, you will scarce credit it, my pursuits are changed and I betake myself to such as I knew nothing of before.'

mutor in is a pregnant use of the verb. Cf. *Met.* 14, 553 *carina mutatur in usum spinae* 'is transformed into and serves as a backbone.' [Lennep, who reads *nitor,* quotes Eur. *Hipp.* 235 ἐπὶ θήρας πόθον ἐστέλλου which he thinks is in favour of *mittor.*]

38. **per saevas feras** 'through the midst of savage wild beasts.' **ire per** with a notion of desperate courage or wild despair, cf. 5, 64.

39. 'The first of the goddesses in my eyes now is she who is adorned with the curling bow,' *i.e.* Artemis, not Venus any longer. **prima,** cf. 117.

40. **Delia:** Artemis born in the island Delos. **subsequor** 'I follow your taste,' *i. e.* I hunt as you do.

41. **pressis in retia cervis** 'driven into the hunting-nets,' cf. Virg. *G.* 3, 412 *montesque per altos Ingentem clamore premes in retia cervos.*

43. **excusso lacerto** 'with the arm thrown well forward'; the position of the arm at the moment the javelin is thrown, opposed to *adducto lacerto,*—cf. *M.* 8, 28 *torserat adductis hastilia lenta lacertis,*—its position when thrown back to take aim.

44. Probably Ovid has two ideas, one that of the hunter's crouching down for concealment in stalking, the other that of the practice of huntsmen camping out for the night [Hor.

Od. 1. 1, 25 *manet sub Jove frigido venator*, and Cic. *Tusc.* 2, 40 *pernoctant venatores in nive*]. He is however translating from Euripides *Hipp.* 212 πῶς ἂν...ἐν κομήτῃ λειμῶνι κλιθεῖσ' ἀναπαυσαίμαν.

39—44. The idea of these six lines is taken from Euripides, where Phaedra first shows her passionate unrest by expressing these longings to join in all the details of the chase in which Hippolytus occupies himself. *Hipp.* 209—222:

> πῶς ἂν δροσερᾶς ἀπὸ κρηνῖδος
> καθαρῶν ὑδάτων πῶμ' ἀρυσαίμαν,
> ὑπό τ' αἰγείροις ἔν τε κομήτῃ
> λειμῶνι κλιθεῖσ' ἀναπαυσαίμαν.
> * * * * *
> πέμπετέ μ' εἰς ὄρος· εἶμι πρὸς ὕλαν
> καὶ παρὰ πεύκας, ἵνα θηροφόνοι
> στείβουσι κύνες,
> βαλιαῖς ἐλάφοις ἐγχριμπτομένα·
> πρὸς θεῶν ἔραμαι κυσὶ θωΰξαι.

Seneca also, who went to the same source as Ovid, has, *Hipp.* 110—111:

> *Juvat excitatas consequi cursu feras*
> *Et rigida molli gaesa jaculari manu.*

45. **versare leves in pulvere currus** 'to turn the light-racing cars on the dusty course.' He is again extracting from Euripides and referring to the chariot races in the games δέσποιν' Ἄρτεμι...γυμνασίων τῶν ἱπποκρότων, εἴθε γενοίμαν ἐν σοῖς δαπέδοις πώλους Ἐνέτας δαμαλιζομένα (*Hipp.* 229). *pulvere* refers to the *pulvis Olympicus.* The greatest test of skill in driving these light cars was to turn round the *meta* close and yet safely, hence *versare.*

46. **fugacis** 'swift,' so Galataea is *volucri fugacior aura M.* 13, 807.

47. **nunc feror** 'at one time I hurry along like the Bacchanals driven by frenzy sent by Bacchus, or like the women who shake their cymbals beneath the hill of Ida.'

Eleleides 'the Bacchanalian women,' from their shout; though ἐλελεῦ is properly a war-cry. **feror** Palmer shows to be used properly of madness, quoting Virg. *Aen.* 4, 376 *Heu Furiis incensa feror.*

48. **quaeque**: *i.e.* the Galli, or emasculate priests of Cybele. Hence the feminine *quae.* *F.* 4, 183 *ibunt semimares et inania tympana tundent.*

49—50. Madness was supposed especially to be caused by a sight of the Nymphs and other country gods, cf. *F.* 4, 761 *nec Dryadas nec nos videamus labra Dianae Nec Faunum, medio cum premit arva die*: hence *lymphatici* *νυμφόληπτοι*. This is another way of saying that such madness is unaccountable. Ovid is again referring to words of Euripides, *Hipp.* 141:

> σὺ γὰρ ἔνθεος, ὦ κούρα,
> εἴτ' ἐκ Πανὸς εἴθ' Ἑκάτας
> ἢ σεμνῶν Κορυβάντων
> φοιτᾷς ἢ ματρὸς ὀρείας.

attonuere 'have driven distracted,' more naturally used with a thing rather than a person for subject, *M.* 3, 531 *quis furor vestras attonuit mentes.* Hor., *Od.* 3, 19, 14, uses *attonitus* for 'inspired.'

51—2. 'When the fit is over my attendants tell me all this; I said nothing: I was conscious that it was love which was torturing me.'

53. 'Perhaps this passion is but as it were a debt that I am paying to the fate of my race,' cf. 8, 65. 6, 51. Ovid is fond of playing with fancies of fatalism, and when in trouble himself often recurs to the idea. *Tr.* 2, 148 &c.

55—60. 'Love has been a cause of woe to my grandmother Europa, and my sister Ariadne.' Europa was mother of Minos by Jupiter. **Aegides**: Theseus. **sororis**: Ariadne. **curva tecta**: the Labyrinth, called *saxea tecta* 10, 128.

61. **ne forte** 'lest by any chance I should fail to be recognised as a real daughter of Minos, cf. 8, 82 *ne non Pelopeïa credar: ne forte* like *nisi forte* seems to belong to a proposition unlikely or impossible.

62. 'Last of my race I fall under the laws which govern it and me.'

Palmer translates 'I fall under the influence of its marriage laws.' And the word is used with this reference, see 5, 126: cf. 4, 17. 5, 126. 3, 109 *Sociare cubilia.* Yet I am inclined to abide by the interpretation of the older commentators; for I think *sociae leges* require a more distinct context before they can be rendered 'marriage laws.' And Ovid uses *socius* as an adjective = 'combined,' 'associated,' cf. *M.* 13, 375 *per spes socias. A. A.* 1, 492 *hic socias tu quoque junge moras.*

63—66. **domus una** 'one family,' *i.e.* Theseus and his son Hippolytus (Theseïdes).

tropaea (*τροπαῖον, τρέπω*) cf. 9, 104. Properly the trophy of arms etc. put up by the victorious army on the spot where they turned the foe to flight. Ovid uses it as equivalent to *spolia. Rem.* 157 (to Augustus) *Vince Cupidineas pariter Parthasque sagittas Et refer ad patrios bina tropaea deos.*

67. Referring to the occasion on which Phaedra had first seen Hippolytus, at one of the yearly celebrations of the Eleusinian Mysteries. These mysteries were celebrated from the 15th to the 23rd of Boedromion (Sept.) and on the 5th, 6th and 7th days included solemn processions to Eleusis and initiations of the uninitiated. In the time of Euripides a young man of the rank of Hippolytus would be certain on some occasion to be among the number. **Cerealis** because the mysteries were connected chiefly with the worship of Ceres and Bacchus, cf. *F.* 4, 507. *M.* 7, 439. **inita** est 'was entered,' *i.e.* in one of the processions. There does not seem to be any allusion in this word to the initiations.

Eleusin: the MSS. vary between this form and *Eleusis.* Servius (*Georg.* 1, 163) maintains the form *Eleusin* to be correct because of the oblique cases *El usinos -na* &c. He compares *delphin, Attin.* Priscian (6, 5) confirms this, quoting also *Trachin.*

68. **Gnosia humus,** *i.e.* Crete, from Gnosus an ancient town in that island, and the capital of Minos.

> τῇσι δ' ἐνὶ Κνωσσός, μεγάλη πόλις· ἔνθα τε Μίνως
> ἐννέωρος βασίλευε Διὸς μεγάλου ὀαριστής.
>
> *Odyss.* 19, 178.

69—70. **nec non tamen ante** 'though you had done so before in some degree.'

in extremis ossibus 'in my inmost bones.'

71. **candida vestis, &c.**: as taking part in the mysteries apparently. Loers quotes *F.* 4, 619 *alba decent Cererem: vestes Cerealibus albas Sumite.* A custom which Ovid may choose to refer to the Eleusinian mysteries from the Roman Cerealia, or which may have been drawn from it.

Hippolytus is represented in Euripides as offering a garland to Artemis. (*Hipp.* 73, sq.)

72. **flava** 'sun-browned,' though Seneca, evidently copying Ovid, seems to take it of the heightened colour of modesty: 651 *Quis tum ille fulsit, presserant vittae comam, et ora flavus tenera tingebat pudor.*

76. **fine modico** 'within moderate limits.'

80. 'I admire the way in which your horse is turned in narrow space.' The allusion is to some feat of horsemanship, not to the 'training-ring' of the Georgics and elsewhere. Cf. *Met.* 12, 468 *armaque concussit certumque equitavit in orbem,* cf. *ib.* 6, 215. There were from very ancient times games at the Eleusinian mysteries, on the 7th day of the ceremony it is said.

81. 'Or if you join in the contest of javelin-throwing' (one of the games of the pancratium) 'it is your rigid arm that attracts all eyes.' **lentum** seems to mean 'quivering,' from the suppleness of the spear-haft. Compare *M.* 8, 38 *torserat adductis hastilia lenta lacertis* with *M.* 13, 800 *lentior et salicis virgis et vitibus albis.* **ferox** 'gallant', an epithet really more applicable to the person than the limb.

83. 'Or whether you hold hunting-spears of cornel wood with broad iron head.' Cornel wood is often mentioned as the material for spears, Virg. *Aen.* 5, 557 *cornea bina ferunt praefixa hastilia ferro,* and other instances there quoted by Conington, and *Georg.* 2, 447 *ut myrtus validis hastilibus et bona bello Cornus.*

86. **materia...tua** 'I do not deserve to be victim to your disposition,' *i.e.* to your aversion from love. **Materiam** seems to be suggested by the previous line, and to be used as nearly equivalent to *indoles* [in this case *duritia*] as in the passage of Cicero quoted by Loers, &c., *Verr.* 5, 68 *fac enim fuisse in illo aut C. Laelii aut M. Catonis materiem atque indolem.*

[*militia*, proposed by Palmer, introduces a fresh idea and is not I conceive much supported by the passage quoted from the Amores, where it suits all the previous words and metaphors.]

87. **studia Dianae,** *i.e.* 'hunting.' **incinctae** 'with her tunic girdled,' *i.e.* for convenience in the chase, so *F.* 5, 675 *incinctus tunicam mercator:* it is more properly *succincta,* cf. *M.* 3, 156 *succinctae sacra Dianae.*

88. **numeros suos** 'her dues.' *Tr.* 1, 8, 4 *ut careant numeris tempora prima suis.*

92. **mollis** [μαλ-ακὸς, μαλ-θ-ακός, μῶλυς] 'slack.' Lennep quotes Herod. 2, 73 τὰ τόξα, εἰ τὸν πάντα χρόνον ἐντεταμένα εἴη ἐκραγείη ἄν. But he refers *mollis* to the bowstring, which I cannot think is right.

93—100. Three men famous as hunters who yet loved, Cephalus, Adonis, Meleager. The story of Cephalus and Procris, the former beloved by Aurora but remaining faithful to Procris, is told in *Met.* 7, 663. **a sene,** *i.e.* Tithonus.

97. **Cinyra creatum**: Adonis son of Cinyras a hero of Cyprus. *Met.* 10, 520 sq.

99. **Maenalia Atalanta**: *i.e.* Arcadian Atalanta, from Maenalus a mountain in Arcadia. *Met.* 10, 560 sq. For the hiatus cf. 9, 87, 133, 141.

100. **ferae**, *i.e.* of the boar killed in the Calydonian hunt.

102. **rustica** 'dull,' 'uninteresting,' cf. 1, 77.

104. **obliquo dente timendus aper** 'the boar formidable for the slanting blow of its tusk.' So of the Calydonian boar *Met.* 8, 344 *canes...latrantes obliquo dissipat ictu.*

105—6. **Isthmon**, *i.e.* of Corinth, cf. 8, 69. But Troezen is at least fifty miles from the isthmus.

107. **Pittheia regna**: Pittheus, grandfather of Theseus, lived at Troezen a town in the S.E. of Argolis.

109. **Neptunius heros**, *i.e.* Theseus, reputed a son of Neptune, see on 2, 37. **tempore** 'opportunely,' 'at this time.' Cf. *Rem.* 131 *vina data tempore prosunt.*

110. **Pirithous**: one of the Lapithae, of whom Theseus was the devoted friend. He lived at Larissa in Thessaly. The noble friendship of Theseus and Pirithous, like that of Pylades and Orestes, is much celebrated in the classical writers. These heroic friendships are the bright side of a somewhat dark picture of manners.

111. **nisi si**, a pleonasm nearly equivalent to *nisi.* Ter. *Haut.* 391 *nisi si prospectum est aliquid interea desertae vivimus.* Cf. Cic. *Phil.* 2, 28 *nisi si tu es solus Antonius.* The *si* perhaps is an adverb to be translated 'truly,' and the phrase is more particularly used in sentences implying an impossible or absurd proposition. Cf. Cic. *Cat.* 2, 2 *Nisi vero si Catilinae similes cum Catilina non sentire putes.*

115. **mei fratris**, *i.e.* the Minotaur.

116. **soror**: Ariadne.

117. **securigeras...puellas**, *i.e.* the Amazons. There are different traditions as to the mother of Hippolytus. According to some she is Hippolyte (so Euripides) who was slain eventually by Hercules for the sake of her girdle; according to others she was Antiopa sister of Hippolyte, to avenge whose capture by Theseus, the Amazons invaded Attica and who was afterwards slain by Theseus in consequence of an oracle. Ovid seems to be following the latter tradition.

109—124. She endeavours to make Hippolytus throw off all scruples of respect for his father by counting up the injuries they have both received: (1) he has preferred Pirithous to his wife, (2) he has killed Phaedra's brother the Minotaur, (3) he has deserted her sister Ariadne, (4) he never wedded Hippolytus' mother, and so left him to be a *nothus*, (5) he afterwards killed her, (6) he then married Phaedra and had sons detrimental to the interests of Hippolytus whom he caused to be reared.

120. **tanto pignore** 'by having produced so mighty a son as you.' Children are often called *pignora* or *pignora amoris*, (see index): here it is especially appropriate when the safety of the mother is in question.

121. **taeda accepta iugali**: 'taken to his home with the bridal torchlight procession,' cf. 6, 134. 8, 35.

124. **tollendi** 'which he, not I, caused to be reared.' This refers to a ceremony which originated in the cruel practice of exposing infants to perish, if the parents did not wish to rear them. The ceremony remained after the custom was gone. The midwife laid the new-born infant at the feet of the father who, if he wished it to be reared, lifted it from the ground (*tollere ἀναιρεῖσθαι*): if he left it lying, it was to be exposed. This is often referred to in Plautus and Terence. See Bekker's *Gallus*, Excurs. Scene 1, p. 182. Naturally the determination to expose an infant was made by the father, often to the grief of the mother who indeed at times secretly took means to rear the child. See Ter. *Hautont.* 627—640 where Chremes lectures his wife in quite an exalted tone of morality for the sin of disobedience to him in thus saving her infant, and only excuses it on the ground of *misericordia* and *animus maternus*. Accordingly when Phaedra says that her husband and not she wished to rear her infants, she seems to boast of her unnatural hardness to them as a proof of her care for the interests of Hippolytus. See on this subject an interesting passage in Professor Mahaffy's *Social Life in Greece*, p. 272.

125. **nocitura tibi**, *i.e.* by producing children who would take what should be your inheritance.

127. **i nunc**: see on 3, 26.

meriti: used ironically.

128. Referring to the absence of Theseus, which she pretends to be a quasi-desertion.

129. **videar coitura**: cf. on 36.

132. **rustica** 'was old-fashioned even in Saturn's reign,' cf. 1, 77.

133—4. **quodcumque iuvaret**: 'whatever one happened to wish.'

omne : cf. 12, 28. **fratre marita**: lit. 'a wife by means of her brother.' Loers cps. Hor. *Od.* 3, 5, 5 *Milesne Crassi conjuge barbara turpis maritus vixit.*

135. The only close and binding tie is not marriage or legality, but love.

137—8. Another topic. 'I have shown you that our love is not against nature; now as to concealing it if necessary. Ask that as a favour from Venus. Our formal connection will serve as a pretext for intimacy.'

nec labor est 'nor will it give you much trouble.' **illa**, *i.e.* Venus, who will favour lovers. **cognato nomine** 'the pretext of relationship.' Cf. *M.* 9, 558 *dulcia fraterno sub nomine furta tegemus.*

[These two lines present great difficulty: which is not much removed even if we adopt Madvig's alteration.]

139. **foedera**, *i.e.* of love, cf. *foedera lecti*, 12, 150.

140. **sic**: see on 3, 135.

150. **iacent** 'Alas! where now lie despised all my pride and lofty words?' for *jacent* cf. inf. 161. 2, 124. For **ubi** cf. 6, 41.

152. **certa fui**, 'I was resolved,' cf. 6, 51—2, *certa fui pellere.*

155. 'I have done with modesty. Modesty is a traitor and has deserted its colours.'

depuduit: the *de* is intensive, 'I have felt all the shame I can feel.' For different shades of meaning of *pudor* vid. index. It may be either that which causes, that which feels, or that which is protected by, shame.

157—160. **quod** 'though.' Although Minos is my father, Jupiter my ancestor, Sol my grandfather, yet pride of birth is conquered by love.

Jupiter is father of Minos by Europa, cf. sup. 55. Another Minos, grandson of the first-named, married Pasiphae the daughter of the Sun, and by her was father of Phaedra, Ariadne, and others. **proavum** 'great-grandfather,' is apparently used loosely for a more remote ancestor.

qui possidet aequora: who rules the seas, *i.e.* as king of an island and seafaring people. The Cretans were early noted sailors. Strabo quotes as a proverb of those who pretend not to know what they know well ὁ Κρὴς ἀγνοεῖ τὴν θάλατταν (10, 4, 17.)

159. **radiis frontem vallatus acutis**, 'his brow adorned by a coronet of pointed rays.' The engraving of Helios on a Rhodian coin given in *Dict. of Ant.* will explain this line best, cf. *ex Pont.* 1, 2, 23 *tecta rigent fixis veluti vallata sagittis.*

161. **miserere priorum** 'ancestors.' It seems somewhat ridiculous to beg a lover though he has no pity for his mistress yet to have some for her—grandfather! **miserere** must be translated 'respect.'

163. **dotalis** 'part of my dowry,' cf. 6, 118. 12, 53. **Iovis insula**: because of Jupiter having been nursed in Crete *A.* 3, 10, 20 *Crete nutrito terra superba Jove.*

Crete could not be said to form part of Phaedra's dowry in the ordinary sense. She does not mean that she possesses Crete, but that it is her home, a home which will be at the service of Hippolytus. So in 6, 118 Hypsipyle says that she is to be counted by Jason *inter dotales, i.e.* among the advantages to be acquired by marriage.

165. **quae plurima mecum est** 'who is very powerful with me.' Ovid was no doubt thinking of Euripides' use of πολλὴ as Palmer points out, *Hipp.* 444 Κύπρις γὰρ οὐ φορητὸν ἢν πολλὴ ῥυῇ. But this meaning is derived from the notion of frequency, cf. *Tr.* 4, 10, 128 *in toto plurimus orbe legor.*

168—169. **sic**: see on 140 and 3, 135.

agilis dea: Diana.

171. **montanaque numina Panes**: the Pans of Roman mythology seem to be a confusion with the Fauni and to stand for all goat-footed country-gods. In earlier mythology there is only one Pan. Virgil classes Fauni and Dryades together (*G.* 1, 10—11), Horace Nymphs and Fauni (*Od.* 1, 1, 31). And this very early induced copyists to alter the reading here to *Fauni.* But Ovid elsewhere speaks of *Panes*, and always in connection with Satyri; vid. *Met.* 14, 638. *F.* 1, 397.

172. **adversa cuspide** 'by a spear aimed straight and hitting it full in the breast.' *Adversus* = 'that which is exactly opposite,' and applied to a javelin &c. comes to mean 'aimed straight at': so in *M.* 12, 312 he speaks of a man falling with an *adversum vulnus*, which he explains to mean from a spear hitting him between the eyes. Cf. *A.* 2, 10, 31 *induat adversis contraria pectora telis Miles.*

175—6. 'I add tears also to these words: the prayers you read: the tears you must imagine,' *i.e.* you cannot see them.

V.

OENONE PARIDI.

Paris was exposed as an infant on mount Ida, because his mother, when about to bring him forth, dreamed that she had produced a firebrand which fired all Troy. The infant however had been saved by shepherds and brought up as a shepherd lad, and had wedded the river-nymph Oenone. After Paris had been made the judge between the three goddesses he was acknowledged by his father Priam, sailed to Sparta, and brought back Helen.

Oenone thus convinced that she was finally deserted writes this letter, reminding Paris of their old love and warning him that Helen will only bring him trouble and disaster.

[The Story of Oenone is not mentioned in Homer and we are referred to Apollodorus * (the Lemprière of the ancients) for Ovid's materials. The poet however had probably other materials to work upon, just as a story in the 'Palace of Pleasure' is not often enough to account for a Play of Shakespear. This will be apparent from the passage of Apollodorus himself, book 3. 'Alexander wedded Oenone the daughter of 'the river Kebren. She had learnt the art of prophecy from 'Rhea and used to warn Alexander not to sail to fetch Helen. 'Failing to persuade him she told him if he were ever wounded 'to come to her, for she alone could heal him. So he carried off 'Helen from Sparta; and in the siege of Troy he was wounded 'by Philoctetes with the bow and arrows of Hercules. There-'upon he went to Oenone on Mt. Ida. She however remembered 'her wrongs and refused to heal him. Then Alexander was carried 'back to Troy and died. But Oenone repented and went after 'him, carrying her healing drugs with her, for she was skilled in 'the arts of healing and song. Finding him dead she hanged 'herself.']

1—2. The abruptness of this opening has been often noticed and admired, and no doubt much of the effect would be destroyed by accepting the introductory couplet found in some copies.

'Will you read my letter, or will your new wife forbid it? You may read it. It is not from the enemy at Mycenae,' *i.e.* from Agamemnon king of Mycenae, who is preparing the expedition to avenge the carrying off of Helen.

3. **Pegasis** 'River-nymph' (πηγή) the feminine of Pegasus, who was so called also from πηγή.—Madvig however ridicules

* Apollodorus of Athens fl. circ. 140. Only one of his books 'the Library' survives. It is an account of Greek mythology and heroes.

this word, which he says could only be the feminine patronymic from *Pegasus*. He would therefore restore *Pedasis*, from *Pedasus* a town on the river Kebren, whose daughter Oenone was. The assumption in Madvig's note is that of calling Pedasus the *oppidum patrium* of Oenone. In Homer (*Il.* 21. 87) Pedasus is said to be on the Satnioeis*.

4. I have been wronged and have somewhat to complain of you,—of you my own, 'if you yourself will let it be so.'

si sinis ipse, *i.e.* not 'if you will let me complain,' but 'if you will allow yourself to be called mine.'

8. **indigno**: the masculine used in general statements of this kind, 'to one who deserves it not.' Cf. on 3, 43.

9. **tantus** 'so great a man as you are now,' *i.e.* acknowledged as son of Priam. See Introd.

10. **edita de magno flumine**, *i.e.* the *Kebren*, vid. Introd. This river was also said to have been the father of Hesperie. *M.* 11, 769.

11--12. **absit reverentia vero** 'let no respect for your rank prevent my speaking the plain truth to you.'

tuli: ἔτλην. 'I condescended.'

17—18. **quis**, not *quae*, on the principle laid down on 8.

saltus 'coverts.' *M.* 5, 578 *una fui, nec me studiosius altera saltus Legit.*

fera 'wolf.'

19—20. 'Often as your attendant have I stretched out the wide-meshed hunting-nets; often have I taken the swift hounds over the long ridges.'

maculis 'meshes.' That *maculae* does not mean 'knots,' may be gathered I think from considering the following passage of Pliny 11, 24, 81: he is speaking of a spider spinning, *texere a medio incipit circinato orbe subtemina adnectens, maculasque paribus semper intervallis sed subinde crescentibus ex angusto dilatans indissolubili nodo implicat.* I think in the two passages, quoted from Varro and Columella by Ramsay, Palmer and others, nets which would keep fowls in and eagles out might still be said to have *maculae grandes*, whereas the 'knots' would make no manner of difference. The passages are Varro *R. R.* 3, 11. Colum. *R. R.* 8, 15.

comes: cf. 4, 103.

* The river Kebren seems only known from Apollodorus l.c. Strabo mentions the town Kebrene (Κεβρήνη, Κεβρὴν) 517, 13 and the district Κεβρηνία 510, 33, but says nothing of a river of that name. Xenophon (Hell. 3, 1, 18) however mentions a fountain in the town.

20. **egi canes** refers to the leading the hounds in leash. These duties of an attendant in the chase are referred to by Tibullus in a very similar passage, 4, 3, 11:

Sed tamen ut tecum liceat, Cerinthe, vagari,
Ipsa ego per montes retia torta feram.
Ipsa ego velocis quaeram vestigia cervae,
Et demam celeri ferrea vincla cani.

per iuga longa: cf. 4, 42. And Propert. 3 (4), 14, 16 *Sectatur patrios per juga longa canes.*

21—30. The custom of carving names and verses on trees is referred to by Virgil *Ecl.* 5, 13 *in viridi nuper quae cortice fagi carmina descripsi,* and 10, 53 *tenerisque meos incidere amores Arboribus, crescent illae, crescetis amores.*

22. Cf. 'As you like it' 3, 2, 'There is a man haunts our forest that abuses our young plants with carving Rosalind on their barks.' Spenser, *Colin Clout.*

'Her name on every tree I will endosse
That, as the trees do grow, her name may grow.'

25—26. 'And with the growth of the trunks grow the letters of my name:—Grow on, and rise up boldly to be my epitaph.' Oenone seems to be thinking of the inscription on a tombstone or memorial pillar. For **in**, see on 4, 16; and for **titulos** cf. 2, 68. 5, 26.

recta seems to refer to *nomina*, it would appear to mean 'straight,' 'bold,' 'clear:' and being joined closely to the verb may be represented in English by an adverb.

[While admitting the difficulty of *recta*, I am unable to accept *rite* as Palmer does. Its lack of all MS. authority is of less weight than the fact that it fails to make any clearer a very obscure conceit.]

28. **carmen** 'inscription,' 2, 146. 7, 194.

30—32. 'Let all the laws of nature be reversed.' This particular mode of expressing the idea is a common one in the Poets, *e.g.* Prop. 3, 7, 31 *Terra prius falso partu deludet arantes ...Fluminaque ad caput incipient revocare liquores.* Hor. *Od.* 1, 29, 10 *quis neget arduis Pronos relabi posse rivos Montibus, et Tiberim reverti.* Eur. *Med.* 414 ἄνω ποταμῶν ἱερῶν χωροῦσι παγαί καὶ δίκα καὶ πάντα πάλιν στρέφεται. Ovid frequently uses it, *Tr.* 1, 8, 1 *In caput alta suum labentur ab aequore retro Flumina, conversis solque recurret equis. Ex P.* 4, 5, 43 *fluminaque in fontes cursu reditura supino. M.* 13, 324 *Ante retro Simois fluet...* For a great number of similar expressions, see Ramsay; and Zingerle 'Ovidius und sein Verhältniss, etc.' p. 110—111.

Xanthus: also called Scamander, *ὃν Ξάνθον καλέουσι θεοὶ ἄνδρες δὲ Σκάμανδρον Il.* 20, 74, by which Homer is supposed to mean that Xanthus is the earlier name.

33—4. 'That day told me my destiny, poor girl: from that day begins the darkest overclouding of a love that has suffered change.' For *mutare* of a sudden change in weather cf. *Tr.* 1, 2, 107 *fallor an incipiunt gravidae evanescere nubes Victaque mutati frangitur ira maris.*

37. **micuere**: see on 1, 45.

40. **constitit esse nefas** 'they all agreed that it was of evil omen.' The idea of crime is generally attached to *nefas;* but it may also refer to that view only of crime which regards it as ominous of evil. So *M.* 15, 785 *ferunt...terribilesque tubas auditaque cornua caelo Praemonuisse nefas.* Hence *dies nefastus* is a day on which it is of evil omen to do business. Oenone consults old witches and wizards. For an account of a witch see *Am.* 1, 8, 13 sq.

41—58. 'Then came felling of timber, building and launching of ships; you departed, but it was with tears and embraces. You could hardly tear yourself away, and often feigned that the winds detained you that you might not leave me. I followed your departing sails with prayers for your return,—little thinking that your return would give you to another's arms!'

The cause of Paris' expedition to Greece was, according to some, merely the fact of Menelaus having been at Troy and asking Paris to return to Sparta with him; according to others, because he had incurred blood-pollution by involuntarily killing Antheus.

42. **ceratas rates** 'smeared with wax and pitch:' for this mixture see the account of a burning ship *Met.* 14, 532 *Iamque picem et ceras alimentaque cetera flammae Mulciber urebat, perque altum ad carbasa malum Ibat.* This would be the last thing done to the ships before launching them, and so Ovid says (*Rem.* 447) *non satis una tenet ceratas anchora puppes.*

44. 'Your present love (for Helen) is the one to make you blush rather than your past love (for me).'

45. **nostros flentis ocellos** 'the eyes of me weeping.' The possessive pronoun is in these phrases in the place of a genitive. This is common enough in such phrases as *mea defunctae ossa cubent* (*A.* 1, 8, 107), but that the plural possessive should be thus joined with a genitive singular is an idiom not to be easily justified. Loers quotes Mart. 7, 51, 7 *Si tenet absentis nostros cantatque libellos.*

48. **nexa**: cf. 2, 141.

50. 'You lingered with me, pretending that the wind was so unfavourable that you could not start; it was favourable all the while, and your real reason was that you could not leave me.'

51. 'How often did you let me go, and then recall me for one kiss more.' The *dimissae* and *repetita* both refer in a manner to the person.

54. **remis canet**: cf. 3, 65. **eruta** 'turned up.' *Am.* 3, 8, 43 *Non freta demisso verrebant eruta remo.* It is applied to land 'turned up' by the plough in *F.* 4, 404 *tunc primum soles eruta vidit humus.*

56. **qua licet** 'as far as I can,' referring not to distance but opportunity, cf. *ex P.* 2, 8, 55 *Nos quoque vestra juvet quod, qua licet, ora videmus*, 'That we see your face as far as we may,' *i.e.* in pictures or busts.

57. **virides Nereidas**: the sea-nymphs, daughters of Nereus, are called *virides* from the colour of the sea, just as *Caerulei di* mean 'sea gods,' cf. *Nereus caerulus* 9, 14.

58. **in mea damna** 'to my bitter loss,' cf. 1, 96. **scilicet**: see on 4, 21.

59. **alii** 'for another's benefit.' **votis meis**: abl. of the effective cause.

ergŏ: this shortening of the final letter of *ergo* is unusual in Ovid, at any rate in his earlier style. It is less surprising to find it in the *Tristia* (1, 1, 87); by that time Ovid allowed himself many more licences, especially as to the quantity of the final *o*.

61. **moles nativa** 'a crag of natural rock.' Cp. 5, 149 *est moles nativa loco.*

64. 'My first impulse was to rush into the water to meet you.' Cf. 4, 38.

69. **quid enim furiosa morabar** 'why was I mad enough to stay to see it?' a touch of nature; she was heart-broken at the sight, but irresistibly drawn on to stay to see it.

71. **rupi sinus** 'I tore open the folds of my dress,' cf. 6, 27 *tunicis a pectŏre ruptis.*

74. **illuc** 'thither—to my own rocky hills—I carried my tears.'

75. **deserta coniuge** 'deserted by her husband.' Ovid often omits *a* with the abl. of agent, see index. But *desertus*

from its sense of loss or want, almost being equivalent to *carens*, may take an ablative. Cp. 12, 161. Munro in Mayor's *Juv.* 1, 113.

77—80. 'A bold woman, who does not shrink from crossing the sea with you, a bad woman who deserts her lawful husband, is now to your taste. Not so once, when you were a shepherd: then you were content with Oenone.' **quae...sequantur... destituant**: the reference is to Helen, of course, though she uses the plural, see on 3, 43.

81. 'I am not dazzled by your wealth or the splendour of your palace, or by the chance of being called daughter-in-law of Priam.'

88. **purpureo toro**, *i.e.* the bed of a prince.

93—96. 'If you are not convinced by me, ask all the wisest men in Troy what they think, Hector, Deiphobus, Antenor, Priam himself, as to the advisability of restoring Helen.'

Polydamas is represented in the Iliad as advising Hector, and sometimes reproving him. It is his censure that Hector most dreads, *Il.* 22, 100 Πουλυδάμας μοι πρῶτος ἐλεγχείην ἀναθήσει. From which passage his name came to be used as a kind of impersonification of public opinion,—a Mrs Grundy, cf. Persius 1, 4 *Ne mihi Polydamas et Troiades Labeonem Praetulerint*, and Cic. *Ep. Att.* 7, 1, 4.

gravis 'weighty.' Antenor advises that Helen should be sent back to Argos, *Il.* 7, 350. **quis** for *quibus*.

98. **vir** 'the husband,' sc. Menelaus.

101. **minor Atrides**: the younger Atrides, *i.e.* Menelaus. **foedera lecti**: cf. 12, 150.

104. **semel** 'once for all.'

106. **viduo toro**: cf. 1, 10.

109. **tum cum**: see on 1, 5.

113. **tua germana**, *i.e.* Cassandra.

116. **littora**, *i.e.* 'the sand of the sea-beach.' To plough the sand was a proverb for wasting labour. *Trist.* 5, 4, 47—8 *Plena tot ac tantis referetur gratia factis, Nec sinet ille tuos litus arare boves.* Juv. 7, 49 *litus versamus aratro.* Palmer would add Juv. 1, 157, but in his view of that passage I am unable to concur.

117. **Graia iuvenca**, sc. Helen. Ovid may possibly have had Cassandra's words in his mind, as Palmer says, from Aeschylus, *Ag.* 1094 ἄπεχε τῆς βοὸς τὸν ταῦρον, referring there to Clytemnestra.

117—118. **quae...perdat**: obs. the subj. 'Of such kind as to be the ruin of.'

122. **diriguere** 'stood on end stiff and singly.' The meaning of the prefix *dis-* or *di-* here may be illustrated by Shakespear: 'I could a tale unfold...would make thy knotted and combined locks *to part*, and *each particular* hair to stand on end.'

124. **saltus** 'pastures,' cf. *Am.* 2, 9, 20 *mittitur in saltus carcere liber equus.*

125. **facie** 'in face.' The ablative of the part concerned or affected, Roby §·1210.

126. **hospite capta** 'captivated by a guest;' for *ab hospite:* see on supr. 75 and index. **socios deos** 'her wedded home,' lit. the gods of her marriage, cf. 2, 33 *socii anni.* Loers quotes *Am.* 2, 11, 7 *Ecce fugit notumque torum sociosque Penates.*

127—8. There was a tradition of Theseus having carried off Helen before her amour with Paris. And Herodotus (9, 73) mentions the expedition of the Tyndaridae (*i.e.* Castor and Pollux) into Attica to recover her. The story was that she was only seven years old when Theseus carried her off and that she was hidden at Aphidnae, which the Tyndaridae besieged and took.

131. Cf. *Met.* 7, 69 *Conjugiumne vocas speciosaque nomina culpae Imponis?* and Virg. *Aen.* 4, 172 *Conjugiumque vocat, hoc praetexit nomine culpam.*

135—6. **celeres**: because of their goat's feet. **proterva** 'wanton.'

137. **pinu acuta** 'sharp-pointed pine leaves.' In *Met.* 1, 699 Pan is said to be crowned with the same. **Faunus**: see on 4, 49.

139. **Troiae munitor** 'the builder of Troy's walls,' sc. Apollo, vid. on 1, 67.

146. **ad sua dona**, *i.e.* to his skill in healing herbs. Apollo is the god of medicine, hence father of Aesculapius. Ovid calls the physician's trade *ars Apollonea*, *Tr.* 3, 3, 10.

147. **utilis medendi** 'useful for healing,' see on 1, 81.

149. Cf. *Met.* 1, 523 *Ei mihi quod nullis amor est sanabilis herbis.*

150. **deficior...ab arte mea** 'though skilled in the art (of simples) I fail in the very art which I call my own.' It is not very easy to be certain as to the construction though the meaning is clear. We may (1) regard *deficio* as a transitive verb, as in *F.* 3, 665 *victus defecerat illos*; whence the passive

defecti 'in want,' ib. 674. And explain *ab arte* as an instance of the Ovidian use of *ab* with the ablative which is nearly instrumental, cp. 4, 32; 10, 9, 138. Or (2) we may regard *deficior* as a kind of middle 'to be wanting in.' It should however in that case be followed by an ablative of defect, cp. Cic. *pro Cluent.* 65 *mulier abundat audacia, consilio et ratione deficitur.* Sueton. *Aug.* 84 *quamvis non deficeretur ad subita extemporali facultate*,—whereas **ab arte** must be 'in respect of my art,' like Horace's *nihil est ab omni parte beatum* (Od. 2, 16, 27) Ovid *Tr.* 4, 10, 6 *insignis ab arte.*

151—2. **repertor opis** 'the inventor of medicinal aid.' **vaccas Pheraeas**: the cows of Admetus, son of Pheres. The version of the Fable used by Euripides represents Apollo as keeping the herds of Admetus when banished from heaven. There was another version however which assigned him a motive of Love. Loers quotes Callimachus, *Hymn. Ap.* 48 ἐξότ' ἐπ' Ἀμφρυσῷ ζευγητίδας ἔτρεφεν ἵππους Ἠιθέου ὑπ' ἔρωτι κεκαυμένος Ἀδμήτοιο. The same version of the story is referred to by Ovid *A. A.* 2, 239 *Cynthius Admeti vaccas pavisse Pheraei Fertur et exigua delituisse casa.*

e nostro igne: *i.e.* from the passion (love) from which I am suffering.

154. **auxilium**, like *opis* in 151, has a special reference to medicine.

VI.

HYPSIPYLE IASONI.

HYPSIPYLE was the queen of Lemnos. A short time before the Argo started on its voyage Lemnos had been the scene of a dreadful tragedy. Aphrodite had, in revenge for neglect on their part, afflicted the women with a curse which made them distasteful to their husbands; who accordingly took in their place women whom they captured in Thrace. In revenge, the women of Lemnos murdered every male in the island (*Lemniadum facinus* v. 139). Hypsipyle alone saved her father Thoas. When the Argo touched at Lemnos the Argonauts landed and remained some time on the island, wedding various of the women there. Jason was entertained by Hypsipyle, and she became a mother by him. When the Argonauts left Lemnos, Jason promised, if he succeeded in his voyage and survived, to come back to Lemnos. Hypsipyle is supposed to have heard of his success and of his marriage with Medea, and to write this letter to reproach him with his breach of faith.

[The story is told in Apollodorus, bk. I. But the spirit of Ovid's poem is from Apollonius Rhodius I. 608—909, so far as it is not his own. He has especially noticed and used the lines of Apollonius relating to the parting between Jason and Hypsipyle, and the prospects of the birth of her child. The fact of her having brought forth twins he found in Apollodorus, who gives their names, Eunaeus and Nebrophonus. The treatment and passion of the theme is Ovid's own; though as usual he calls all his knowledge to bear to give a vraisemblance to what he writes: notice in this respect especially Hypsipyle's curses upon Medea.]

μνώεο μὴν ἀπεὼν περ ὁμῶς καὶ νόστιμος ἤδη
Ὑψιπύλης.

1. **Thessaliae**: Jason lived at Iolchus in Thessaly.

3—4. **hoc tamen ipso...tuo** 'I ought however on this very subject to have been informed by a letter of yours.' [*hoc ipso* is rather peculiar, but not so hard to understand as Palmer's *hoc ipsum* which he construes as the accusative after *certior factus esse* as though it were *scire*. Surely this is a strange construction. To say nothing of the fact tnat it is entirely unsupported by MS. authority.]

scripto is a substantive as in Hor. *Sat.* 2, 3, 2.

4—9. 'I ought at least to have had a letter from you. Stress of weather may have prevented your coming back past Lemnos, but no weather could prevent your writing a letter which would have reached me at least as soon as the news which I have *heard* of you.'

5. **pacta** 'pledged to you as part of my marriage-portion,' infr. 117 *dos tibi Lemnos erit.*

6. **ventos** 'the winds you wanted,' 'favourable winds.'

7. **signatur** 'can be written,' cf. 13, 66.

8. **missa salute** 'of having a greeting sent.'

10. **Martis boves**: the fire-breathing bulls, which Jason had to use for ploughing the field before sowing it with dragon's teeth, cf. 12, 41.

iuga panda 'curved yokes.' There were two forms of yoke to couple beasts used,—one a mere flat bar; the other shaped like a bow. See the pictures in Rich. It is the latter which Ovid calls *panda.* He applies the word elsewhere to the keel of a ship *panda carina A.* 2, 114, and a bow-backed ass *pandus asellus A. A.* 1, 543, to the horns of heifers *juvencae pandis cornibus M.* 10, 271; to dolphins *pandi delphines, Tr.* 3, 10, 43; and to boughs weighed down with fruit *pandos autumni pondere ramos M.* 14, 660.

11. **adolesse**: for *adolevisse, adolesco.*

12. **in necem** 'for death,' 'to be killed.' **non eguisse**, *i.e.* because they killed each other.

13. **pecudis spolium**: the sheep's skin, *i.e.* the golden fleece. For *spolium* see index.

15—16. 'If I had been able to say to those who doubted of the truth of these facts "I have it from his own hand," how great a woman I should have been!'

17—18. **officium** 'attentions,' cf. *A. A.* 1, 151 *Etsi nullus erit pulvis, tamen excute nullum: Quaelibet officio causa sit apta tuo.*

obsequium is a stronger word, 'indulgence,' cf. *Am.* 3, 4, 11 *Desine crede mihi vitia inritare vetando, Obsequio vinces aptius illa tuo.*

The sense is, Why complain that I am left without the proper attentions of a husband? I shall consider myself treated not only with attention but with indulgence if I am allowed to remain yours.

19. **venefica** 'witch' (*venenum facio*).

21. **credula res amor est**: repeated in *M.* 7, 826.

23. **Haemoniis** 'Thessalian,' cf. 12, 127. 13, 2.

24. 'He had scarcely got well over the threshold.' For *tangere=inire* cf. 1, 142, and see index.

25. **Aesonides**: Jason, son of Aeson.

26. **opposita** 'with his eyes fixed straight upon the ground.' *Opposita* is expressed by *adversa* in *M.* 13, 541 and like it refers more to the position of the eyes than of the ground.

27. **tunicis...ruptis**: cf. 5, 71.

29. '"He lives," said he. A lover is a timid thing, I forced him to swear. His calling the god to witness could scarcely make me believe that you were alive.'

For *timidum quod amat* (which I think the best reading of the many proposed), cf. *res est solliciti plena timoris amor* 1, 12.

35. **civili marte** : *i.e.* 'in fighting with each other.'

36. **diurna** 'begun and ended in one day.'

37. **devicto serpente** 'when the victory over the serpent had been narrated.' For this pregnant use of *devicto* cf. on 2, 69. 3, 13. [The whole passage 31—38 is condemned as spurious by Merkel and Palmer, chiefly on the ground that these particulars have been just given in 10—14: and also from the difficulty of *devictus serpens*, which is the common reading for *devicto serpente*. The latter is from the second or late Eton MS. and though resting on such feeble authority seems to me a good reading, if the verses are to be retained at all.]

39—40. 'In the excitement and hurry of speaking he unintentionally reveals my sorrow.' For *ingenio suo* 'naturally' *sponte*, Loers quotes Petron. 126 *crines ingenio suo flexi* 'curling naturally.'

41. **pacta**: cf. 2, 4. **iura** : cf. 2, 31.

42. 'And a brand which was more fitted to be put to a pyre that was going to be lighted.' For this contrast of things funereal with things matrimonial, see on 2, 120.

43. 'My marriage with you was open and regular, there was nothing clandestine about it.' For **pronuba** cf. 2, 117. For **Juno** and her connection with marriage see on 2, 41. Cf. Virg. *Aen.* 4, 166 *pronuba Juno.*

45. **Erinys**: 2, 119. **praetulit**: carried in front of me in the bridal procession, see on 2, 120. **infaustas**: 2, 115.

47. 'What had I to do with the Minyae or with the ship of Pallas? What had you to do with my country, oh! mariner Tiphys?'

Minyae: a name given to the Argonauts again, in 12, 65. Minyas was the traditional founder of Orchomenus in Boeotia. From his daughters many of the Argonauts were descended, and the name therefore is applied to them generally.

Tritonide pinu, *i.e.* the pine-built ship of Pallas. *Tritonis* is an epithet applied to Pallas, and consequently to everything belonging to her. And the Argo was built at her suggestion, *'Αθηναίης ὑποθημοσύνῃσιν* Apollon. 1, 19. *Tritonis* was said to be a nymph of a lake in Africa and mother of Pallas.

48. **Tiphy**: Tiphys was the steersman of the Argo, *ἐσθλὸς μὲν ὀρινόμενον προδαῆναι κῦμ' ἁλὸς εὐρείης, ἐσθλὸς δ' ἀνέμοιο θυέλλας καὶ πλόον ἠελίῳ τε καὶ ἀστέρι τεκμήρασθαι* Apollon. 1, 105.

49—56. 'You need never have come to Lemnos: the golden fleece was not there. And indeed I had at first made up my mind not to receive you; we Lemnian women were quite capable of taking care of ourselves if you had tried to come forcibly. However I *did* receive you, and you stayed two years.'

49. **spectabilis**: a very favourite word with Ovid, see index.

50. **Aeetes**: king of Colchis and father of Medea.

51. **sed me mala fata trahebant**: see on 4, 53, and cf. 12, 35, and *Tr.* 2, 341, *ib.* 3, 6, 15 for a repetition of the same phrase of fatalism.

52. **hospita castra** 'the foreign soldiers.' The neut pl. *hospita* (which is also fem. sing.) seems to imply a form *hospitus*, which is now non-existent. In *F.* 1, 340 we have *hospita navis*. Stat. *Theb.* 4, 842 *hospita flumina*. As a feminine of *hospes* it occurs in these Epistles 2, 1, 74. 7, 107. As a feminine adjective again Virg. *Aen.* 3, 539 *terra hospita*.

53. 'Lemnian women know, only too well, how to conquer men.' Referring to the murder of all the males by the Lemnian women, vid. introd.

54. 'My life (if I had repelled and refused to receive you) might have been protected by so valiant a soldiery,' *i.e.* as these Lemnian women.

fuit: for *esset*, cf. infr. 148: see on 1, 108.

55. The connection is 'Though I might have safely repelled him, I did assist the man with the hospitality of my city, I did receive him under my roof and into my chamber.'

Juvare aliquem aliquo 'to help a man by giving him anything,' cf. 2, 55.

[I have adopted Palmer's emendation *juvi* for *vidi* in the text. But there are some considerations which favour the old reading. There is no need of the many passages he quotes to justify the construction or the phrase as Ovidian, but that being admitted there seem other objections. Not the least is the absolute unanimity of all copies. Nor have Editors altered it, though Burman proposed in his notes *Urbe virum et vidi*, and Heinsius *urbe virum vidua*. And perhaps there is more point in *vidi* than Palmer will allow. The sense would then run: 'I had resolved to repel the Argonauts; I might have done so safely; but I saw a man in my city, and (at once) I received him into my house and chamber.' We must remember that the city is empty of men, and that *virum vidi* therefore is no common-place. And Ovid may be thinking of the excitement caused by the appearance in the town of this splendid young man as described in Apoll. 1, 775—785.]

57. 'It was the third year of your stay.' This certainly is against the authority of Apollonius, who says that the Argonauts would have stayed a long time had not Hercules chided them, 1, 862 *δηρὸν δ' ἂν ἔλιννον αὖθι μένοντες εἰ μὴ ἀολλίσσας ἑτάρους ἀπάνευθε γυναικῶν Ἡρακλέης τοίοισιν ἐνιπτάζων μετέειπεν.* In Apollodorus no indication of the time spent by Jason is given. Ovid must be using some other authority, which he does not however use consistently, for v. 123 implies that Jason left before the birth of the children.

58. **implesti** 'you filled up the pauses in these words with tears.' *Implere* 'to take the place of,' cf. *Am.* 2, 6, 39 *Optima prima fere manibus rapiuntur avaris Implentur numeris deteriora suis.* And so may be used of a musical accompaniment as Palmer remarks.

67. 'The blue wave ripples from beneath the keel as it is driven on.' **subducitur** prettily describes the apparent withdrawal of the water under a ship as she makes way.

74. **nunc quoque** 'even now'—when, though you are safe, I am deserted.

77—8. **feram...concidat**: deliberative subjunctives.

80. **pater** 'your father,' sc. Aeson.

Argolica and **Argolidas** 'Greek,' not Argive.

81. **barbara**, *i.e.* not a Greek.

83. **carmina** 'incantations,' *ἐπῳδαί.*

84. 'She cuts with knife, which has been duly prepared with charmed herbs of dread potency.' A number of such herbs is alluded to in Hor. *Epod.* 5, 17 sq. Ovid has given us another elaborate description of a witch in *Am.* 1, 8, and in *Met.* 7, 180 sq.

85—6. 'She tries to bring down the resisting moon from her course, and to hide the Sun's horses with darkness,' *i.e.* to bring on an eclipse. The moon was believed to be especially subject to witchcraft, cf. Hor. *Epod.* 5, 45 *Quae sidera excantata voce Thessala Lunamque caelo deripit.* Virg. *Ecl.* 8, 70 *Carmina vel caelo possunt deducere lunam.* Sen. *Hipp.* 791 *tractam (lunam) Thessalicis carminibus rati tinnitus dedimus.*

87. **obliqua** 'flowing down.' Hor. *Od.* 2, 3, 11 *obliquo laborat lympha fugax trepidare rivo.*

89. **passis capillis**: the hair in disorder seems a necessary arrangement for a witch, *M.* 7, 183 *nudos humeris infusa capillos.*

90. **ossa**: cf. Lucan 6, 533 *Fumantes juvenum cineres ardentiaque ossa E mediis rapit illa rogis.* Tibull. 1, 2, 46 *et tepido devocat ossa rogo.* (Loers.) **tepidis** 'still warm,' where the body has just been burnt.

91—92. **devovet** 'dooms to death with her enchantments.' **cerea**: a common mode of thus devoting a person to destruction was to form a likeness of them in wax, and either stab or melt it. Cf. *Am.* 3, 7, 29 *Sagave poenicea defixit nomina cera, et medium tenuis in jecur urget acus.*

93—4. **male** 'ill is it to seek for love by magic herbs which should be won by charms of mind and beauty.'

[I believe *male* to be the right reading. Nearly all the MSS. however have *mage.* If this were admitted into the text I should not regard it as the vocative of *magus*, but as an archaic form of *magis*, which Ovid elsewhere uses. *Tr.* 2, 479.]

98. **feros anguis**: alluding to the dragon guarding the fleece, which Jason put to sleep by drugs supplied by Medea. She however chooses to use the plural as though this were only one of many such acts of power on Medea's part.

99—100. 'Besides she contrives that her name should be put in the inscription which records the achievements of yourself and of your nobles, and so the wife eclipses the honour of her husband.' The thought is that of a tablet, or a statue with an inscription detailing Jason's deeds and those of his fellow Argonauts. Cf. 2, 67—74. Hypsipyle says that Medea contrives to have her name put in the inscription, and thus by getting the credit of the deeds, she eclipses her husband's honour (*titulus*). **titulo**: elsewhere when used in the sense of 'honour' the plural is employed, cf. 7, 76. 9, 1. But here the honour meant is especially that of the *titulus* or inscription.

[If this view is right it does away with all necessity of finding allusion to legal formulas as Palmer does: and for his reading *se cavet*, which I cannot like. As to the reading in the text *se facit* is the most ancient emendation of the unintelligible *se favet* known to us, and I think the best.]

101—2. **aliquis Peliae de partibus** 'some one of the party of Pelias.' *Partes* a political party. Pelias uncle of Jason deprived his brother Aeson of the throne of Iolcos, but offered to surrender it to Jason, on the condition of his bringing the golden fleece.

acta venenis imputat 'puts your achievements down to the powers of magic drugs.' *Imputare* is the word used in keeping accounts.

103. **Phasias Aeetine** 'the Phasian daughter of Aeetes.' Phasias, *i.e.* Colchian, from the river and town Phasis. For the patronymic *Aeetine* Heinsius quotes *Neptunine*, *Nereine*, *Oceanine*, *Adrastine*, *Nonacrine*, *Evenine*, though without saying by whom used. And the other editors have followed him without adding to our information. I cannot find that they are any of them employed by Ovid. The MSS. know nothing of the word, which is due to Heinsius. In Catullus 64, 28 the reading varies between *Neptunine* and *Nereine*, Mueller adopting the latter.

104. **Phrixeae ovis** 'the sheep that carried Phrixus.'

105. **consule**: cf. 5, 95—6.

106. **a gelido axe**: *i.e.* from the North.

107. **illa**: sc. Medea.

Tanai (abl.). The Tanais (Don) is far enough from Colchis; but it is somewhere in the north, and that is sufficient for Ovid, or indeed any Roman poet.

114—116. The descent which Hypsipyle boasts is this: Minos, Ariadne, Thoas. Bacchus wedded Ariadne, whom he afterwards made into a constellation.

feror 'I am spoken of as.'

117. **ingeniosa** 'productive,' cf. *F.* 4, 684 *ad segetes ingeniosus ager*. See on 2, 22.

118. **dotales inter** 'among those whom your marriage with me will put into your hands.' Palmer quotes Virg. *Aen.* 4, 102 *dotalesque tuae Tyrios permittere dextrae*. Nevertheless what he calls 'the worthless reading' *res tales* has some point, referring to *ingeniosa* in its sense of 'fertile.' 'Me too you may count as fertile.'

121. **prolemque gemellam**: Apollodorus gives the names of the two boys, Nebrophonus and Eunaeus, though he does not call them twins.

123. **cognosceris illis** 'you are recognised in them,' *i.e.* their likeness to you strikes all. Loers quotes *M.* 4, 290 *Hujus erat facies in qua materque paterque Cognosci posset.* Cf. Longfellow:

'Dear babe, sweet image of thy father's face.'

126. **saeva noverca**: the thought of their cruel step-dame Medea.

127. **plus est** 'Medea is worse than a step-dame.' Stepmothers are the ideal of wickedness in the Roman poets. See Virg. *G.* 3, 282.

128. **faciunt** 'Medea's hands are fitted for any crime,' cf. 14, 56 *non faciunt molles ad fera tela manus.*

129. Medea cut up her brother Absyrtus to prevent her father's pursuit. *Tomi*, the place of Ovid's exile, had from its name 'the Cuts,' τέμνω, got the credit of being the scene of this tragedy (*Tr.* 3, 9, 32); though probably the real origin of the name was from some cuttings or canals in the neighbourhood.

130. **pignoribus**: cf. 4, 120.

131. **hanc** 'such a woman as this.' **ablate** 'deceived,' cf. *R.* 343 *auferimur cultu*, and Virg. *Ecl.* 8, 41 *Ut vidi ut perii! ut me malus abstulit error.*

134. **taeda** 'marriage,' cf. 4, 121 *taeda jugalis*, and 8, 35.

135. **Thoanta**: her father Thoas, see introd.

137. 'What good is it to be better than she? She wins her husband by the very fact of her wickedness.'

139—140. 'When I think of your perfidy I begin to understand the crime of the Lemnian women, though I blame it. Jealousy uses any arms it can to revenge itself in its wrath.'

quaelibet iratis 'the very sting (of despised love) puts arms of any kind you please into the hands of angry impulse.' Cp. Tr. 4, 9, 8 *induet infelix arma coacta dolor.* Verg. Aen. 1, 150 *furor arma ministrat.*

[Palmer adopts the emendation *quamlibet infirmis* made by comparing *Am.* 1, 7, 66. But the two passages are widely different in intention. Here Hypsipyle is not thinking of the contrast between woman's ordinary weakness and the strength given her by jealousy; but she is suggesting *ira* and *dolor* as an explanation or excuse for their *conduct.*]

141. **ut oportuit** 'as I wish you had done!'

142. **comesque**, *i.e.* Medea.

144. **nempe** 'doubtless:' *pe* is a form of *que* (*nam-pe*, cf. *namque*), Roby § 517.

hiscere: cf. 3, 63. **roganda fuit**: cf. supr. 54. 10, 112.

146. **dignus eras**=*dignus esses*, see on 1, 108, and index.

150. **quosque** 'and the face which she has inveigled,' *i.e.* yours. For **abstulit** see supr. 131.

151. **quod** introduces an imprecation.

153—154. 'May the intruder upon my marriage-bed feel all the sorrow which Hypsipyle is sighing over, and herself suffer by the example she has set.' **subnuba** is probably like *prosocer*, in 3, 74, a legal term, but it does not appear to be used elsewhere. **sentiat** 'feel the full misery of,' cf. 9, 46.

leges: cf. 5, 134 *et poteras falli legibus ipse tuis.*

156. **cum totidem** 'may she, with the same number of children as I have, be abandoned by her husband.' As Medea in fact was, cf. 12, 148 sq.

[I have no doubt of the correctness of this reading; but it is more ancient than Lindemann to whom Palmer attributes it, as will be seen in the critical note.]

157. **nec male parta diu teneat** 'nor keep long what she gained by such ill means.' There was a proverb, which Ovid perhaps is thinking of, *male parta male dilabuntur* 'ill got, ill spent,' cf. Cic. *Phil.* 2, § 65. I had marked this, and now see that Lennep refers to the same passage.

peiusque relinquat 'and leave them even more miserably' than I have done.

159—160. 'May she prove as disastrous a wife as she did a daughter and sister,' cf. 129. This seems rather a curse upon Jason and his children than on Medea.

161. **consumpserit** 'has used up,' has exhausted all the facilities for flight which they give. This is a bold and elegant use of *consumere*, which Ovid employs elsewhere to mean 'exhaust by using,' *consumere omnem materiam ficti*, *M.* 9, 768.

aera temptet: referring to the legend of Medea being carried in a chariot drawn by dragons from Corinth to Athens. *M.* 7, 219 sq.

162. **inops, exspes**: very anciently this was altered to *inops mentis*, but there are parallel passages in *M.* 14, 217 *Solus inops exspes leto poenisque relictus*, and *Ibis* 113 *Exul inops erres alienaque limina lustres.* See also 14, 114.

VII.

DIDO AENEAE.

Dido, driven from her home by the persecutions of her brother Pygmalion, who had killed her husband Sychaeus, took refuge in Africa, and there purchased land and founded the city of Carthage. While the town was still in process of building Aeneas was driven on shore there by contrary winds as he was trying to make his course along the western shore of Italy. Dido entertains him, falls in love with him and yields to his embraces. Aeneas after a time obeys his destiny in seeking once more his promised Italian settlements, and sails away without the knowledge of Dido. When she discovers it she resolves on suicide, and Ovid supposes her to write this letter to Aeneas, full of sorrow and remonstrance, before she destroys herself.

[The story is well known from Vergil. And Ovid has been content to take all facts from him, as well as the spirit in which he conceives the character of Dido. He elsewhere briefly tells the same story, *Met.* 14, 75—81,

Hanc (Scyllam) ubi Trojanae remis avidamque Charybdim
Evicere rates, cum jam prope litus adessent
Ausonium, Libycas vento referuntur ad oras.
Excipit Aenean illic animoque domoque,
Non benè discidium Phrygii latura mariti,
Sidonis. inque pyrâ sacri sub imagine factâ
Incubuit ferro, deceptaque decipit omnes.]

1—2. The notion of a swan singing, and especially just before its death, is as old at any rate as Aristotle, who states it as a fact in natural history. The **Maeander**, a river in Phrygia, (mod. Mendere) which like the Cayster had as many swans as the Thames. *M.* 2, 252 *Et quae Maeonias celebrarant carmine ripas Flumineae volucres medio coluere Caystro. Tr.* 5, 1. 11:

Utque jacens ripa deflere Caystrius ales
Dicitur ore suam deficiente necem.

abiectus is a strong word, 'cast down helpless,' *i. e.* dying.

4. **movimus ista** 'I have begun this appeal with heaven against me:' for Ovid's use of *movere* see index.

5. **merita** 'my services to you,' 'the favours I have granted you.' cf. 12, 192.

7. **certus es ire**: cf. 6, 51.

8. **venti vela fidemque ferent**: see on 2, 25.

9. **solvere** is used in an actual and metaphorical sense 'to break away from your moorings and your contract at once.' In 10, 78 we have *solvere fidem* in the latter sense, and in 7, 55 *solvere retinacula* in the former.

10. **Itala regna sequi**: this was the reason of Aeneas' departure. Mercury thus urges him to go, *Aen.* 4, 274, *Ascanium surgentem et spes heredis Iuli Respice, cui regnum Italiae Romanaque tellus Debentur.*

ubi sint nescis. Aeneas had been sent to Italy by oracular warnings, but had twice already mistaken their meaning, and founded a city in the wrong country.

11. **nova Carthago—crescentia moenia.** When Aeneas lands in Africa he finds the Tyrian settlers engaged in building the new town of Carthage, *Aen.* 1, 423—428, and he exclaims *O fortunati quorum jam moenia surgunt.* This Vergil has arranged to suit his own purposes; but the truth seems to be that Carthage was not founded till long after the period of the Trojan war legend, and perhaps not more than half a century before the founding of Rome.

12. **summa** 'chief power,' cf. *M.* 13, 192 *dati summa sceptri.* Loers also quotes Plautus *Truc.* 4, 2, 15 *solus summam hic habet apud nos.*

13—14. 'You are of a roving, discontented, restless nature. Whatever you have accomplished you wish to abandon, and ever look forward to something still to be done. No sooner have you acquired one country than you must search the whole world for another.'

15. **ut** 'ever supposing that,' cf. on 1, 116. And see index.

habendam 'in possession,' see infr. 163.

18. **quam iterum fallas** 'to break as you have broken before,' **fides** 'plighted word.'

19. **quando**: see on 1, 11.

21. **ut**, cf. on 13. Though everything turn out according to your wishes, and the accomplishment of your prayers does not keep you waiting, whence will you have a wife to love you as I have done?

tua vota 'the accomplishment of your prayers,' the reaching the destined Italian home.

[Palmer reads *di tua vota morantur* from Lennep, who argues that a personal subject to *morantur* is required. To his illustrations of this he might have added Juv. 14, 250 *jam nunc obstas et vota moraris.* Nevertheless this pregnant use of *vota* for 'the accomplishment of prayers' is so much in Ovid's manner that I should be unwilling to change without some authority.]

25. **inducto** 'waxed torches tipped with brimstone' as appears from *M.* 3, 373 *non aliter quam cum summis circumlita taedis Admotam rapiunt vivacia sulpura flammam.* Cf. Juv. 13, 145.

uror 'I am on fire with love,' cf. 4, 19.

27—30. 'Though he is unkind, and though if I were wise I should care nothing for losing him, yet I do love him all the same.'

27. **male gratus** 'ungrateful', see index for *male.*

30. **peius**: cf. on 6, 157, and see index.

31. **nurui**, *i.e.* herself, as having wedded Aeneas, the son of Venus and therefore the brother of Cupid.

32. **castris militet** 'let him serve in your camp,' *i.e.* let him be in love. Loers quotes *Am.* 1, 91 *Militat omnis amans et habet sua castra Cupido.*

33—4. 'Or at any rate let him, whom I have begun to love (and I am not ashamed of the fact), afford a subject for my passion,' *i.e.* let him allow me to go on loving him though he does not love me. The connection is 'let him fall in love with me (31—2) or at least let him so behave as to allow me to love him.' The editors all quote *Am.* 1, 3, 2 *aut amet aut faciat cur ego semper amem. Ah nimium volui! tantum patiatur amari.* We may quote verse 19 in the same poem to show more fully the view meant to be expressed: the poets says to his unwilling mistress *Te mihi materiam felicem in carmina praebe etc.* 'Only let me have the privilege of singing of you, and I will make you famous' etc. *i.e.* Suffer yourself to be the subject of my love even if you do not return it.

ego is out of its place to mark the emphasis which belongs to it, and draw the contrast sharply with *ille* in the previous line.

[I cannot agree to retain *quae* for *quem*, and thus admit a very awkward anacoluthon. Nor do I feel able to take Madvig's emendation into the text, *i.e. amorem* for *amare*. The sense seems to me complete without it. 'I am not ashamed to own that I began to love him first, I only ask that he will let me go on doing so.']

36. **matris**, sc. Venus.

37—40. The idea is suggested by *Aen.* 4, 365 where Dido says to Aeneas: *Nec tibi diva parens, generis nec Dardanus auctor, Perfide; sed duris genuit te cautibus horrens Caucasus, Hyrcanaeque admorunt ubera tigres.* Cf. *M.* 9, 613 *neque enim te tigride natus: Nec rigidas silices solidumve in pectore ferrum, Aut adamanta gerit nec lac bibit ille leaenae.* Tibullus 3, 4, 85 *Nam te nec vasti genuerunt aequora ponti...nec te conceptam sacra leaena tulit*, cf. also 10, 131—2. It occurs first in Homer, *Il.* 16, 33, οὐκ ἄρα σοίγε πατὴρ ἦν ἱππότα Πηλεὺς...οὐδὲ Θέτις μήτηρ· γλαυκὴ δέ σε τίκτε θάλασσα ..πέτραι δ' ἠλίβατοι. Cp. Theocr. 3, 15.

40—3. He is again using Vergil *Aen.* 4, 309 *quin etiam hiberno moliris sidere classem Et mediis properas aquilonibus ire per altum.*

42. **eversas** is proleptic. 'See how Eurus is rousing the waters and making them rough.' *evertere aquas* would be to make the waves tumble.

43. **malueram** for *maluissem*, as we have *erat* and *fuit* for *essem:* cf. on 1, 108. 'I should have preferred if I had had the choice.'

44. **iustior** 'kinder.' See on 3, 133.

45—6. **tanti** 'worth so much.'

quid non tu reris inique 'what is there that you do not estimate wrongly?' For the use of *reor* with the idea of 'estimation' cf. *Tr.* 5, 6, 35 *elige nostrorum minimum minimumque laborum Isto quod reris grandius illud erit.*

[The readings proposed for this line are almost as many as there are editors. The best MS (P) has *quid non terreris*, with the first syllable of *terreris* indistinct, I have therefore guessed *tu reris* as being the nearest to this word, which would have no meaning.]

46. **ut pereas** depending on *tanti*, cf *Am.* 2, 5, 1 *Nullus amor tanti est—abeas pharetrate Cupido—Ut mihi sint totiens maxima vota mori.* **dum me fugis**: cf. Virg. *Aen.* 4, 313 *Mene fugis?*

47. **constantia magno** 'that will cost you dear.' **dum me careas** 'so long only as you can get rid of me.'

vile 'of small account.' Cf. 12, 187.

49. **ponent** 'will subside.' The intransitive use of *ponere* seems confined to this particular connection, *Aen.* 7, 27 *venti posuere. Ib.* 10, 103 *Zephyri posuere.*

50. **caeruleis**: the colour attributed to sea-gods, and hence to whatever belonged to them. *M.* 2, 8 *caeruleos habet unda deos.* Virg. *G.* 4, 388 *caeruleus Proteus.*

Triton curret, *i.e.* there will be calm. The idea is from Virgil *Aen.* 1, 144—147, where Cymothae and Triton busy themselves with remedying the damage done by the storm, and Neptune their father, after calming the disturbed waters, *rotis summas levibus perlabitur undas.*

52. **duritia**: cf. 4, 85.

53—4. 'What would you have done if you had known nothing of what the power of the angry sea was?' How ill is it that you trust the water whose nature you have so often learnt before!

male 'to your own misfortune,' cf. 9, 99.

expertae: *expertus* as a passive seems nearly unexampled before the Silver Age.

55. **ut** 'although,' as in 15. **pelago suadente**: the reverse of *pelago negante* 2, 100. **retinacula solvas**: cf. sup. 9, 'hawsers.'

57—58. Cf. Hor. *Od.* 3, 2, 26 *Vetabo qui Cereris sacrum Vulgarit arcanae sub isdem Sit trabibus, fragilemque mecum solvat phaselum.*

59. **laesus** for *laesus fuerit*, see index under *sum* omitted.

60. **Cytheriacis aquis.** The sea near the island of Cythera, Hes. *Theog.* 192 *πρῶτον δὲ Κυθήροισι ζαθέοισι ἔπλητ', ἔνθεν, ἔπειτα περίῤῥυτον ἵκετο Κύπριν.*

61—2. 'I fear that my ruin (wrought by you) may prove your own, and that so unwillingly I may be the cause of your destruction.'

63. **sic melius,** *i.e.* by your living with all the pangs of an uneasy conscience. Ovid's Dido is no less eager for Aeneas' punishment than Virgil's (*Aen.* 4, 382), but Ovid represents her, with perhaps more of refinement though less of nature, desire that his punishment should not be death but the pangs that come from remorse, and the evil reputation of being the cause of her death.

64. **ferere** 'you will be said to be.'

65. **pondus** 'significance,' see index.

66. **quid mentis** 'what will be your feelings?' Cf. 12, 5 *quidquid vitae.*

68. **Phrygia fraude** 'Trojan perfidy,' cf. 1, 55.

69—70. In Virgil she threatens that her ghost shall haunt him, *Omnibus umbra locis adero, Aen.* 4, 386.

71. What can make it worth your while that you should then have to say 'I am guilty: pardon me!'?

The use of *concedite* absolutely is not common. We have *veniam concedere Trist.* 2, 44, and *concede A. A.* 1, 1, 523.

[The line as it stands in the text is due to the restoration of Palmer, as should have been stated in the critical note.]

72. 'And that you should think that whatever thunderbolts shall fall were aimed at you.'

73. **spatium** 'a time to relax.' Cf. *Aen.* 4, 433 *tempus inane peto requiem spatiumque furori*, and inf. 178—180.

74. **grande morae pretium**: cf. *Am.* 3, 13, 5 *grande morae pretium ritus cognoscere.* 'It is well worth while.'

75. **curae**: dat. of predicate, 'for a care.' *Es* omitted, see on 59.

76. **titulum** 'the credit,' cf. 6, 100, a sense doubtless arising from the custom of describing a man's exploits in the inscription on his statue or tombstone, see 2, 67—74.

78. **ereptos**, *i.e.* from the flames of Troy.

82. **primaque plectar ego** 'nor am I the first to suffer at your hands': for *que* in the second of two negative clauses cf. 2, 90. Roby § 2242.

83—4. **mater Iuli**, Creusa, whose loss is briefly narrated by Aeneas, *Aen.* 2, 738:

> *Heu! misero conjunx fatone erepta Creusa*
> *Substitit, erravitne via, seu lassa resedit*
> *Incertum; nec post oculis est reddita nostris.*

85—86. 'You had told me this story; but (instead of putting me on my guard) it touched me, as I deserved it should. The punishment I am going to suffer (*i.e.* death) will be too light for my frailty.'

merentem seems a sudden outbreak of petulant self-condemnation for having been foolish enough to be affected by the false story told by Aeneas as to the loss of Creusa.

illa: that which is in my mind to inflict.

[This is a most vexed and difficult passage. For the various readings adopted, see the critical note. If *ure* is to be read instead of *illa*, which I now think probable, I believe it should be translated 'burn me on my funeral pyre,' not 'break my heart' as Palmer explains it.]

87—8. **nec mihi...quin...damnent**: this refers to *culpa* in the preceding line. My fault was great, but I am certain that you too have offended heaven, else you would not be in your seventh year of fruitless wanderings.

88. **septima**: Loers quotes *Aen.* 1, 759 *nam te jam septima portat Omnibus errantem terris et fluctibus aestas.*

89—90. **eiectum** 'driven ashore.' Ovid is again using Virgil (*Aen.* 4, 373) *ejectum litore egentem Excepi et regni demens in parte locavi; Amissam classem, socios a morte reduxi.*

91. **officiis** 'kindnesses,' cf on 6, 17.

93—96. *Aen.* 4, 160—172.

95—96. 'I thought it was only the cry of nymphs, it was really the shriek of the Furies foreboding my fate.' For the presence of the Eumenides cf. on 2, 117. In both the other instances in these epistles of *ululare* it is used in a sense not joyful 2, 117. 8, 107. Nor do I think that it is so used here. Dido's mistake was that she thought it was *only* nymphs, a less dreadful omen than it really was.

97. 'Exact your penalties, O violated chastity, and ye shades of Sychaeus, to which unhappy one! I go overwhelmed with my shame!' *Sychaeus* the first husband of Dido to whose memory she had resolved to be faithful. *Si mihi non animo fixum immotumque sederet, Ne cui me vinclo vellem sociare jugali, Postquam primus amor deceptam morte fefellit.* (*Aen.* 4, 15.) It is her breach of this resolution which is weighing on her mind. For **pudor** and **pudoris** see on 4, 155.

[This is another vexed passage, as will be seen by referring to the critical note. Palmer supposes two lines to be lost. *Umbraeque* appears to be a conjecture of Merkel's.]

99—102. Again from Virgil *Aen.* 4, 457—461. **vellera alba**: the fillets (*infulae*) used to decorate a temple or altar on a festal occasion; it was made of wool dyed red and white, knotted at intervals with a riband (*vitta*). See Rich. For **oppositae frondes** Loers quotes *Tr.* 3, 1, 39 *cur tamen opposita velatus janua fronde?*

106—7. 'The lover for whose sake I broke my resolution was a worthy one,' cf. 4, 33—34.

107. 'The fact that you had a goddess to your mother, and had been loyal to your father.' **sarcina**, see on 4, 34.

109. **si fuit errandum** 'if I was bound to go wrong.'

110. 'Only you keep your word, and I shall have nothing to regret in it.' With *pigendus* understand *error.*

111—128. 'I have always been unfortunate; my husband was murdered; my brother seized his goods; I am an exile; I have built a city, but I am harassed by surrounding foes, and plagued by suitors; complete my misfortunes by giving me up to Iarbas, or my brother.'

113. **occidit internas** 'my husband fell murdered at the altars within his house.' Dido's brother Pygmalion killed her husband Sychaeus, *Aen.* 1, 348 *ille Sychaeum Impius ante aras atque auri caecus amore Clam ferro incautum superat securus amorum Germanae.*

[*Internas* is a conjectural reading for *in terras* which the best MSS. have: other readings proposed have been *Herculeas* and *Herceas*. The principal objection to *internas* is that *internus* seems a word characteristic of the Silver Age.]

116. **hoste sequente** 'pursued by my enemy,' *i.e.* my brother.

117. **adplicor ignotis** 'I land on unknown shores.' Cf. *F.* 1, 543 *ecce boves illuc Erytheïdas applicat heros.*

118. **litus emo**: cf. *Aen.* 1, 367 *Mercatique solum, facti de nomine Byrsam, Taurino quantum possent circumdare tergo.* Dido purchased so much ground as could be covered by a bull's hide, which she then had cut into narrow slips, that it might cover a wide range.

120. 'An object of jealous dislike to neighbouring countries,' cf. *Aen.* 4. 39 *Nec venit in mentem, quorum consederis arvis? Hinc Gaetulae urbes, genus insuperabile bello, Et Numidae infreni cingunt et inhospita Syrtis.*

121. **peregrina et femina** 'both as a foreigner and a woman,' *i.e.* by enemies and by suitors. For *femina* cf. 14, 55.

122. **vix** 'only just in time.' The surrounding hostile tribes attack her and she has only just time to put up rough temporary gates.

123—4. *Aen.* 4, 320 *Te propter Libycae gentes Nomadumque tyranni Odere, infensi Tyrii*... cf. *ib.* 535.

nescio quem: see on 3, 78. Cf. 13, 63.

125. **Gaetulo Iarbae.** Iarbas is the only one of Dido's suitors named by Virgil, see *Aen.* 4, 36, 196 and 326 *aut captam ducat Gaetulus Iarbas.* He was king of the Numidians, and is therefore called *Gaetulus* from the *Gaetuli*, a nomad tribe of Numidia. Juvenal calls Aeneas *Zelotypo juvenis praelatus Iarbae* 5, 45.

127—128. **frater,** *i.e.* Pygmalion, see on verse 113.

129. **pone deos** 'lay by those gods,' *i.e.* which you brought from Troy, cf. 77—8.

131—2. 'If they escaped burning only to be worshipped by you, surely the gods will be sorry they did escape.'

133. **Didon**: the MS. authority seems in favour of this form and not *Dido* for the accusative, cf. 7. Virgil seems not to use any oblique case of the word; Conington looks upon *Dido* in *Aen.* 4, 383 as a vocative. The gen. Διδοῦς in Strabo on the other hand would seem to point to *Dido* as correct.

forsitan: see on 4, 53.

137. **parente** 'mother.'

139. **sed iubet ire deus** 'but,' you say, 'the god bids you go.' In Virgil Mercury is sent down to Aeneas to bid him depart and go to Italy, *Aen.* 4, 219—295.

140. **Punica** 'Carthaginian,' so the people are called *Poeni.* Both words are Latinised forms from Φοίνιξ.

141. **nempe**: see on 6, 144: it is here ironical. 'Is the god you mean the one under whose favour you are tossed by contrary winds and spend long years on the swift-flowing sea?' *i.e.* The god you appeal to does not seem to be of much service to you. Cf. 86.

143—4. 'It would have given you no more trouble to go back to Troy, if Troy were still existing.'

145. **Simoenta**: cf. 1, 33. **Thybridas.** Thybris is a feminine adj. formed on the analogy of *Argolis* (6, 81),

Sithonis (2, 6), *Tritonis* (6, 47), *Inachis* (14, 23) etc. Sometimes it is used as the name of the river itself. *Tr.* 5, 1, 31 *quot flavas Thybris arenas...habet.*

146. **nempe ut** 'and yet even supposing;' for **ut** see supr. 15. **Nempe** like *scilicet* has different shades of meaning according to the context, in 141 it was ironical, here it introduces a result not contemplated by the agent. So in 9, 41 it may be translated 'little as you would think.' **hospes** 'a stranger.' Not an honoured husband and ruler as you might be at Carthage.

147. **utque** 'and considering how the land hides itself and shrinks back from your ships.' Ovid seems to have in his mind the words of Aeneas to Helenus, envying him his *parta quies* as contrasted with his own hunt after a shore that ever seemed to recede from him, *Aen.* 3, 496 *Arva neque Ausoniae semper cedentia retro Quaerenda.*

148. **tibi continget** 'will reward your pains.' *Contingere* of good, *accidere* of bad luck. See Mayor *Cic. Phil.* 2, § 17.

149. **in dotem** 'as my dowry,' *Aen.* 4, 103—4 *liceat Phrygio servire marito Dotalesque tuae Tyrios permittere dextrae.*

ambage remissa 'your endless wandering o'er.' *Ambages* (*amb* ἀμφί—*agere*) is generally used in the sense of circumlocution. But Ovid elsewhere uses it of a path winding in and in and crossing itself; *e.g.* of the labyrinth, *Met.* 8, 161 *ducit in errorem variarum ambage viarum.*

150. **advectas Pygmalionis opes**, see on 113. The ghost of Dido's husband warns her to fly, *Auxiliumque viae veteris tellure recludit Thesauros ignotum argenti pondus et auri...... portantur avari Pygmalionis opes pelago*, *Aen.* 1, 358.

151. **felicius** 'with better fortunes than it had before.'

152. **sceptraque sacra.** The sceptre is called sacred from the notion of kings being especially under the care of Jupiter.

[*Sisque* is a conjecture of my own. For the variety of readings, see critical note. None of them are satisfactory; nor do I expect my own to meet with much more approval. It has the advantage of being easy; but I am more inclined to believe that Ovid really wrote *inque loco regis regia sceptra tene*, just as in all probability in *F.* 6, 305 he wrote *ante focos olim longis considere scamnis.* And Propertius (5, 4, 48), *tu cape spinosi rorida terga jugi*, where see Paley's note.]

154. **eat** 'may go in procession.' Ovid is thinking of the Roman mode of triumph.

156. **capit** 'admits of,' 'has room for.' Cf. *Am.* 3, 6, 86 *nec capit admissas alveus altus aquas. A. A.* 3, 365 *parva tabella capit ternos utrimque lapillos.*

157. **fraternaque tela** 'the weapons of your brother Cupid,' see 2, 40.

160. **Mars ferus, &c.** 'and may that fierce war be the limit of your losses,' *i.e.* may you lose nothing more than you have already lost in the Trojan war.

162. **molliter ossa cubent**: a common poetical wish, cf. Virg. *Ecl.* 10, 33 *O mihi tum quam molliter ossa quiescant.*

163. **quae...habendam** 'which gives itself up entirely into your hands,' cf. supr. 15.

165—6. **non ego sum Phthias...Mycenis** 'I am not sprung from Phthia (whence came Achilles), not from Mycenae,—the home of Agamemnon, nor have husband or father of mine been your enemy.' Phthia or Phthiotis was the south district of Thessaly.

For **stetĕrunt** see on 2, 141, and for the sentiment see *Aen.* 4, 425 *Non ego cum Danais Trojanam exscindere gentem Juravi, etc.*

167. **hospita** 'hostess' 2, 1. Cf. on 6, 52.

170. **dantque negantque**: cf. 2, 100.

171. **carbasa**: neut. plur. from *carbasus* fem., which is from a Sanskrit word meaning 'cotton.'

172. 'At present a mass of light seaweed hems in your stranded ship.' A quantity of seaweed ashore is a sign of rough weather at sea. Loers quotes Virgil 7, 590 *Saxa fremunt laterique illisa refunditur alga.* Hom. *Il.* 9, 4 *ὡς δ' ἄνεμοι δύο πόντον ὀρίνετον ἰχθυόεντα...... ἄμυδες δέ τε κῦμα κελαινὸν κορθύεται πολλὸν δὲ παρὲξ ἅλα φῦκος ἔχευαν.*

173. **serius ibis** 'you shall go, but later in the season.' The emphasis is on *ibis.*

177—180. The sentiment is again founded on Virgil (*Aen.* 4, 433), *Tempus inane peto, requiem spatiumque furori, Dum mea me victam doceat fortuna dolere....*

siqua debebimus ultra 'and by the further favours I shall owe you if you remain.' Cf. 2, 110. [Palmer however explains it as a reference to her loss of chastity supr. 5—6 and illustrates by the words of Lucretia, *F.* 2, 825 *hoc quoque Tarquiniis debebimus?* I prefer however the old explanation, nor is there any necessity to change the word to *praebebimus* as Burman did and Loers wished to do.]

179. **usu** 'by becoming habituated to the idea.' *Am.* 1, 8, 75 *nullum patiendi colligat usum amor. Rem.* 503 *intrat amor mentes usu dediscitur usu.*

dum is not 'until,' which would require the subjunctive, but 'while.'

I now see that Heinsius had suggested the same emendation as I have done in the critical note.

181. **si minus** 'otherwise' *εἰ δὲ μή*. Roby § 1563—5.

183. **imago** 'appearance.'

184. **Troicus ensis.** Aeneas left his sword with Dido, and she had hung it up in her thalamus (*Aen.* 4, 495, 507); with this she killed herself on the funeral pile (*Aen.* 4, 646—665).

187—188. 'How conveniently does your present come in to complete my fate.! It is a cheap way on your part to provide for my obsequies.' For v. 187 cp. the Greek epigram *Ἕκτωρ Αἴαντι ξίφος ὤπασεν, Ἕκτορι δ' Αἴας ζωστῆρ'· ἀμφοτέρων ἡ χάρις εἰς θάνατον.* The point of v. 188 seems to be: 'truly this is a cheap way of providing for a wife's obsequies—you leave her a sword.'

sepulchra 'funeral rites' not 'tomb,' see 10, 124.

191. **culpae** 'my frailty with Aeneas,' cf. supr. 86. Cf. *Aen.* 4, 172 *conjugium vocat, hoc praetexit nomine culpam.*

Anna soror: *Aen.* 4, 9—53.

193—4. 'I will not venture to be inscribed on my tomb as the wife of Sychaeus, to whose memory I have not been faithful as I had intended to be.' Cf. supr. 97 sq.

carmen 'inscription,' cf. 5, 28.

195—6. Ovid elsewhere nearly repeats this couplet *A. A.* 3, 39 *et famam pietatis habet, tamen hospes et ensem Praebuit et causam mortis, Elissa, tuae.* And in *F.* 3, 549 the same recurs word for word. (Loers.)

VIII.

HERMIONE ORESTAE.

Hermione, daughter of Menelaus and Helen, growing up during the absence of her father at the Trojan war and her mother's flight with Paris, was betrothed by her grandfather Tyndareus to Orestes son of Agamemnon. But her father had meanwhile promised her to Pyrrhus, son of Achilles, and upon his return bestowed her on him, rejecting Orestes on account of his pollution by the murder of his mother (Eur. *Andr.* 977—981 Hom. Od. 4, 1—59.). In Euripides' *Andromache* we find Hermione living unhappily with Pyrrhus, with just cause for jealousy on account of his connection with Andromache. This hint is enough for Ovid, as in the case of Briseis. He imagines her from the first to have been attached to Orestes and to be writing this letter expressing her misery, reproaching him for not coming to rescue her and claim his affianced bride, and declaring her determination to be faithful to him.

[Whether the legend had appeared definitely in the shape in which Ovid indicates it is not of much importance. For he treats the story quite generally, and makes Hermione speak as any woman detained by one she detested from one she loved might be supposed to speak. And there is no such appearance of a conscious following of any model as in the case of most of the previous Epistles.]

Ἑλένῃ δὲ θεοὶ γόνον οὐκέτ' ἔφαινον
ἐπεὶ δὴ τὸ πρῶτον ἐγείνατο παῖδ' ἐρατεινὴν
Ἑρμιόνην, ἣ εἶδος ἔχε χρυσέης Ἀφροδίτης.

Odyss. 4, 12.

1. **imagine patris** 'after the likeness of his father,' cf. 12, 89.

2. **contra iusque piumque** 'against all justice human and divine.' Cf. *A. A.* 1, 200 *stabit pro signis jusque piumque tuis.*

5—6. **quod potui** ''twas all I could do,' cf. 10, 53 *quae possum.* 13, 41 *qua potui.*

non invita 'with consent on my part.'

7. **Aeacide**: see on 1, 35. **vindice** 'some one to claim my freedom,' a legal term, see infr. 16 and 12, 158.

8. **tibi** 'let me tell you': ethic dative.

9. **surdior freto**: see on 3, 133. **clamantem nomen** 'as I shrieked out the name of Orestes.'

10. **inornatis** 'disordered' 'disarranged,' more than 'not adorned.' Cf. *Am.* 3, 9. 52 *inornatas dilaniata comas.* So of Ceres in grief for her daughter, *M.* 5, 472 *inornatos laniavit diva capillos.* Yet in *M.* 1, 497 it is merely 'not arranged,' *Spectat inornatos collo pendere capillos Et 'Quid si comantur?' ait:* so also in *M.* 9, 3.

11—12. Alluding to the constant habit of selling the women of conquered towns as slaves or distributing them among the victorious chiefs. See 3, 69. **barbara**: see on 3, 2. **nurus**: 'brides,' used generally for 'women,' cf. *ex P.* 3, 8, 10 *Palladis uti Arte Tomitanae non didicere nurus.*

13—14. **Achaia victrix**, *i.e.* the victorious Greeks. **Phrygias**: Trojan, see 1, 54. 7, 68.

15. **pia** 'natural' as from a lawful husband.

16. **inice manus.** The *injectio manus* was the legal term for the arrest of a defendant in a suit, who had been condemned to a certain payment, and had not paid it within thirty days. The prosecutor could then claim the person of the defendant, who had no power of resistance except by appealing to a *vindex* (see sup. 7). Cf. *Am.* 2, 5, 30 *Iniciam dominas in mea jura manus* and 12, 158. *Inicere* not *injicere* is the correct form. The preposition remains long though *j* is omitted, yet from Ovid downwards even this was sometimes neglected, *e.g.* *ădĭci.* Roby § 144.

18. **lentus** 'patient and inactive' 3, 22.

21—22. **si socer**...'If your father-in-law (Menelaus) had been a reclaimer of a stolen bride after your sort, my mother would have still been the wife of Paris, as she was before.'

si repetitor, sc. *esset.* For the omission of *sum* see index.

23. **nec tu...pararis** 'But do not *you* get ready.' **mille rates**: cf. *Aen.* 2, 198 *non anni domuere decem non mille carinae.* See on 13, 97.

25—6. **sic quoque eram** 'even so,' *i.e.* if you must needs bring an army to do it. **eram repetenda** 'it was your duty to have rescued me.' **toro** 'wife.'

27—8. Atreus, son of Pelops, was father of Agememnon and Menelaus. Helen and Orestes are therefore first cousins.

frater 'cousin,' Loers quotes *M.* 13, 31 where Ajax calls Achilles *frater* as having the same grandfather Aeacus. See also 14, 115, 117, 130.

30. **instant** 'make a claim on.' **officio**: see on 6, 17.

31—32. **me tibi**. See introduction. **neptis** 'over a granddaughter.' *nepos* and *neptis* both refer to grandchildren or children of a brother or sister. The same root appears in ἀνεψιός.

33. **at** 'But it will be said,' introducing supposed objection: often *at enim*, cp. the use of ἀλλὰ or ἀλλὰ νὴ Δία. **Aeacidae**, *i.e.* Pyrrhus great-grandson of Aeacus, as his father Achilles, the grandson of Aeacus, is elsewhere also called: cf. 1, 35. 3, 87.

inscius acti implies an answer to the objection. 'Yes he did so, but it was in ignorance of what had already been done,' *i.e.* that Tyndareus had already promised me to you.

34. 'Besides, as being the senior, my grandfather should have the greater weight.' Thus Lennep and Jahn both understand the line. Loers and Palmer refer *quoque* to *prior*, 'Let my grandfather, who has the precedence in order of time (*i.e.* of betrothing me), also carry the preference.' I prefer the former explanation, first, because it is simpler; and, secondly, because it brings out more fully that *inscius acti*, though grammatically belonging to the subject of *promiserat*, is in sense a separate sentence, and an answer to the objection introduced by *at*.

35. **mea taeda** 'my marriage,' cf. 4, 121 *taeda jugalis*. 6, 134 *taeda pudica*, and cf. on 6, 42.

36. **mihi**: the dative of the agent, 'by me.' Cf. 2, 115 and index.

37—40. 'The love my father had for his wife Helen will cause him to pardon mine for my husband.'

40. **proderit** 'will stand me in good stead.' **mater amata** 'the fact that my mother was loved by him.' **exemplo** 'precedent.'

41—2. **Dardanius advena**, Paris. **partes egerat**: see on 2, 78; the plural *partes* is always used in this sense.

43—48. 'And you are as good as Pyrrhus. If he boasts the deeds of his father Achilles, you can point to those of Agamemnon, who was the chief of all the chiefs, while Achilles was only a subordinate. You can also claim Pelops as a grandsire and the father of Pelops, Tantalus, as an ancestor. And, if you choose to make a still more particular calculation, you are fifth in descent from Jupiter.'

The descent of Orestes was, Jupiter and Aegina (3, 73), Tantalus, Pelops, Atreus, Agamemnon, Orestes.

45. **Tantalides**: Agamemnon. So Orestes is also called infr. 122.

46. **dux erat ille ducum.** Agamemnon was chief of all the chiefs, *ἄναξ ἀνδρῶν*.

48. **melius**: cf. 2, 7 *Tempora si numeres bene quae numeramus amantes*, 'more closely' or 'accurately.'

a Iove quintus: cf. Persius 6, 57 *quaere ex me, quis mihi quartus Sit pater: haud prompte, dicam tamen: adde etiam unum, Unum etiam: terrae est jam filius.*

49—54. 'You have shown your spirit also. It is true that the duty you performed has brought on you some odium, and I could have wished you a better subject for the display of your powers. But still it was a duty, and you fulfilled it.'

She carefully avoids any direct mention of his mother Clytemnestra; her death however necessary could bring only pain and not honour to Orestes. To kill Aegisthus however was not only his duty, but a deed of prowess. The rest is veiled under the general term *causa*.

49. **virtute** 'personal courage.' **invidiosa** 'likely to cause a feeling against you,' cf. 2, 145. She is referring of course to his killing his mother as well as Aegisthus.

50. 'But what were you to do? 'twas your father put those arms upon you,' *i.e.* the Manes of your father crying for revenge forced you upon your task. In the *Electra* of Sophocles and the *Choephoroe* of Aeschylus the action opens with propitiatory offerings by Clytemnestra on the tomb of her murdered husband; and all through both dramas Orestes is represented as acting in obedience to impulse from the same direction. In Sophocles however he has no doubts as to the righteousness of his cause and the absolute propriety of the deed he has to do. This is the view Hermione here takes. In the *Choephoroe* on the other hand Orestes is plagued with doubts, which revive when the deed is done. And it is these doubts which Hermione may be supposed to be here endeavouring to quiet, as well as to be arguing against the representations of his enemies. See Professor Jebb's interesting introduction to Sophocles' *Electra* pp. xi—xiii.

As to the form of the sentence, it really amounts to the protasis and apodosis of a conditional sentence under the guise of a statement and a question. 'If your father did thus, you would have done as you did.' For which latter clause is substituted 'What were you to do?' or 'You should have done—what?' cf. 10, 45. 12, 117, 146.

51. **materia**: cf. *materiam caedis* 3, 152. **vellem** 'I could have wished,' *i.e.* if I had had any choice in the matter. **fuisses**: dependent on *vellem*, cf. *id velim mihi ignoscas* Cic. *mallem Cerberum metueres* Cic. *Vin te faciam fortunatum* Plaut. Roby § 1336. 1607. So with *facio:* see index.

52. 'You did not choose an object for the display of your strength: it was assigned you by destiny' [or, by Phoebus, Eur. *Or.* 28]. For **operi** cf. *M.* 8, 393 *Discite femineis quid tela virilia praestent O juvenes operique meo concedite!*

53. **hanc tamen implesti.** 'This task however, good or bad, you nobly fulfilled.' *Hanc* has some idea of disparagement, cf. *F.* 4, 842, Remus says contemptuously of the walls of Romulus *His populus tutus erit?* Cf. infr. 104. 10, 104. Hence she uses **implesti** which implies making good something lacking, as if Orestes had made up for whatever was lacking in his cause by the manner of his supporting it; cf. *Tr.* 4, 3, 73 *Materiamque tuis tristem virtutibus imple*, where Ovid means that his friend in interceding with Caesar for him is to make his own excellences supply what is wanting in the goodness of Ovid's own cause. See also on 6, 58.

55—60. 'With this deed Pyrrhus reproaches you, and yet dares look me in the face. I rage inwardly when I hear him, and long for strength and a sword to slay him.'

55. **Aeacides**: Pyrrhus, cf. supr. 7.

59—60. 'Has any one dared to utter a reproach against Orestes in Hermione's presence,—and I lack strength and a sword?'

obicit requires an accusative of the subject of reproach. Its omission seems to add effect to the vehemence of Hermione's feelings. As though she had said 'Has any one dared to utter a reproach, no matter what or how small, against Orestes in my presence?' An equally bold use of *obicior* occurs in *Am.* 2, 7, 17 *sollers ornare Cypassis Obicitur dominae contemerasse torum*, 'is reproached for having violated.'

vires, *caedere* or some such word understood, cf. 1, 109 *vires pellere.*

61—64. 'At least I can weep. It is the only outlet for my pent-up wrath. In this consolation I ever indulge.'

diffundimus: a metaphor from draining off and dispersing a body of water. Loers rightly shows that it expresses the full meaning as *defundimus* could not do. *Defundimus* 'I pour out' is much less significant than *diffundimus* 'I disperse by pouring,' and so lessen and weaken, cf. *Met.* 9, 142 *flendo dolorem diffudit.*

64. **perenne** for *perenni* Ovid uses again in *F.* 6, 158; it occurs also in Lucretius 1, 161. For explanation see note on 4, 34.

65—82. 'Can there be some strange fate that dogs our race and brings it to pass that all the women of our family should suffer violence? Not to mention Leda; there was Hippodamia; the first violent seizure of Helen by Theseus and her second flight with Paris; and now I am forcibly detained by Neoptolemus.'

Tantalides is the plur. of the fem. adjective *Tantalis*, cf. infr. 122, and must not be confused with the masc. patronymic in 8, 45. **matres** 'matrons.'

69—70. **Hippodamia** was daughter of Oenomaus king of Elis, who offered her as a prize to whoever should beat him in the chariot race: this Pelops did, by the treachery of Oenomaus' charioteer Myrtilus, and carried off Hippodamia, who may be said to be *rapta* because she was won unfairly. The course was to be from Pisa to the isthmus. The chariot is called *rotae peregrinae* 'foreign,' because Pelops was son of Tantalus king of Phrygia. Verse 70 is from Propert. 1, 2, 20 *avecta externis Laodamia rotis.*

distinet 'keeps apart,' cf. 12, 104.

71—2. Alluding to the carrying off of Helen by Theseus when she was quite young, and the expedition of Castor and Pollux to recover her, see 5, 126. They are both called *Amyclaeo* from *Amyclae* near Sparta of which Tyndareus was king.

Mopsopia urbe 'Athens.' So Triptolemus is called *Mopsopius juvenis*, *M.* 5, 66. And *Mopsopios muros* are 'the walls of Athens' *M.* 6, 423. And Seneca who is fond of imitating Ovid calls the art of Daedalus *ars Mopsopia*, Hipp. 121. Attica is said by Strabo (10, 18 and 23) to have been called Mopsopia from an ancient king Mopsopus.

Taenaris soror: their sister Helen. *Taenaris* is simply 'Laconian,' a feminine adjective from Taenarum (Cape Matapan), see on 6, and 1, 46.

77. **Phoebe**: Loers quotes Eurip. *Iphig. Aul.* 49 ἐγένοντο Λήδᾳ Θεστιάδι τρεῖς παρθένοι, Φοίβη, Κλυταμνέστρα τ', ἐμὴ ξυνάορος, Ἑλένη τε. This Phoebe, daughter of Leda, however is so seldom mentioned that she was forgotten and the reading was changed to *Phaebique soror*. Here as elsewhere Ovid shows the minuteness of his knowledge of Greek mythology.

79. **scissa capillos**: cf. 3, 79. **non longos etiam tum** 'which were still not very long,' *i.e.* because she was so young.

81—82. **nam coniunx aberat** is parenthetical. 'And lest I should fail to be thought one of the family of Pelops I became an easy prey to Neoptolemus, for my husband was absent,' as Menelaus was when Paris carried off Helen.

Neoptolemus is another name for Pyrrhus; which latter does not appear in Homer. He was said to have been called Pyrrhus from his red hair, Neoptolemus because he came late to the Trojan war.

83. **Pelides**, *i.e.* Achilles, who was killed by an arrow of Paris, which Apollo directed. *Aen.* 6, 56 *Phoebe......Dardana qui Paridis direxti tela manusque Corpus in Aeacidae.* His death is not described in the Iliad, but Hector when dying prophecies it (*Il.* 22, 359) ἤματι τῷ ὅτε κέν σε Πάρις καὶ Φοῖβος Ἀπόλλων ἐσθλὸν ἐόντ' ὀλέσωσιν ἐνὶ Σκαιῇσι πύλῃσι. The most detailed statement in Homer as to his death is in *Odyss.* 24, 36—97: but there there is no mention of Paris or Apollo.

84. **proterva** 'wanton and violent:' with a reference to sensuality, cf. 5, 136. Hor. *Od.* 1, 25, 1—2 *Parcius junctas quatiunt fenestras Ictibus crebris juvenes protervi.* So *A. A.* 1, 599 *dicere protervius* under the influence of wine.

85—86. **nec quondam placuit**, referring to the rage and grief of Achilles when deprived of Briseis by Agamemnon.

88. **sidus** 'unfavourable planet.' The use of astrology among the Romans of the imperial period was very general, see Mayor on Juvenal 14, 248. The influence of the planet under which one is born is often referred to. *Tr.* 5, 10, 45, *O duram Lachesin, quae tam grave sidus habenti Fila dedit vitae non breviora meae.* Propert. 1, 6, 36 *vivere me duro sidere certus eris.* Pers. 5, 45 *Non equidem hoc dubites amborum foedere certo Consentire dies et ab uno sidere duci.* The influence of one planet could counteract another, *ib.* 50 *Saturnumque gravem nostro Jove frangimus una*

90. 'And though both are living still, I was already deprived of both.' Her mother Helen had fled with Paris, her father Menelaus was at Troy.

92—102. 'As a baby I knew no mother's fondling, as a girl no mother's care; as a young woman no mother lovingly prepared my wedding-chamber; I met Helen when she returned, but I only guessed that it was she from her exceeding loveliness; and she did not know me: the only happiness of my girlhood was to have been plighted to Orestes; him even I shall lose unless he defends his rights.'

I think Ovid never wrote lines more simple and beautiful. *Te tamen esse Helenam quod eras pulcherrima sensi*, is an exquisite touch. The girlish pride in her mother's beauty survives so much neglect and unkindness.

incerto...ore 'with a baby's imperfect words.'

93. 'I never tried to clasp your neck with arms too short to go round it.' The tentative *captavi* and the epithet *brevibus* vividly represent to us a pretty picture.

95. **pacta** 'betrothed,' see on 2, 34 [where it should have been stated that the custom referred to was a Latin not Roman one, and that it ceased when the Latins obtained the full *civitas* by the Lex Julia B.C. 90].

matre parante. It appears that the mother was accustomed to carry the *lectus genialis* into the *atrium* on the day of her daughter's marriage and prepare it. Cf. Cic. *Cluent.* 5 § 14 *itaque...lectum illum genialem quem biennio ante filiae suae nubenti straverat, in eadem domo sibi ornari et sterni jubet.* See Becker's *Gallus* Excurs. I. sc. 1, p. 166.

101. **pars haec una**: 'this one stroke of fortune in my life.' **bene cessit**: securing Orestes as husband 'was one favourable stroke for me.' She is evidently using the phraseology of some game of chance, see 4, 33. 10, 141.

104. **hoc** 'that is all the good I get from the destruction of Troy.' For *hoc* see supr. on 53.

105. **instat** 'stands upon his car,' cf. *Aen.* 11, 529 *sive instare jugis et grandia volvere saxa (velis). Instare* 'to press or hurry on' seems to be used absolutely (cf. Verg. *G.* 3, 106 *illi instabant verbere torto*), or with accusative of the thing pressed. Though in a hostile sense it takes the dative, *Met.* 12, 134 *cedentique sequens instat turbatque ruitque.*

equis is for horses and chariot, then, for chariot alone. Cf. *ex Pont.* 2, 8, 49 *Sic tibi fraterni mature funeris ultor Purpureus niveis filius instet equis.* *i.e.* in a triumph.

106. Though still unhappy I have then the luxury of more freedom in my trouble.' Her lot is still an unhappy one but it is more free in the absence of Pyrrhus. That she should call her *malum* '*liberius*', when she means that she herself is '*liberior*' is intelligible. But Loers interprets it more literally as = *minus urgente*.

109. **lacrimis oculi funguntur obortis**: 'instead of sleeping as they should, all the duty that my eyes perform is to weep.'

fungi: so an altar is said *fungi igne*, *F.* 4, 824. A man is said *fungi dapibus*, *F.* 2, 791. **obortis** 'that rise and cover them.' Cf. *F.* 4, 845 *lacrimas introrsus obortas devorat.* Cf. 13, 23.

110. **quaque licet** 'and as well as I can,' cf. 5, 55.

112. **Scyria membra** 'the limbs of Pyrrhus,' who was born and brought up at Scyros, of which his grandfather Lycomedes was king.

117. **generisque parentem**, *i.e.* Jupiter, who was father of Tantalus, great-great-grandfather of Hermione. See on 45.

119—120. 'By the bones of Agamemnon, which owe it to you that they lie well-avenged as they do.' *i.e.* by your killing of Aegisthus and Clytemnestra.

The distinction between *ultus* as a passive or a middle in such a sentence is not wide. A person may be *ultus* 'in a state of having had his vengeance satisfied' whether that be by his own means or another's. This consideration may make us hesitate to accept Palmer's decisive remark in favour of *se* for *sic*. Moreover the passive use of the past participle of a deponent verb is very common, and Facciolati quotes an undoubtedly passive use of *ultus*, though in a somewhat different sense, Liv. 2, 17 *ob iras graviter ultas.*

sub tumulo 'under their funeral mound,' *βωμός*.

121. **praemoriar** 'die beforehand,' *i.e.* before you can recover me.

122. **Tantalidae Tantalis**, see on 66.

IX.

DEIANIRA HERCULI.

The last expedition of Hercules was against Eurytus of Oechalia in Euboea. He took Oechalia, killed Eurytus and his sons, and carried off his daughter Iole. He stopped on his way home at Cenaeum, a promontory of Euboea, and having there built an altar to Jupiter, he sent Lichas to Trachis in Thessaly, where his wife Deianira was, to fetch a white robe wherein to sacrifice. Deianira had heard that Hercules had become enamoured of Iole, and she sent as a love-charm the white robe dipped in the poisonous blood of the Centaur Nessus. This letter is supposed to be written by her after sending the robe, to reproach Hercules with his infidelity to her, and the shame which he is bringing upon himself. At verse 143 she is supposed to hear of the fatal effects of the robe, and of the approaching death of Hercules. She thereupon resolves to die, and ends with a passionate farewell to all that belong to her.

[In some respects this Epistle appears to me to be less effective and artistic than the others. It is laden with learning and allusion, and the long digression about Omphale (55—118) seems a clumsy contrivance to bring in an enumeration of the 'Labours.' In this passage, too, there are many minor irregularities, *e.g.* no less than four cases of hiatus; a doubtful use of *Nympha* (103); a confusion of metaphors in legal matters in which Ovid was well informed (107—8); very probably the unparalleled licence of *tegendŏ* (126); and many other minute matters which might be alleged to make us suspicious of the genuineness at any rate of the greater part of the passage from 55 to 118.]

[The *Trachiniae* of Sophocles supplied Ovid with much of his material, though he would know the story from many sources. We have also the advantage of being able to compare his treatment of the same subject in *Met.* 9; as well as that of Seneca in his *Hercules Oeteus*, who as in the case of the 'Phaedra Hippolyto' not only used the same materials as Ovid, but imitated his treatment of them.]

1. **titulis** 'our honours,' from the practice of inscribing a man's achievements on his statue, see on 6, 100, cf. 10, 130 and index. By **nostris** she associates herself with her husband's actions.

Oechaliam. There are several towns of this name mentioned, in Thessaly, in Messenia, and Euboea. The last is probably meant by Ovid, following Sophocles *Tr.* 74 Εὐβοΐδα χώραν φασίν, Εὐρύτου πόλιν, ἐπιστρατεύειν αὐτόν.

3. **Pelasgiadas** 'Grecian.' The Pelasgi were the most ancient inhabitants of Greece, see 14, 23. The fem. adjective *Pelasgias* is formed from *Pelasgus* as *Lemnias* from *Lemnos* (6, 139).

4. **decolor** 'disgraceful.' Ovid nowhere else uses the word in any but a physical sense. Virgil (*Aen.* 8, 326) has *Deterior donec paulatim ac decolor aetas*, but that has reference to the change from the gold to the bronze age.

factis infitianda tuis 'a report which your great achievements should disown,' *i.e.* one that is unworthy of a hero of your mighty achievements. The *facta* are, as it were, personified and stand for the man who accomplished them. Loers quotes *M.* 2, 34 *progenies Phaethon haud infitianda parenti:* but his explanation (*quam negari debeat esse factorum tuorum*) is neither good Latin nor good sense.

6. **fregerit** the subj., 1st because it is oratio obliq. dependent on *fama*, and 2nd because **quem** = 'the sort of man whom.'

numquam fregerit 'has ever failed to crush.'

7—8. Eurystheus, king of Argos, at whose bidding Hercules performed his twelve labours. He was from birth the rival of Hercules, being ordained by the fraud of Juno to reign over the descendants of Perseus (see *Class. Dict.* 'Hercules'), and therefore may be supposed to rejoice at any disgrace that befell him.

germana Tonantis...noverca, *i.e.* Juno. For *noverca* see 6, 126 and *M.* 9, 181 *decet haec dare dona novercam.* For the form of expression Loers quotes *Aen.* 2, 104 *hoc Ithacus velit et magno mercentur Atridae*, and *Il.* 1, 255 ἦ κεν γηθήσαι Πρίαμος Πριάμοιό τε παῖδες.

10. 'Was not enough for the begetting of so mighty a one as you.' **tanti** should mean 'of so great value' or 'price,' and is not easy to reconcile with the sense required. Most of the old editors read *tanta*.

12. **humili** 'humiliating.' So *pingue serum*, *pingue flumen* (Virg. *G.* 3, 406. *Aen.* 9, 31) mean 'fattening,' 'fertilizing.' *Exsangue cuminum* (Hor. *Ep.* 1, 19, 18), 'cumin that makes pale.'

13. **vindicibus viribus** 'your strength that had been its protection,' so in *Met.* 9, 241 *timuere dei pro vindice terrae.* And Sen. *Herc. Oet.* 321 *vindicem tellus suum defendet omnis.* (Loers.)

14. **qua** 'wherever.' **caerulus Nereus**, *i.e.* the ocean. *M.* 1, 187 *Nunc mihi qua totum Nereus circumtonat orbem Perdendum est mortale genus:* for *caerulus* cf. 7, 50, for *Nereus* cf. 3, 74. For this and following line cf. Seneca *Oet.* 3—4 *protuli pacem tibi quacunque Nereus porrigi terras vetat.*

15. 'To you are owing the security to be found on land and the (safe) state of the whole sea.' This is well enough implied in *tota aequora* without changing to *tuta*, see on 7, 21. The real difficulty in the line is that it seems to attribute to Hercules some feats against sea-monsters or pirates, which are not elsewhere recorded.

16. *i.e.* 'east and west,' Loers quotes Seneca *Herc. F.* 1061 *novit tuas utrasque domos. Herc. Oet.* 2 *Sator deorum cujus excussum manu Utraeque Phoebi sentiunt fulmen domus.*

17—18. Cf. *F.* 1, 565 *nititur hic humeris, coelum quoque sederat illis.* Hercules held up the heavens while Atlas went to fetch the golden apples from the gardens of the Hesperides for him. For one of the legends of Atlas see *M.* 4, 630—662. The correct form is doubtless *Atlans*, Ἄτλανς hardened in oblique cases into Ἄτλαντ-ος, though probably the *n* was omitted in pronunciation of the nominative.

19—20. 'What good are all your achievements except to add greater notoriety to your shame, if you put a finishing stroke to them by the stigma of seduction?' It is true, as Palmer says, that there was no *stuprum* in the case of Iole; but Deianira believed that there was. See *Met.* 9, 141 *credit amans venerisque novae perterrita fama Indulsit primo lacrimis flendoque dolorem Diffudit.* For **cumulas** see 2, 57. It conveys the idea of something excessive or superfluous, cf. *Rem.* 541 *dum bene te cumules et copia tollat amorem.*

21—2. **tene ferunt** 'can it be you that they say gripped the snakes?' Cf. *A. A.* 1, 107 *Parvus erat manibusque duos Tirynthius angues Pressit et in cunis jam Jove dignus erat.*

25. **Stheneleius hostis**, sc. Eurystheus, son of Sthenelus, who was son of Perseus and Andromeda, see on 7.

27. **quia nominer** 'because, as they say, I am called the wife of Hercules.' *Nominer* the subj. is evidently right here because it is not her reason, but the reason of *feror*, *i.e.* of those who say that she is *bene nupta.*

28. **sitque socer qui**, *i.e.* Jupiter.

30—2. **magno...minor**, *i.e.* in regard to rank. The passage of Callimachus (*Epig.* 1, 16) which Palmer quotes refers to the man, whom it warns to wed within his own degree.

31. **species** 'mere show.' **onus ferentis** 'those who have to bear it as a burden.' She means herself, but uses the plural to make the statement general, vid. on 3, 43. There is some slight play on the sound of the words *honor* and *onus*, as in *verba* and *verbera* 10, 38.

35. **operata** 'busying myself with chaste prayers.' *operatus* is peculiarly used of religious exercises. Cf. Liv. 1, 31 *operatum iis sacris se abdidisse. Fast.* 2, 261 *Nympha mone, nemori stagnoque operata Dianae. Ib.* 6, 249 *Vesta fave! tibi nunc operata resolvimus ora.*

38—9. **iactor** 'I am tossed in imagination.' **terna per ora**: referring to Hercules carrying off Cerberus. Verse 38 refers to three of the labours of Hercules—his destruction of the Hydra, the Erymanthian boar, the Nemeaean lion.

39—40. 'In my terror I try various methods of divination, by the entrails of sheep, dreams, magic.'

fibrae 'the entrails,' especially the liver, used in divination by the haruspex. For a description of such a proceeding see *Met.* 15, 573—582.

simulacra somni: see 13, 111.

40. **ominaque arcana nocte**: witches chose midnight when the moon was full for their operations, see a full description of the doings of Medea in this way *Met.* 7, 180—192. She begins her prayer to Hecate thus, '*Nox*,' *ait*, '*arcanis fidissima*,' &c.

41. **aucupor** 'I catch at,' cf. 13, 107. Cicero has *inanem aucupari rumorem;* it properly means 'to go fowling' (*avis*).

43—4. **mater abest** 'your mother Alcmena is away,' *i.e.* at Tiryns; Deianira is writing from Trachis. **Amphitryon** according to most accounts was dead. **Hyllus** had been sent by Deianira in search of his father, in accordance with a suggestion of her maid. Soph. *Trach.* 58 sq.

45—6. **arbiter** 'minister' or 'agent.' It is a bold use of the word drawn from the meaning 'manager,' 'chief administrator,' cf. *Tr.* 5. 2, 47 *arbiter imperii.*

nobis sentitur 'is felt by me,' *i.e.* in imagination, as much as though I were actually the object of it, cf. *jactor* in 38. For *sentitur* cf. 6, 154. *Nobis* is dative, see 2, 115 and index.

47. **parum**: cf. on 3, 25.

49—54. The loves of Hercules. A similar enumeration is made by the nurse in Sen. *Herc. Oet.* 365 sq., doubtless taken from this.

Auge: daughter of Aleus, king of Tegea, whom Hercules caught on Mt Parthenius, in Arcadia, and became by her the father of Telephus.

Ormeni nympha: Astydamia, grand-daughter of Ormenus, king of the Dolopes. *Ormeni* is vocative of fem. patronymic *Ormenis.*

Theutrantia turba: Thespis a king in Mysia, son of Teuthras, had fifty daughters who were bestowed on Hercules as a reward for his slaying the lion of Cithaeron.

53. **una**: Omphale, queen of Lydia, to whom Hercules was sent as a slave by Mercury. **unde ego sum Lydo** 'by whom I have been made the stepmother to the Lydian Lamus.'

55—118. A digression on the subject of Omphale. Deianira had heard that Hercules had submitted to the greatest ignominy in her service; had been dressed in a robe of a wanton girl, and worn her ornaments; had been set to work at the loom, and borne the scoldings and blows of his mistress; how could he venture in such humiliating circumstances to speak of all his mighty deeds? Omphale has appropriated to herself the credit of them all, and is the victor's victor: she was the man, since Hercules failed to be one.

55. 'The Maeander that is so often a wanderer in the same district, and who often sweeps round upon itself its slackened waters.'

The Maeander, whose tortuous course has given a word to our language, is often described, *e.g.*

Met. 2, 246 *quique recurvatis ludit Maeandros in undis.*
„ 9, 451 *...Maeandri totiens redeuntis eodem.*
„ 8, 162 *Non secus ac liquidus Phrygiis Maeandros in arvis*
Ludit, et ambiguo lapsu refluitque fluitque
Occurrensque sibi venturas aspicit undas
Et nunc ad fontes, nunc ad mare versus apertum
Incertas exercet aquas.

Which Seneca has as usual imitated: *Herc. F.* 633
qualis incerta vagus
Maeander unda ludit, et cedit sibi
Instatque, dubius litus an fontem petat.

56. **lassas** seems to refer to breaking or slackening of the stream by the many windings. It has been commonly altered to *lapsas*, which makes good sense enough, but is not necessary. Loers quotes among other passages Lucan 5, 466 *neuter longo se gurgite lassat.* And *Met.* 1, 582 *In mare deducunt fessas erroribus undas.*

58. **cui caelum**: see on supr. 17--18. **sarcina**: see on 3, 68.

61—2. Ovid is using Sophocles *Trach.* 1090.

> ὦ νῶτα καὶ στέρν', ὦ φίλοι βραχίονες
> ὑμεῖς ἐκεῖνοι δὴ καθέσταθ' οἵ ποτε
> Νεμέας ἔνοικον, βουκόλων ἀλάστορα,
> λέοντ', ἄπλατον θρέμμα κἀπροσήγορον
> βίᾳ κατεργάσασθε.

And Seneca copies Ovid in this passage and *Met.* 9, 197 *his elisa jacet moles Nemeaea lacertis*: see *Herc. Oet.* 1235 *His ne ego lacertis colla Nemeaei mali elisa pressi.* Lennep.

nempe: see on 6, 144. 7, 141, indignation rather than irony is expressed by it here.

63. **mitra** 'a woman's snood.' A scarf wound round the head and tied under the chin. In Italy it was principally used by aged people, Ov. *F.* 4, 517 *simularat anum mitraque capillos Presserat.* In Asia it was worn by men as well as women, but seemed to the Romans a mark of effeminacy, *Aen.* 4, 215 *et nunc ille Paris cum semiviro comitatu Maeonia mentum mitra crinemque madentem Subnexus.*

redimire 'to tie with its long ends.' So the Latin Remulus reproaches the Trojans (*Aen.* 9, 616) *et tunicae manicas et habent redimicula mitrae.* Seneca again copies Ovid *H. Oet.* 375 *crinemque mitra pressit.*

64. **populus alba**: λευκή. Theocr. 2, 121 Ἡρακλέος ἱερὸν ἔρνος, so in Virgil, *Ecl.* 7, 61. *G.* 2, 66. *Aen.* 8, 276. Hercules is said to have made a wreath for himself of it on his way from the infernal regions,—a way of accounting for its use as a prize-garland in the games. It is in this last capacity that Deianira here calls it *aptior* to Hercules. So the youth in the *Nubes* (1007), if he will listen to the δίκαιος λόγος, is to live in the gymnasia μίλακος ὄζων καὶ ἀπραγμοσύνης καὶ λεύκης φυλλοβολούσης.

65—6. **Maeonia** 'Lydian.' The Maeones were the earlier race supplanted by the later Lydians. Herod. 1, 7 says that the people were formerly called Maeonians, but took the name Lydians from *Lydus* the ancestor of their kings. Homer knows only of the name 'Maeonian,' *Il.* 2, 864—6 Μῄονας ἦγον ὑπὸ Τμώλῳ γεγαῶτας. See Rawlinson's Her. vol. I. p. 291.

incingi: cf. 4, 87.

67. Diomede king of Thrace fed his mares with human flesh (or 'horses' *M.* 9, 104 *Thracas equos humano sanguine pingues*); those it was Hercules' eighth labour to lead off or kill.

crudi 'savage,' an epithet doubtless suggested by the horrible food of his horses, cf. *Pont.* 1, 2, 121 *Non tibi Thermodon crudusque rogabitur Atreus, Quique suis homines pabula fecit equis.*

69—70. **Busiris**, a king of Egypt who used to sacrifice all strangers, was killed by Hercules. Cf. Verg. *G.* 3, 4 *quis aut Eurysthea durum, Aut inlaudati nescit Busiridis aras?*

nempe: see sup. 62.

71. **redemicula**: the ends of the scarf which formed the *mitra*, see on 63.

72. **molli** 'effeminate,' so *Tr.* 2, 411 *mollis Achilles.*

73. **Ioniacas**, *i.e.* Lydian. Ionia stands generally for Asia Minor. Ovid has nearly repeated the lines in *A. A.* 2, 219 *Inter Ioniacas calathum tenuisse puellas Creditur et lanas excoluisse rudes. Paruit imperio dominae Tirynthius heros.*

76. **rasilibus calathis** 'baskets made of smooth osiers.' Ovid applies *rasilis* to a 'buckle' in *M.* 8, 318 *rasilis huic summam mordebat fibula vestem* (radere 'to scrape'). The example given by Rich represents the *calathus* 'wool-basket' as very much like an ordinary waste-paper basket.

77. 'Do you draw off from the distaff thick and clumsy threads with your stalwart hand?' Just the reverse of the effect of skilful manipulation, see on 3, 70.

78. **aequa**, *i.e.* like a slave girl who is required to produce exactly the same weight as was dealt out to her.

79. **torques**: cf. *M.* 12, 474 *columque, I, cape cum calathis et stamina pollice torque.*

81—2. **scuticae habenis** 'the thongs of the whip.' σκυτικὸς leather, see Rich. It was less severe than the *flagellum*, Hor. *S.* 1, 3, 119 *Ne scutica dignum horribili sectere flagello.* And both these and the ferula were used for slaves, Juv. 6, 478 *hic frangit ferulas, rubet ille flagellis, Hic scutica.* For severities to maid-servants see on 3, 78.

83—100. 'You tell her of all the monsters you have conquered: the serpents throttled in your cradle; the Erymanthian boar; the fierce man-eating mares of Diomede;

Geryon, the monster with three bodies; the three-headed Cerberus; the Lernean Hydra; Antaeus, the son of earth; the Centaurs. Do you venture to tell of all these deeds dressed in a woman's robe?'

82. The sameness of the ending of this line with that of 74 justly brings it into suspicion. The idea of it is that of a slave-girl throwing herself at her mistress' feet to entreat to be spared a flogging.

83. 'You told the utmost glories of your triumph with all its splendid pageants and deeds which now you should disown,' *i.e.* because in your present effeminate employment, cf. supr. 4.

eximiis pompis is a descriptive ablative qualifying *triumphi*.

praeconia: lit. 'the proclamations of a *praeco* or herald.' Ovid uses the word several times rather for the 'publication of fame' than for 'fame' itself, *Pont.* 4, 8, 45 *Carmina vestrarum peragunt praeconia laudum. Tr.* 5, 1, 8 *ut cecidi, subiti perago praeconia casus. Pont.* 1, 1, 55 *talia caelestes fieri praeconia gaudent.* **narrare praeconia** therefore is not the usual Ovidian use, nor indeed an intelligible one at all unless we suppose *praeconia* to be used metaphorically for 'glory' or 'splendour.' This and the unusual ablative *eximiis pompis*, coupled with the fact that this verse and 81 are only written in the margin of the best MS., make it very probable that the text has been thrown into confusion and awkwardly patched by some not very skilful hand.

85—6. **scilicet** 'to wit,' introducing an enumeration of circumstances or details, see on 4, 21.

elisos faucibus 'throttled,' lit. crushed in the throats: abl. of the part affected, see supr. 21, 22. *Elisus* expresses the effect of a powerful grasp, *M.* 9, 197 *his elisa jacet moles Nemeaca lacertis.* Lennep who reads *cunis* for *caudis* quotes Theocr. 24, 27 *ἄμφω δὲ βαρεὶ ἐνεδήσατο δεσμῷ | δραξάμενος φαρύγος. M.* 9, 67 *cunarum labor est angues superare mearum.*

infantem 'wound their coils round your infant hand.' Cp. *infantia pectora* F. 6, 145, &c.

87. **ut...incubat...laedit**: 'you tell how the Tegeaean boar lies low and dints the ground with his huge weight.'

cupressifero Erymantho, for the hiatus see 4, 99 and infr. 131, 133, 141. Erymanthus is a high range of mountains in Arcadia, famed for its wild beasts, *Monstriferumque Erymanthon* (Statius). **Tegeaeus**, *i.e.* 'Arcadian' from Tegea in the S.E. of Arcadia.

88. **ora** 'human skulls,' of the bodies with which Diomede fed his mares, cf. 68. The heads are nailed up over the doors like the heads of wild beasts, cf. Eur. *Bacch.* 12, 12 αἰρέσθω λαβὼν πηκτῶν πρὸς οἴκους κλιμάκων προσαμβάσεις, ὡς πασσαλεύσῃ κρᾶτα τριγλύφοις τόδε λέοντος ὃν πάρειμι θηράσασ' ἐγώ. Loers quotes Virgil's description of the cave of Cacus, *Aen.* 8, 196 *foribusque adfixa superbis Ora virum tristi pendebant pallida tabo*, which Ovid has copied *Fast.* 1, 557 *Ora super postes affixaque brachia pendent Squalidaque humanis ossibus albet humus.*

91—2. **armenti dives Hiberi** 'rich in Spanish cattle.' Geryones, a monster with three heads, was a king in Spain, or as Ovid implies in *F.* 1, 542 of Erytheia an island in the straits of Gibraltar, or the peninsula on which Cadiz stands. It was his cattle that Hercules was driving off when some were stolen by Cacus.

armenti dives, the genitive of respect, see on 1, 81: it is especially used with words expressing abundance. In the same connection he constructs *dives* with abl. *M.* 15, 12 *dives ab oceano bubus Jove natus Hiberis*, &c. But the gen. is almost equally common in poetry, cf. Verg. *Ecl.* 2, 20 *quam dives pecoris*, Roby § 1211, 1334.

93—94. **digestus**: cf. 10, 67 'branching out into,' separation with connection is implied by this word, cf. *M.* 7, 773 *septem digestum in cornua Nilum.* Cerberus is described by Virgil as having snakes on his neck, *Aen.* 6, 419 *cui vates, horrere videns jam colla colubris*, &c. For his three heads, cf. ib. *latratu trifauci*, and *Met.* 7, 414 *implevit pariter ternis latratibus auras.*

95—6. The Lernean Hydra, whose heads grew as fast as Hercules could knock them off. *Met.* 9, 70 *vulneribus fecunda suis.* For the position of *ab* and *ipsa* cf. 12, 18 and 13, 116. And for the use of *ab* see on 4, 32, and index. **Lerna** was a lake in the S.W. of the Argive plain; it was drained by the Argives; hence the legend.

97—8. Antaeus, who recovered his strength directly he touched his mother Earth. Hercules therefore held him away from the ground to kill him.

99—100. The Centaurs, who lived in Mt Pelion in Thessaly.

forma bimembri...agmen equestre refer to their double bodies, human and equine. The combat of Hercules with them seems to be a separate legend from that of their fight with the Lapithae.

101—2. **Sidonio amictu,** *i.e.* a robe dyed with Tyrian murex, or purple. *M.* 10, 267 *collocat hanc stratis concha Sidonide tinctis.* [Ovid seems to be borrowing the line from Propertius who (4, 9, 47) makes Hercules say, *Idem ego Sidonia feci servilia palla Officia, et Lyda pensa diurna colu.* (Loers).]

cultu 'dress.'

103. **Iardanis**: Omphale, daughter of Iardanus, see on 5, 3. For **nympha,** which again is used somewhat loosely for 'a bride,' see on 1, 27.

104. **nota tropaea** 'a well-known triumph.' *Tropaeum* is properly the trophy of arms, etc. put up at the spot where the enemy was turned to flight (*τρέπω*). It is used poetically for any triumph. **nota** referring to the notoriety of Omphale's conquest over Hercules seems singularly inappropriate, as indeed does much of this episode.

105—6. **i nunc**: see 3, 26. **vir** 'a real man.' For this emphatic use of *vir* cf. Cic. 2 *Ph.* § 34 *quod non fecisti ignosco; virum res illa quaerebat.* § 96 *ille vir fuit, nos contemnendi.*

[The old reading *quod* for *quum* which both Palmer and Merkel retain seems unintelligible.]

107—8. **maxime rerum**: cf. 5, 125. 'And you are inferior to her in proportion as it was a greater achievement to conquer you than to conquer those whom you have conquered.'

109—110. 'The value of your achievements is now reckoned to her credit: surrender your goods; your mistress is the heir to your glory.'

procedit is used in a technical sense, in which it was among other cases frequently employed in military affairs, of reckoning pay or time of service, Liv. 5, 7 *aera militibus procedunt.* But there is no reference to military matters here. The words **rerum mensura tuarum** and **cede bonis** very likely are, as Palmer says, suggested by the legal process known as *cessio bonorum,* which was an informal (*extra jus*) arrangement ('composition with creditors') by which a man delivered all his property to his creditors, thereby avoiding public bankruptcy (*emptio bonorum*), and securing some small fragment of his property. The words **heres laudis** however introduce a new metaphor; and we must conclude that it is not possible to push too closely metaphorical language suggested to the poet from various quarters, and quite intelligible, though involving a confusion of metaphors.

111. **costis exuta**, between this reading and *costas* it is perhaps difficult to decide. On the one hand the MSS. are all for *costas*. On the other Madvig seems right in assuming that *exutus* has the accus. only when used in middle sense. He refers us to his Lat. Gr. § 237.

112. **molle**, *i.e.* a woman's.

114. **feri.** Ovid several times uses *ferus* instead of *fera*, *F.* 1, 550 *traxerat aversos Cacus in antra feros*. Cp. Verg. Aen. 2, 51.

119. **audieram** 'I had *only* heard,' *i.e.* not seen.

120. **mollis** 'softened.' Hor. *A. P.* 180 *segnius irritant animos demissa per aures Quam quae sunt oculis subjecta fidelibus. Pont.* 3, 4, 21 *Scilicet affectus similes, aut impetus idem Rebus ab auditis conspicuisque venit?*

123. **non sinis averti** 'you do not allow me to avert my eyes;' lit. 'to turn oneself away.' Cf. *M.* 5, 214 *sibi proxima tangit Corpora: marmor erant. Avertitur, atque ita supplex Confessasque manus tendens*, &c. The full phrase is *avertere vultum*, cf. *Am.* 3, 9, 45.

126. 'Confessing her change of fortune, while her face tries to hide it.' *i.e.* Her disorderly appearance shows that she is a captive while she still tries to maintain an impassive look.

[This seems the only meaning to be got out of the line as it stands, and as it appears in the best MS.; but it is very far-fetched for Ovid. Lennep's emendation *decente* makes all things easy; but is on that account to be received with caution. The common reading *tegendo* is objectionable on the score of prosody, and gives after all a very weak meaning.]

128. **qualiter**: cf. supr. 59. **sublimis** 'high on her triumphal car as though Hercules had been conquered,' cf. *Tr.* 4, 2, 27 *Hic qui Sidonio fulget sublimis in ostro, Dux fuerat belli. Sublimis* has a double reference (1) to the lofty car, (2) to her exultation of mind, cf. 12, 179.

131. **Aetolide Deianira.** Deianira was daughter of Oeneus, king of Calydon in Aetolia. Soph. *Tr.* 7 Αἰτωλὶς γυνή. For the hiatus, see supr. 87.

133. **Eurytidos** 'of Eurytis,' *i.e.* daughter of Eurytus. **insani Alcidae** 'mad Hercules.' Perhaps the worst breach of artistic propriety to be found in this letter, which is full of them. So that one would be glad enough to accept *Aonii* if it had any authority; but in such an absolute unanimity of MSS. and old edd., a guess however plausible is to be received with extreme caution. If **Aonii** is accepted it will mean 'Boeotian,' Aonia being the ancient name of Boeotia. Hercules is called *Aonius* in *M.* 9, 112.

135. **perambulat artus**: cf. Sen. *Herc. O.* 706 *vagus per artus errat excussus tremor.*

137. **cum multis** 'among your many amours.'

139—140. Hercules fought for the possession of Deianira with Achelous, who took the form of a bull. In the contest one of the bull's horns was broken off, the Naiads picked it up and filling it with fruit and flowers made it into a Cornucopia. *Met.* 9, 85:

Nec satis hoc fuerat: rigidum fera dextera cornu
Dum tenet infregit, truncaque a fronte revellit.
Naiades hoc, pomis et odoro flore repletum,
Sacrarunt divesque meo Bona Copia cornu est.

legit 'picked up.'

141—2. Nessus the Centaur undertook to carry Deianira over the river Evenus, but in the middle of the stream offered her violence, and was shot by Hercules. *Met.* 9, 104—133.

sanguis equinus, *i.e.* the blood of the Centaur Nessus, cf. 100.

letifero Eueno: for the hiatus see above 87. The Evenus is in Aetolia (mod. Fidhari).

144. **tunicae tabe**: the shirt steeped in the blood of Nessus, which was *mixtus Lernaei tabe veneni*, *M.* 9, 130: and which she imagined to be a love-charm, *dat munus raptae velut irritamen amoris*, ib. 133. **perire** 'that my husband is perishing.' Hercules did not die at once, but was in his lacerated state brought to Trachis.

147. **Oeta**. The range of mountains between Thessaly and Locris, through which the only pass is that of Thermopylae. Thither Hercules went from Trachis to die and be burned.

149. **siquid facti**, partitive gen. Cf. 7, 66 *quid mentis.* 4, 152 *siquid certi.*

151. **Meleagre**: see on 3, 95.

153—4. **Agrios** the brother of Oeneus deprived him of his throne for a time, until he himself was slain by Diomede grandson of Oeneus. **devota domus**: for Ovid's fatalism see 4, 53 and index.

155. **Tydeus**, son of Oeneus and father of Diomede; in consequence of some murder he fled to Argos, where Adrastos received him and gave him his daughter Deiphyle.

157. **mater.** Althea, who killed herself in remorse for having been the cause of her son Meleager's death.

161—2. See on 144.

165. **Gorge.** This mention of Deianira's sister is another instance of Ovid's curious knowledge of mythology. She is mentioned in Apollodorus as having married Andraemon.

166. **frater.** Meleager.

168. **sed o possit**: i.e. *valere*. On this double meaning of *valere* see on 4, 1. **Hyllus** was ordered by his father on his deathbed to marry Iole.

X.

ARIADNE THESEO.

Minos king of Gnosus in Crete exacted a cruel tax from Athens. Seven youths and seven maidens were every nine years (according to Diodorus) to be sent by the Athenians to be devoured by the Minotaur. Theseus son of king Aegeus was among the second batch. On his arrival at Crete he gained the love of the king's daughter Ariadne, who betrayed to him the clue whereby to guide himself through the Labyrinth. Theseus killed the Minotaur, and fled with Ariadne. But having landed on Naxos, on their voyage home, he abandoned her in the night and went on to Athens by himself. Ariadne is supposed to write this letter to him in her first anguish at being deserted on a strange island, far from her own home, which she had abandoned for his sake.

[The story of Ariadne had been told by many writers with great variety of detail. It seems to have been especially interesting to Ovid, for he three times treats it at some length, though in each case taking a different phase of it. Here we have the simple tale of Ariadne's desertion; in the *A. A.* 1, 517—564 he tells how Bacchus came to her relief and wedded her; in *Fast.* 3, 461—516 we find her again deserted by Bacchus, but finally removed to the heavens and transformed into a constellation by that god. Apollodorus, whom Ovid often uses, had a full account of it, but that portion of his work has been lost. Homer, *Odyss.* 11, 320—5, has a somewhat different version of the story:—

Φαίδρην τε καὶ Πρόκριν τε ἴδον καλήν τ' Ἀφροδίτην
κούρην Μίνωος ὀλοόφρονος, ἥν ποτε Θησεὺς
ἐκ Κρήτης ἐς γουνὸν Ἀθηνάων ἱεράων
ἦγε μέν, οὐδ' ἀπόνητο· πάρος δέ μιν Ἄρτεμις ἔκτα
Δίῃ ἐν ἀμφιρύτῃ Διονύσου μαρτυρίῃσιν.]

2. **credita eram** for *essem*, see on 1, 108 and index.

ulli: sc. *ferae*.

6. **per facinus** 'wickedly:' so *per scelus, per vim, per officia* (Loers). Cf. *per moras* 2, 94. *per insidias* 1, 99.

8. **et tectae fronde queruntur aves** 'and when the birds are piping, still sheltered 'mid the leaves,' *i.e.* before they have begun to fly about. Cp. 'The earliest pipe of half-awakened birds.' (Tennyson.)

9—10. **a somno languida** seems to combine the ideas of 'from sleep' as a cause, and 'after sleep.' Cf. infr. 138, and index. Roby § 1811.

incertum vigilans, Loers quotes Hor. *S.* 2, 5, 100 *certum vigilans.*

movi manus. Cp. Tennyson's 'In memoriam':

'Tears of the widower, when he sees
A late-lost form that sleep reveals
And moves his doubtful arms, and feels
Her place is empty, fall like these.'

semisupina 'half turning on my side.' *Am.* 1, 14, 20 *Saepe etiam nondum digestis mane capillis, Purpureo jacuit semisupina toro.* The MSS. all have *semisopita*, but there is no authority for shortening the first syllable of *sōpio.*

16. **utque erat** 'just as it was,' without stopping to tie it up. A favourite expression with Ovid, *A. A.* 1, 529 *Utque erat e somno tunica velata recincta, Nuda pedem, croceas inreligata comas Thesea crudelem surdas clamabat ad undas.* *M.* 4, 474 *Tisiphone canos ut erat turbata capillos Movit.* Ib. 9, 113 *Mox ut erat pharetraque gravis spolioque leonis.* Ib. 12, 22 *ille ut erat virides amplexus in arbore ramos Fit lapis.* *F.* 1, 503 *utque erat immissis puppim stetit ante capillis.* Ib. 5, 455 *Inde domum redeunt sub prima crepuscula maesti, Utque erat in duro procubuere toro.* The Greek ὡς εἶχε answers to this use.

25—6. Cf. 2, 121. **hinc** 'from this there is an overhanging projection of rock fretted below by moaning billows.' Loers cps. *M.* 11, 783 *Dixit et e scopulo quem rauca subederat unda*

Se dedit in pontum. *Rauca* is an appropriate epithet in both passages from the specially moaning sound produced by a wave running into hollowed rocks.

28. **metior** 'I take in the broad seas in every direction in my view.' **metior** (1) I measure. (2) Metaphorically with the eyes, as here, or with the mind as in *M.* 2, 187 *multum caeli post terga relictum, Ante oculos plus est. Animo metitur utrumque.* (3) 'to go over,' *M.* 9, 447 *celerique carina Aegeas metiris aquas.*

31. 'I either did actually see them, or at any rate when I thought I saw them I turned colder than ice and half-dead.'

36. **numerum suum** 'its full number:' used especially of a ship's crew, as Burmann shows from Cic. *Verr.* 5, 51 *si suum numerum naves haberent.*

38. **verbera cum verbis**: for the paronomasia see on 9, 31 *onus* and *honor*, and infr. 82 *mora mortis.* It is rather the case of one word suggesting the other unconsciously than a deliberate play on words, though it is used as a conscious pun in the Comedians. See Plaut. *Men.* 5, 6, 13. Ter. *Haut.* 356.

41. **velamina**: plur. for sing. 'a veil.' It is a general term for any loose covering. Thisbe drops it on her flight, *M.* 4, 101. Cf. *F.* 6, 579 *vultus velamine celat amatos.*

42. **scilicet** belongs closely to **oblitos** 'those who had *forgotten* me,' as I tried to believe, whereas in real truth they had purposely abandoned me. See on 4, 21.

43—4. **tum denique** 'then and not till then:' *tum demum* is the more usual phrase. Cf. *nunc denique* 12, 105.

genae 'eyeballs.' *Pont.* 2, 8, 66 *patiar fossis lumen abire genis.* **torpuerant**: cf. *Pont.* 1, 2, 29 *fine carent lacrimae nisi cum stupor obstitit illis: Et similis morti pectora torpor habet.*

45—6. **quid facerent...deslerant**: see on 8, 50 for the construction.

48. **Ogygio deo**: Bacchus. *Ogygius* means 'Theban,' from Ogyges a mythical king of Thebes. Bacchus is Theban from his mother Semele the daughter of Cadmus. Ovid has employed the simile of the Bacchanal before, see 4, 47, and he again does so in 13, 33. Cf. *A. A.* 1, 312 *fertur ut Aonio concita Baccha deo.*

53. **quae possum** ''tis all I can touch in room of thee' *qua possum* 13, 41, 'as best I can:' cf. *quod potui* 8, 5, ''twas all I could.'

58. **ubi**: cf. 4, 150.

60. **hominum...facta boum**: Burmann quotes Hom. *Od.* 10, 98 ἔνθα μὲν οὔτε βοῶν, οὔτ' ἀνδρῶν φαίνετο ἔργα.

61—2. **nusquam**, sc. *est*. **ambiguas** 'dangerous,' cf. *M*. 15, 333 *est lacus Arcadiae...ambiguis suspectus aquis, quas nocte timeto.*

64. **quid sequar?** 'What object am I to make for?'

65—6. **ut......ut**: 'even supposing,' see on 1, 116 and index.

Aeolus, the god of the winds, *Aen.* 1, 52 *vasto rex Aeolus antro Luctantes ventos tempestatesque sonoras Imperio premit ac vinclis et carcere frenat.*

67—8. **digesta**: see on 9, 93. Crete is said to be separated into a hundred cities because each city was an independent community with separate laws and government. The exact number of these states however is not so certain. Homer *Il.* 2, 649 calls Crete ἑκατόμπολις. Of course the Roman poets follow him, and we have Virgil's *centum urbes habitant magnas, uberrima regna Aen.* 3, 106: and Horace's *centum nobilem Cretam urbibus, Epode* 9, 29. But in the Odyssey the number is said to be ninety, 19, 174 ἐν δ' ἄνθρωποι πολλοί, ἀπειρέσιοι, καὶ ἐννήκοντα πόληες.

puero cognita terra Iovi: referring to the tradition of the birth of Jupiter and his concealment near Lyctos, on Mt Dicta in Crete, which Ovid accordingly calls (4, 163) *Jovis insula.*

69. **iusto regnata parenti** 'governed by my just father.' Ovid seems to refer to Minos who became a judge in the infernal regions. But this Minos was great-grandfather to Ariadne, her father Minos being, according to tradition, grandson of the other. For the dative *parenti* Loers quotes *Aen.* 3, 14 *acri quondam regnata Lycurgo.* For the dative of the agent after passive participle or gerundive, cf. 2, 115. 8, 36. Roby § 1146.

71. **tecto recurvo**: the Labyrinth. Cf. 4, 60, and infr. 128. It was made by Daedalus wherein to keep the Minotaur.

72. According to Virgil Daedalus himself gave Theseus the clue in pity for Ariadne's love, *Aen.* 6, 28 *Magnum reginae sed enim miseratus amorem Daedalus ipse dolos tecti ambagesque resolvit Caeca regens filo vestigia.*

73. **per ego ipsa pericula iuro.** This position of the pronouns was common in oaths, and solemn formulae of the like sort. Cf. *F.* 2, 841 *per tibi ego hanc juro fortem castumque cruorem.*

76. **sepulta** 'consigned to gloom and oblivion.' Cf. *Pont.* 1, 5, 85 *vosque, quibus perii, tunc cum mea fama sepulta est,* 'was as good as buried.'

77. **fratrem**: the Minotaur. **mactasses** 'you should have slain:' so in 12, 15 **isset** 'he should have gone,' or 'Oh that you had slain!' 'Oh that he had gone!'

78. 'The pledge which you had given would have been 'redeemed,' because he had sworn that she should be his while they both lived; if she died therefore he would be free.' **solvere fidem** (1) 'to keep one's word' from the notion of 'paying' involved in *solvere*, (2) to be free, by having fulfilled an engagement. In 7, 9 *solvere foedus* means 'to break an engagement.'

79—80. 'I call to mind not only the things which I personally am to suffer but everything that any woman thus abandoned might possibly encounter.' The indicative is used because there is no doubt of these dangers existing and she has the picture of them vividly before her mind.

79. **recordor**, 'turn over in my mind,' used of the future is rare.

82. **mora mortis**: see on 38.

85—6. **Dia** is the old name of Naxos. Diod. Sic. 4, 61 *κατῆρεν εἰς νῆσον τὴν ποτὲ μὲν Δίαν, νῦν δὲ Νάξον προσαγορευομένην.* *A. A.* 1, 528 *Gnosis in ignotis amens errabat arenis Qua brevis aequoreis Dia feritur aquis.* Cp. Theocr. 2, 46.

[I regard this restoration of Heinsius as almost certain. *Quis scit an et saevas tigridas insula habet* is intolerable, principally because of *habet*, which should be *habeat.* The argument from the metrical irregularity of *insula habet* at the end of the pentameter is strong, but still such an ending may be paralleled in Ovid, see *Tr.* 4, 1, 54 *quadrijugos cernes saepe resistere equos.*]

88. **gladios.** It has been suggested this should be translated 'swordfish,' a sense in which the word occurs in Pliny *H. N.* 9, 54. 32, 15, the Greek *ξιφίας.* But to say nothing of the fact that Ariadne would have nothing to fear from swordfish while she remained on shore, the next verse shows that she is referring to the 'swords' of men. She prefers, she says, to be killed rather than taken captive and made a slave. Cf. *Tr.* 1, 11, 25 *Attigero portum, portu terrebor ab ipso: Plus habet infesta terra timoris aqua. Nam simul insidiis hominum pelagique laboro Et faciunt geminos ensis et unda metus.* Two dangers which he again classes together, *ib.* 3, 2, 25 *Cur ego tot gladios fugi totiensque minata Obruit infelix nulla procella caput?*

90. **pensa**: cf. on 3, 75. **serva** as an adjective, cf. *Am.* 1, 6, 26 *nec tibi perpetuo serva bibatur aqua*, and Horace's *Oh imitatorum servum pecus.*

This was the common way of employing captive girls, see 9, 73—82, and Eur. *Bacch.* 514 where Pentheus threatens to enslave the women who join in the revel ἐφ' ἱστοῖς δμωΐδας κεκτήσομαι.

91. **filia Phoebi**, Pasiphae.

95. **caelum restabat** 'There only remained the sky for me to try,' *i.e.* I can only hope to escape by flying. Cf. 6, 161 where though an actual occurrence is referred to, yet escape by flight is thought of as the last resource of despair.

timeo simulacra deorum, *i.e.* (when I think of flight) 'phantoms of the Gods dismay me.' **simulacra** is used in these epistles for the phantoms seen in dreams 9, 39. 13, 111. The line has been objected to on the ground that the sense requires some reference to the state of the island, and that a sudden reference to the sky and to phantoms was out of place. But the sequence of thought is quite just. 'Whether I try sea or land the dangers of either appal, if I think of the sole remaining means of flight, the air, I am equally terrified by dim phantoms.' [As in the passage from *Ep.* 6, quoted above *Quum mare quum terras consumpserit aera temptet.*] Then in despair she concludes 'so then I must be left here a prey to wild beasts.'

97. **sive**, referring to *feris*. 'If on the other hand there are human inhabitants, I feel no confidence in them either.'

98. **externos**: because Theseus was a foreigner.

99—100. **Androgeos** brother of Ariadne, who going to Athens and joining in the games of the Panathenaea and proving successful, was treacherously and from envy killed at the suggestion of Aegeus. It was on this account that Minos warred on Athens and laid upon it the contribution of young men and maidens to the Minotaur.

Cecropi, voc. of *Cecropis*, cf. *Inachi* 14, 105 &c.

102. **parte virum parte bovem**, the Minotaur. **ardua** 'upraised to strike,' an appropriate word to the action in using a club, as **adductas**, which refers to another part of the same action (*adductaque clava trinodis F.* 1, 575), viz. the drawing back the hand when raised; Milton's 'heavèd stroke.'

104. 'The clue repeatedly passed through your hands one over the other.' The action of a man hauling in a rope hand

over hand is described very neatly by this line, which is so difficult to express neatly in English. Much the same alternate action of the feet in treading out the grapes is expressed by the word *adductus* in *Pont.* 1, 9, 32 *Musta sub adducto si pede nulla fluent.* The phrase used elsewhere seems to be *legere filum.*

105. **si** 'if, as in fact it does,'—hence the indicative *stat.*

106. **belua**, the Minotaur.

108. **ut** 'even though,' see on 1, 116. **eras** for *esses*, cf. on 1, 108.

pectore 'by the hardness of your heart,' equivalent to *duritia pectoris* or *duro pectore*, so below 117, *fides = mala fides.*

109—110. **illic**, *i.e.* in your breast. Cf. 2, 137, *M.* 9, 614 *neque enim de tigride natus. Nec rigidas silices, solidumve in pectore ferrum, Aut adamanta gerit, nec lac bibit ille leaenae.* It is a very common metaphor in Ovid. *Tr.* 1, 8, 41 *Et tua sunt silicis circum praecordia venae, Et rigidum ferri semina pectus habet.* So Tibullus 1. 1, 63 *Flebis; non tua sunt duro praecordia ferro Vincta, nec in tenero stat tibi corde silex.* See also Propert. 1, 15, 29. 1, 9, 31. Ovid *A.* 1, 11, 9. *M.* 14, 712.

112. **aut** refers to a condition implied in the previous line. 'I either ought to have awaked in time to prevent the escape of Theseus, or to have slept for ever.' **fui** for *essem*, with gerund, cf. 6, 54, 144.

114. 'And ye breezes so eager to cause my tears to flow.' **officiosa**, like **parati** in the previous line, is meant to imply that the winds were conscious and ready agents in bringing about her distress. *Officiosus* refers not only to obedience, as in *A. A.* 3, 324 *Saxa tuo cantu...Fecerunt muros officiosa novos*, but to alacrity in obedience. For the construction *officiosa in* cf. on 4, 16.

117. **fides** 'treason:' *fides = mala fides*, see supr. 108.

119—120. Comp. Pope's 'Elegy in memory of an unfortunate Lady:'

'By foreign hands thy dying eyes were closed,
By foreign hands thy decent limbs composed,
By foreign hands thy humble grave adorned,
By strangers honoured, and by strangers mourned.'

120. **lumina condat**: the natural office of the nearest relative, cf. 1, 113.

122. **unguet**: *i. e.* in preparation for the funeral pyre. Cf. *F.* 4, 852 *arsuros artus unxit.*

124. **haec** 'such as this,' cf. 8, 53, 104. **sepulchra**: funeral rites, cf. 7, 188. 14, 128. **officiis meis** 'my kindness to you in the matter of the Minotaur.' See index.

125. **ibis portus**: for *ibis ad*, cf. *Aen*, 6, 637 *devenere locos* (Loers).

126. **turbae celsus honore tuae** 'elated by the cheers of your fellow-citizens.' *celsus*, though properly used of physical exaltation, here implies the mental condition as well, cf. *sublimis ut Hercule victo* 9, 129. The idea seems to be of a triumphal entry followed by a speech or address to his fellow-citizens. For *honor* cf. Cic. *Phil.* 2, § 31 *cur ludi Appollinares incredibili M. Bruti honore celebrati?* 'with immense cheering for Brutus.' Cf. *Pont.* 2, 1, 29 *cum magnae vocis honore.*

[This is a case in which the latest and generally received reading seems preferable to that of the better MSS. It was very early received into the printed editions. *Steteris turbae celsus in arce tuae* seems absolute nonsense. Palmer makes it easy by accepting a correction *urbis* for *turbae*. But this has no more authority than *honore*, and does not seem to me to make such good sense. Why should Theseus stand on the citadel? There is every reason for his being received at Athens in triumph, as having delivered the town from its dreadful tax.]

128. **saxea tecta**: the Labyrinth, cf. supr. 71. **per dubias vias** 'cut into intricate paths,' almost an adverb 'intricately,' like *per insidias* 1, 99: see supr. 6.

130. **titulis**: cf. 2, 67—74, where the idea is precisely the same, of the achievements of a man being inscribed on his statue.

131—132. **Pittheidos Aethrae**, Aethra daughter of Pittheus. For the form *Pittheis* cf. *Tantalis*, *Iardanis*, etc.

auctores saxa fretumque: cf. 7. 37.

135—6. **qua potes** 'as best you may,' cf. sup. 53. 13, 41.

haerentem. Palmer well explains this, of the appearance a figure would present to one looking from far out at sea.

137—8. **demissos**: cf. sup. 47. As a sign of mourning see 9, 125.

ab imbre gravis: see 4, 32, and index.

139—140. 'My whole frame trembles like a field of corn ruffled by the north wind.' **labat** 'sprawls,' 'is unsteady.' Cf. Tennyson, 'Princess:'

> 'and I sat down and wrote,
> In such a hand as when a field of corn
> Bows all its ears before the roaring East.'

143. **sed nec poena quidem** 'but not punishment either,' as sometimes *ne quidem* is used. See Ter. *Haut.* 896. Cic. *Phil.* 2, 5. 11 *non tractabo ut consulem, ne ille quidem me ut consularem.* Sen. *Epist.* 5 *non splendeat toga, ne sordeat quidem.*

145. **plangendo**: cf. supr. 15.

147. **qui superant** 'which remain after my tearing of them, see supr. 16.

149. **verso velo**: the reading which Palmer has properly, I think, preferred to *verso vento;* he compares 13, 134.

150. **ossa feres** 'you will take my ashes in their urn with you.' This was the custom Aeschylus refers to, *Ag.* 428 Ἄρης... φίλοισι πέμπει βαρὺ ψῆγμα δυσδάκρυτον Ἀντήνορος σποδοῦ γεμίζων λέβητας εὐθέτου. Loers well quotes *Tr.* 3, 3, 65 *Ossa tamen facito parva referantur in urna: Sic ego non etiam mortuus exul ero.*

XII.

MEDEA IASONI.

When Medea had helped Jason by her drugs to overcome the various dangers and difficulties of obtaining the golden fleece, she fled with him to his home Iolchos in Thessaly, and in order to stay her father's pursuit of them, she cut up her brother Absyrtus and scattered his limbs on the sea. At Iolchos she had two sons by Jason. After a while they removed to Corinth, where Jason determined to divorce Medea and marry Creusa the daughter of Creon, the king of the place.

This letter is supposed to be written soon after this marriage has taken place. She reproaches Jason with her services and sacrifices for him. She reminds him that he was once in her power, and that she pitied him and saved him, and finally she hints darkly at the fearful vengeance she will take. As in

Euripides, some feeling for Medea is excited by the prominence given to Jason's wrong: while the violent and ghastly nature of her revenge is kept in the back ground: the worst of all, the murder of her children, being only darkly hinted in the last line, *Nescio quid certe mens mea majus agit.*

[The story of Medea no doubt Ovid knew so well as scarcely to be conscious of using any one authority. The most detailed accounts of the fable we have, which were likely to be in Ovid's hands, are that of Apollodorus, lib. 1, and that of Apollonius, lib. 3. Ovid no doubt also was well acquainted with the *Medea* of Euripides. And we are able again to notice how Seneca has followed in Ovid's steps, in his tragedy of *Medea*. Cf. *Met.* 7, 1—424. Ovid's own tragedy *Medea* is unhappily lost.]

1. **At** answers some supposed excuse of Jason. 'Ah, well, but whatsoever you may say, I, when queen of Colchis, had leisure to attend to you.' So the man carrying the babes Romulus and Remus says suddenly, as if answering his own thoughts, *At quam sunt similes! at quam formosus uterque*, *F.* 2, 395.

2. **ars mea**: *i.e.* my skill in magic.

3, 4. **evoluisse fusos** 'to have unrolled my spindles,' means that it was time for her to die. The metaphor is to be explained thus: the life of each of us is represented by a certain weight (*pensum*) of wool which the Fates are to spin, and when that is spun our days come to an end. Now the spindle spins the yarn till the thread is long enough to reach the ground from the distaff: the thread is then wound round tho spindle and the process repeated until the spindle is full, the throad is then cut and the wool wound off the spindle into a ball (*glomus*). This is repeated with the same spindle or another, until the whole *pensum* from the *colus* is exhausted, and all wound off into separate balls. When the Fates have done that, a man's life is brought to an end, and they may be said *evoluisse fusos*. **dispensant** (*pensum*), a word derived from the same idea.

7—10. Ovid is no doubt thinking of the opening lines in the *Medea* of Euripides:

> εἴθ' ὤφελ' Ἀργοῦς μὴ διαπτάσθαι σκάφος
> Κόλχων ἐς αἶαν κυανέας Συμπληγάδας
> μηδ' ἐν νάπαισι Πηλίου πεσεῖν ποτε
> τμηθεῖσα πεύκη, μηδ' ἐρετμῶσαι χέρας
> ἀνδρῶν ἀριστέων.

Pelias arbor: timber cut on Mt Pelion, cf. 3, 126.

Phrixeam: the fleece of the ram that carried Phrixus.

Magnetida 'Thessalian:' *Magnetis* is a feminine adjective formed from Magnetes, the people of Magnesia, the eastern district of Thessaly in which is the range of Pelion.

turba Graia 'the Greek crew.' **Phasiacam** 'Colchian.' The river Phasis (mod. Rion) divides Colchis from Asia Minor.

13—15. **aut semel**: cf. 10, 112. *Aut* refers to the implied statement of the preceding passage, as if it had been—The Argonauts should never have come to Colchis, or, if they must come as they did, then Jason should have had no help from me. **praemedicatus** 'previously anointed' with the drug which Medea gave him to make him proof against the fiery breath of the bulls. φάρμακον δίδωσιν.. ᾧ ἐκέλευσε ᾽χρίσαι τήν τε ἀσπίδα καὶ τὸ δόρυ καὶ τὸ σῶμα. Apollod. 1. **nova**: see on 23.

16. **ora adunca** 'the horned heads.' For this meaning of *ora*, cf. 9, 88, where it means 'skulls.'

18. **cultor ab ipse suo**: for the position of *ipse*, cf. 9, 96. And for *ab* with instrumental ablative, see 4, 32, and index.

21. **meritum** 'all one has done for him,' cf. 7, 5, and Sen. *Med.* 120 *Durus merita contempsit mea.* Palmer compares Eur. *Med.* 473 ἐγώ τε γὰρ λέξασα κουφισθήσομαι κακῶς καὶ σὺ λυπήσει κλύων.

23. **inexpertam** 'untried before.' Because this was the first voyage of the Argo, and the Argo was said to be the first ship ever built: cf. supr. 13 *nova puppis.*

24. **beata** 'wealthy.' The searches for the gold and silver of Colchis were explained by Strabo (2, 39) to be the origin of the story of the Argonauts, ὁ πλοῦτος τῆς ἐκεῖ χώρας ἐκ τῶν χρυσείων καὶ ἀργυρείων καὶ σιδηρείων δικαίαν τινα ὑπαγορεύει πρόφασιν τῆς στρατείας καθ᾽ ἣν καὶ Φρίξος ἔστειλε τὸν πλοῦν τοῦτον.

27. **Ephyren**: *i.e.* Corinth. There were several cities of this name in Greece; and it is mentioned in Strabo as an ancient name of Corinth (Strabo 8, 5). **bimaris** 'with two sea-boards,' cf. Hor. *Od.* 1, 7, 2 *bimarisque Corinthi*, see inf. 104; 8, 69; 4, 105—6 *et tenuis tellus audit utrumque mare.*

27—28. She says her father ruled all the country along the Northern shore of Pontus (*Black Sea*) up to Scythia, which would mean, I suppose, up to the Tanais (Don), a great deal further than the district called Colchis extended. But Scythia in Ovid's mouth is a synonym for all the country north of the Pontus, that he did not know otherwise. So Virgil (*Georg.* 3,

349) speaks vaguely of all these countries as *Scythiae gentes*. Ovid had occasion to learn this part of his geography better before he died. **laeva plaga**: the N.W. district.

29. **Aeeta**: the Aeolic nominative of Aeetes. Ovid uses it in *M*. 7, 170; and the gen. *Aeetae* 6, 50 and *Pont*. 3, 120. Below, v. 51, we have *Aeetes*.

30. **pictos**: cf. 52, covered with fine *vestes stragulae*. Thus *purpureus torus* in 5, 88 'royal.'

31. **quis esses** 'what influence you could exert,' cf. *Am*. 3, 6, 24 *flumina senserunt ipsa quid esset amor*.

33. **et vidi et perii**: although Virgil (*Ecl*. 8, 41) wrote *ut vidi ut perii*, there is no valid reason for altering *et* into *ut* here, against all authority. Ovid may have chosen to vary the phrase, even though he had Virgil's in his mind.

35. **et me mea fata trahebant**: see on 6, 51, and 4, 53.

36. **abstulerant** 'had riveted my gaze on themselves,' cf. 6, 131. Ovid has still in his mind, perhaps, Virgil's line l. c., *Ut vidi ut perii ! ut me malus abstulit error*.

39. **lex** 'condition,' *i.e.* the condition on which you were to take the golden fleece, cf. 7, 156.

40. **vomere**: properly 'the ploughshare,' then 'the whole plough,' and finally any part of it as here 'the yoke.'

premeres: the imperfect subj. depending on the historic present *dicitur*, Roby § 1512. Conversely the historic present may be in the subordinate clause, *Aen*. 2, 120 *obstipuere animi gelidusque per ossa cucurrit Ossa tremor, cui fata parent quem poscat Apollo*.

41. **plus quam per cornua saevi** 'whose danger was not confined to butting with their horns,' *i.e.* their fiery breath was an additional danger. Ovid is fond of an instrumental *per*, see index. But he is also probably thinking of the well-known expressions in Euripides, *Bacch*. 742 ταῦροι δ' ὑβρισταὶ κεἰς κέρας θυμούμενοι, *Hel*. 1558 κυρτῶν τε νῶτα κεἰς κέρας παρεμβλέπων, which Virgil has imitated in his *irasci in cornua*, *G*. 3, 232, *Aen*. 12, 104.

43—44. 'Their feet were of solid bronze, bronze too was wrought upon their nostrils; this also was blackened by their own breath.'

aere pedes solidi seems to mean that the whole hoof was of bronze 'solid with bronze' (abl. of material). **praetenta aera** seems to refer to some sort of bronze armour-plating. *praetendere* is said to be a military word 'to put in front of for defence.' Ovid is borrowing from Apollonius 3, 230 *τεχνήεις Ἥφαιστος ἐμήσατο θέσκελα ἔργα. καὶ οἱ χαλκόποδας ταύρους κάμε, χάλκεα δέ σφεων ἦν στόματ', ἐκ δὲ πυρὸς δεινὸν σέλας ἀμπνείεσκον.* But the touch of minute description implied in *nigra per adflatus* is all his own. For **per** see on 41.

47. **qui peterent**: for tense, see on 40. **natis secum telis** 'with weapons born with him,' for they sprang ready armed from the earth.

49. **custodis**: *i.e.* the dragon.

52. 'And the high table is removed from the purple couches,' *i.e.* when the banquet is over, and the moveable table taken away. Ovid is thinking of Roman customs, see on 1, 31—2.

purpurei tori: *i.e.* royal, see on 30, and cf. 5, 88.

53. **regnum dotale** 'the royalty which Creusa is to bring you as her dower.' Jason was not actually to receive the kingdom of Corinth with his wife, but still he would have with her some of the advantages of royalty (*regnum*), cf. 4, 163, where in exactly the same sense Phaedra calls Crete *tellus dotalis*, though it was not hers to bring to her husband.

57. **male saucia** 'with love's wound rankling in my breast to my sorrow,' cf. *Aen.* 4, 1 *At regina gravi jamdudum saucia cura.*

58. **quanta fuit** 'all its dreary length,' see on 3, 49.

per lacrimas 'in tears,' cf. *per moras* 2, 94 and on 10, 6.

61. **hinc...hinc** 'on the one side'...'on the other.' Her love urges her to help Jason, her fear of her father to leave him to his fate.

62. **soror**, Chalciope, Apoll. 3, 667.

63. **adversaque in ora iacentem** 'lying upon my face which was pressed to the pillow.' No doubt Ovid is here representing the *λέκτροισι πρηνὴς ἐνικάππεσεν εἰλιχθεῖσα* of Apollonius (3, 655). But the common reading *aversa* has much to be said for it, 'with my face turned to the wall.'

65. **Minyis** 'for the Argonauts,' see on 6, 47.

petit altera &c. 'The one sister asks for the aid, the other had it in her power to grant.' Quintilian (8, 5, 6) quotes a line from Ovid's play 'Medea:' *Servare potui; perdere an possim rogas?*

69. **delubra**: plur. for sing. 'a shrine,' used in a general sense. *delubrum* is properly 'a place of purification,' (*de-luo*): *templum* (*tem-no*) 'a place cut off and set apart.' **Dianae**: *i. e.* of Diana, Trivia or Hecate, the patroness of Medea as a witch. *M.* 7, 194. Ἑκάτης ἱερὸν, Apoll. 3, 914.

70. **barbarica**: Medea speaks of the hand of her own people as *barbarica*, as Briseis (3, 2) of her own; simply in the sense of non-Hellenic.

71. **excidĕrunt**: see on 2, 141 for this quantity. For the meaning, on 2, 105. [The reading *noscis an exciderunt* was either changed by early editors or found in their MSS. changed to *nescio an exciderint* 'I rather think you have forgotten.' But this seems to me to weaken the passion and irony of the words; and as *noscis an exciderunt* presents no real difficulty and is apparently closest to the two best MSS. I have retained it.]

78. **cuncta videntis avi**: *i.e.* the Sun, who was the father of Aeetes. Ἥλιος πανόπτης. Ennius *Med.* fr. 14 *tuque adeo Sol, qui omnes res suspicis.*

79. **per triplicis...Dianae**: cf. 69. So (in *M.* 7, 194) Medea prays to *triceps Hecate*. The three-headed goddess Trivia is a kind of infernal Luna or Diana: and thus connected with witchcraft, which dealt especially with the moon (see on 6, 14). The origin of the name *Trivia* is said by Varro (*L. L.* 7, 16) to be the fact that a figure of Ἄρτεμις was used at the junctions of three roads in Greek towns, with the heads of a horse, a lion and a dog pointing down the several roads. Cf. *F.* 1, 141 *Ora vides Hecates in tres vergentia partes, Servit ut in ternas compita secta vias*: where consult Paley's note. Senec. *Med.* 6, *Tacitisque praebens conscium sacris jubar Hecate triformis*: which gives a reason for witches worshipping the moon. **arcana sacra** 'magic rites,' *M.* 7, 192 *Nox ait arcanis fidissima.*

80. 'And by the gods peculiar to them, if such there be, that your (*ista*) race has.' Lit. 'If your race has some gods.' It was customary to end all prayers in which particular gods were mentioned by some general phrase to include the other deities, lest any one of them who ought to have been mentioned should be offended. So in his prayer on laying the foundation stone of Rome, after mentioning Jupiter, Mars and Vesta, Romulus concludes *Quosque pium est adhibere deos, advertite cuncti. F.* 4, 829. It was on this same principle that there was at Athens an altar to the Unknown God.

85. 'But how can I expect to be so favoured by the gods as that?'

faciles 'good-natured,' 'well-disposed.' **meos**: cf. 2, 126. For the case cf. 2, 53.

87. **Iuno**: cf. 6, 45. **maritis**: cf. 2, 41 *Junonemque toris quae praesidet alma maritis.*

89. **haec** 'such words as these.' **quota** 'and how small a part are they of all you did say.' For **movere** cf. 7, 85.

93—102. Cf. the passage in 6, 31—38. **inadusto** 'unscorched.'

97. **ipsa ego**: cf. *M.* 7, 134 *Ipsa quoque extimuit, quae tutum fecerat illum: Utque peti vidit juvenem tot ab hostibus unum, Palluit et subito sine sanguine frigida sedit.*

98. **subitos** 'born in an instant full grown,' cf. Sen. *Med.* 469 *hostis subiti tela.*

101. **strictas**, properly applied to weapons drawn from a sheath etc., is applied to hands when used in a hostile manner. Cf. *Am.* 1, 6, 14 *Nec timeo strictas in mea fata manus.*

inter se: *M.* 7, 141 *Terrigenae pereunt per mutua vulnera fratres Civilique cadunt acie.*

103. **ubi**: cf. 4, 150 and index.

104. See on 8, 69.

106. **barbara**: see on 70. **nunc denique**: cf. on 10, 43. **illa ego**: cf. *Tr.* 4, 10, 1 *Ille ego qui fuerim, tenerorum lusor amorum.*

107—8. **flammae** 'I withdrew from you by a drugged sleep the fiery eyes.' Cf. *M.* 7, 149 *Pervigilem superest herbis sopire draconem...hunc postquam sparsit Lethaei gramine suci...somnus in ignotos oculos sibi venit, et auro Heros Aesonius potitur.* **tuta**: see the passage quoted on 97.

110. **munus quodlibet** 'ever so great a favour.' Loers quotes Seneca, who doubtless is copying Ovid. *Med.* 491.

Jas. *Lacrimis meis evictus, exilium dedit.*
M. *Poenam putabam: munus, ut video, est fuga.*

quodlibet 'as great as you please.' Palmer illustrates by *quamlibet aptus* 'as fitted as you please,' *i.e.* 'well fitted.' *Am.* 1, 18, 14. A writer in the Athenaeum says that the meaning is 'I have earned as my reward to be whatever you please in exile'. If so, it seems a very fatuous remark of Medea's, to say nothing of the fact that *quodlibet* should be *quidlibet* in that case. Medea means 'my reward for all these services (and a great one it is!) is to be in exile.'

112. **soror** : see on 62.

113. **germane**: her brother Absyrtus, whose limbs she cut up to delay her father's pursuit. See introd. and 6, 129.

116. **dilaceranda fui** 'I ought to have been dismembered myself.' For the tense see on 6, 54, 144. 10, 112.

sed tecum : *i.e.* but you ought to have been punished in the same way with me. On the principle of *cui prodest scelus Is fecit* (Sen. *Med.* 500) she insists on the guilt of this cruel act being Jason's as well as hers.

117—118. **credere me pelago...iamque nocens**: 'Nor yet did I shrink to trust myself,—a woman and now too a guilty one,—to the deep.' *jamque* completes the climax, not only is there the natural timidity of a woman, but the restless fears of a guilty one also, to make her shrink from the sea, which was supposed to punish guilt, *Nec violasse fidem temptantibus aequora prodest*, 7, 57.

119. **numen** : *i.e.* the Providence which punishes guilt.

121. **elisissent**: see 9, 85. This spondaic ending of a hexameter is not very frequent in Ovid. He has however used it four times before in these epistles, but in all cases with proper names 6, 103. 8, 71. 9, 133. 9, 141. **Symplegades** 'the clashing rocks' [σύν, πλήσσω], two islets at the northern mouth of the Bosphorus. *Odyss.* 12, 69 sq.

123. 'Or would that ravening Scylla had sent us to her hounds to devour!' Scylla is the monster on the Italian side of the straits of Messina. *Aen.* 3, 420 *Dextrum Scylla latus, laevum implacata Charybdis Obsidet.* According to Ovid Scylla is converted into this monster by Circe, *M.* 14, 64 *et corpus quaerens femorum crurumque pedumque Cerbereos rictus pro partibus invenit illis.* Cf. Hom. *Odyss.* 12, 85—100.

Medea may be supposed to have passed through this strait when the Argonauts were driven into long wanderings by Jupiter, angry at the cruel murder of Absyrtus. Apollodorus says that they coasted along the shores of Libya, Gaul, Sardinia and Etruria, and landing on Aeaea, the island of Circe, were by her purified from the pollution of the murder.

124. **debuit ingratis &c.** This may arise from confusing Scylla the sea-monster with Scylla daughter of Nisus of Megara, who betrayed her father to Minos, and was yet killed by Minos himself. But there is also a legend of Scylla, the sea-monster, who Circe transformed from jealousy of her lover Glaucus, who refused to give her up. She may therefore be angry at all unfaithful lovers.

125. **quaeque vomit,** *i.e.* Charybdis, on the Sicilian side. Ovid is reproducing Homer *Odyss.* 12, 104—106 *τῷ δ' ὑπὸ δῖα Χάρυβδις ἀναρροιβδεῖ μέλαν ὕδωρ. Τρὶς μὲν γάρ τ' ἀνίησιν ἐπ' ἤματι, τρὶς δ' ἀναρροιβδεῖ δεινόν.*

127. **Haemonias urbes,** *i.e.* Thessalian Iolchos. See on 6, 23.

129—130. **pietate nocentes** 'guilty from sheer filial affection;' the ablative of efficient cause in the agent, cf. 4, 17. Medea persuaded the daughters of Pelias to cut up their father and boil his limbs, promising to restore him to youth, and having first shown a specimen of her magic power in this way on an animal.

131. **ut** 'though,' see on 1, 116, and index.

134. **cede domo** 'depart from my house,' apparently the words of a husband divorcing his wife, Mart. 11, 104, 1 *vade foras, uxor.* Cf. Cic. *Phil.* 2, § 69 *illam mimam suas res sibi habere jussit, ex duodecim tabulis claves ademit, exegit,* where see Mayor's note. The last word *exegit* would describe the action of the husband in using this formula. The woman was said *decedere.* Ter. *Andr.* 568.

Aesonia, *i.e.* of Jason, son of Aeson.

135. **natis comitata duobus.** Ovid always uses *comitatus* with ablative of person without preposition, *solo comitatus Achate, F.* 3, 602. *Satyris comitatus* ib. 737. Cf. *Aen*, 1, 312 *uno comitatus Achate.* Roby § 1220.

137. **Hymen** 'the marriage-hymn,' see on 6, 44.

138. **lampades**: for the torches at a marriage-procession see on 2, 120.

139. **socialia carmina** 'marriage-songs,' cf. *socialia foedera* 4, 17. *Livia sic tecum sociales compleat annos, Tr.* 2, 161.

140. **funerea flebiliora tuba.** The *tuba* was a straight instrument with bell mouth, it was used at funerals: cf. Pers. 3, 103 *hinc tuba candelae tandemque beatulus...in portam rigidos calces extendit.* For this contrasting of marriage with funeral ceremonies, see on 2, 120. Loers quotes Prop. 2, 6, 12 *Tibia funesta tristior illa tuba.*

141. **tantum scelus,** *i.e.* that you really meant to marry at once.

143. **Hymen Hymenaee**: the refrain of the marriage-hymn, cf. 14, 27. **frequentant** 'repeat with their many voices.' *frequentare* conveys the notion of a crowd as well as that of repetition. Cf. 14, 29 *comitum clamore frequentes.* This hymn

was sung in the solemn procession conducting the wife to her new home.

144. **hoc** 'in that proportion' answering to *quo*. For **pejus** see index.

145. **diversi** 'standing aloof from me,' *i.e.* lest I should see the sorrow on their faces.

149—152. 'When our younger child,—in his eagerness for play and for seeing the spectacle he took his place on the very threshold of the front door,—says, "Come this way, mother; our father Jason is leading a procession, and all shining with gold is driving a team of horses."'

149. **studio**: abl. of efficient cause, supr. 129.

150. **geminae foris** 'of the double door,' *i.e.* the front or street door, which would consist of two swing doors. Cf. Livy 1, 14 *fores portarum*. Cf. 13, 87—8.

152. **aureus**: cf. *A. A.* 1, 214 *Quatuor in niveis aureus ibis equis.* (Loers.)

153. **abscissa veste** 'tearing the bosom of my dress,' cf. *F.* 4, 448 *ipsa suos absciderat que sinus.* **planxi**: cf. 10, 15 *protinus adductis sonuerunt pectora palmis.* 5, 71.

154. **tuta a digitis**: cf. *A. A.* 3, 707 *Ut rediit animus, tenues a pectore vestes Rumpit, et indignas sauciat ungue genas.*

156. **sertaque compositis demere**, *i.e.* 'to snatch the garlands from the bride's neat locks,' such a contrast to her own, which are torn and dishevelled.

157. **sic** 'even as it was,' 'even though I was so deserted and helpless and the attempt would have been hopeless.' *Sic* refers to the whole situation, not to *laniata capillos.* See 13, 137.

158. **iniceremque manus**: cf. on 8, 16. Add *Am.* 1, 4, 40 *Et dicam 'mea sunt,' iniciamque manus.* Ib. 3, 9, 20 *omnibus obscuras inicit illa* (sc. *mors*) *manus.* *F.* 4, 90 *Quem Venus injecta vindicat alma manu.*

160. **inferias** 'offerings to the deities below' to propitiate the Manes. Cf. *F.* 5, 421 *Ritus erit veteris, nocturna Lemuria, sacri: Inferias tacitis Manibus illa dabunt.* **umbrae** 'ghost,' plur. for sing.

162. **qui nobis omnia solus erat** 'who by himself was all these four to me,' *i.e.* kingdom, country, home, and husband. Cf. on 2, 51. At the same time *omnia esse alicui*

'to be all in all to any one' is a general phrase, cf. Livy 40, 11 *Demetrius iis unus omnia est*, corresponding to the Greek *πάντα εἶναι*. See Lidd. and Sc.

163. **igitur** 'so then it seems' *ἄρα*. Cf. *Pont.* 4, 10, 7 *Tempus edax igitur praeter nos omnia perdit.*

168. **Hecates**: see on 79. The form of the genitive in *-es* seems taken simply from the Greek, cf. Hypsipyles 6, 132, though one of the ancient varieties in the genitive of *-e* stems was that in *-es*. Roby § 357.

169. **noctes vigilantur amarae** 'the bitter nights are spent in wakefulness.' So in *F.* 4, 167 *vigilata nocte. A. A.* 1, 735 *attenuant juvenum vigilatae corpora noctes. Vigilo* is properly intransitive, but like other similar verbs of the first conjugation has a passive in use, especially a passive participle. See F. A. Paley on *F.* 3. 357; where he quotes as instances *regnatus, clamatus, triumphatus, ululatus, cessatus, lacrimatus, bacchatus.* Cf. Roby § 1421.

170. This line has been admirably restored by Palmer from *Tr.* 4, 3, 22. *Pont.* 3, 2, 12. *tener* must be taken to mean 'light' in the sense of easily dissolved or broken, cf. on 2, 143. In *A. A.* 2, 546 it seems to mean 'light sleep' in the same sense.

175—6. **stultae** (dat.), an epithet born of angry jealousy. She contrasts her rival's common-place feminine character with her own unlawful cunning.

iniustis 'unfriendly to me,' so in 7, 44 *justior* is 'more friendly.'

179. **Tyrio in ostro** 'in her royal couch of Tyrian purple,' cf. supr. 52. **Tyrio**, *i.e.* dyed with the *Tyrian murex*, cf. 13, 37. **sublimis** refers partly to mental elevation, partly to physical, see on 9, 129.

180. **adusta**: cf. on 4, 33 'penetrated by the fire.' The garland and robe sent Creusa by Medea burnt into her flesh and destroyed her. Eur. *Med.* 1184—1202.

184. 'Now if ever listen to words that are all too humble for my pride.' So *Tr.* 2, 214 *et sunt notitiâ multa minora tuâ* 'too small for you to know them.'

187. **vilis** 'held cheap,' cf. 3, 41.

188. **noverca**: see on 6, 126—7.

189. **similes**: cf. 6, 123. **imagine** 'the likeness to you.' Cf. 8. 1.

191. **per avitae lumina flammae**, see supr. 78.

192. **meritum** 'my services to you,' supr. 82. **pignora**: see on 6, 122.

194. **adde fidem dictis** 'keep your promises,' cf. 7, 110.

197. **quem nobis ipse dedisti**: referring to Jason's own words, see on 82 and 86.

200. 'Which had to be ploughed as a condition of your carrying away the golden fleece.'

202. 'As to which dowry if I should now say to you "Pay it back," you would decline.' Ovid again makes Medea refer to procedures under Roman law. In the case of a divorce arising from a mere caprice of the husband's, without reasonable cause to be alleged against the wife, he was bound to pay back the whole of the *Dos*. Ramsay *Rom. Antiq.* p. 254. Cf. Sen. *Med.* 487 *Tibi patria cessit, tibi pater frater pudor, Hac dote nupsi, redde fugienti sua.*

203. 'My dower is the safety which I secured for you, and for the other Grecian youths.'

204. **i nunc**: cf. on 3, 26. **Sisyphias opes** 'the wealth of your new Corinthian wife Creusa.' *Sisyphias* stands for Corinthian because Sisyphus was said to have founded Ephyra, afterwards called Corinth. I do not know on what authority Loers calls Sisyphus the father of Creon.

205. **potentis** 'of princely rank,' cf. 5, 85.

206. 'The very power itself of being ungrateful you owe to me,' *i.e.* it is all my doing that you are alive at all.

207. **quos equidem actutum**: the threat is all the more significant for not being completed, cf. *Aen.* 1, 135 *quos ego...*

208. **parturit ira** 'my wrath is in labour with immense threats.' Seneca imitated Ovid's use of the word by making Medea (v. 25) say, *Partu jam parta ultio est; Peperi.*

In these last lines Medea is hinting at the dreadful vengeance she means to take upon her husband, the complete extent of which we may suppose her as not yet to have conceived.

209. **quo feret ira** 'whithersoever rage shall hurry me.' *fero* is used often in connection with violent excitement, cf. 4, 47.

211. **viderit ista deus** 'let the God see to that.' 'That is God's affair, not mine,' cf. *A. A.* 2, 371 *viderit Atrides; Helenen ego crimine solvo*, ib. 3, 671 *viderit utilitas, ego coepta fideliter*

edam. Rem. 249 *Viderit, Haemoniae siquis mala pabula terrae Et magicas artes posse juvare putat. M.* 10, 624 *Viderit! intereat.... F.* 2, 782 *Viderit, audentes forsve deusve juvet. Tr.* 5, 2, 43 *Viderit! ipse sacram quamvis invisus ad aram Confugiam. Pont.* 1, 2, 11 *videris. Aen.* 10, 744 *At de me divom pater atque hominum rex Viderit.*

versat 'tortures,' cf. *Am.* 1, 2, 8 *Et possessa ferus pectora versat amor.*

212. **nescio quid**: see on 3, 78.

XIII.

LAODAMIA PROTESILAO.

The story of Protesilaus is briefly this. There was an oracle to the effect that the first man of the Greek host who touched Trojan soil should immediately be killed. Protesilaus of Phylace, in Thessaly, led the warriors of several Thessalian towns, and in spite of this oracle was the first to leap on the shore of Troy, and was killed, according to the tradition followed by Ovid, by Hector. *Met.* 12, 67 *Hectorea primus fataliter hastâ, Protesilae, cadis.* His wife Laodamia is supposed to have heard of this oracle while the host is still at Aulis, and to write this letter to warn him of it; telling him of her own evil forebodings and dreams, and entreating him to abstain from being too forward to land.

[We have no materials in our hands which Ovid could have used except the passage in Homer, *Il.* 2, 698—702:

τῶν αὖ Πρωτεσίλαος Ἀρήιος ἡγεμόνευεν
ζωὸς ἐών· τότε δ' ἤδη ἔχεν κάτα γαῖα μέλαινα.
τοῦ δὲ καὶ ἀμφιδρυφὴς ἄλοχος Φυλάκῃ ἐλέλειπτο
καὶ δόμος ἡμιτελής· τὸν δ' ἔκτανε Δάρδανος ἀνὴρ
νηὸς ἀποθρώσκοντα πολὺ πρώτιστον Ἀχαιῶν.

But we can gather from the poem that Ovid has used various traditions which suit his purpose. For instance he knows the story of her being found by her husband, when allowed to return to earth, embracing his image, see 151 sq. The tale however has been often told, and with many variations, by later writers; among others by Lucian, 'Dialogues of the Dead,' 23. And it is made more interesting to us by having formed the subject of one of the finest poems of our own Wordsworth. One stanza of his gives the story briefly:

'Thou know'st, the Delphic oracle foretold
That the first Greek who touched the Trojan strand
Should die; but me the threat did not withhold;
A generous cause a victim did demand;
And forth I leapt upon the sandy plain;
A self-devoted chief—by Hector slain.']

1—2. 'Thessalian Laodamia to her Thessalian lord sends greeting and health, and lovingly wishes that health may indeed go where she sends it.'

The point of the lines, not a very great one after all, depends on the double use of *salutem*, first as a complimentary formula, and secondly to mean literally 'health:' a like use we have noticed before, see on 4, 1—2.

Haemonis Haemonio 'Thessalian,' see on 6, 23. 12, 127.

6. 'That was the right time for the waters to rage.' So in *F.* 6, 223 *Junius utilis nuptis, utilis viris* means that 'June is a right time for maids and men to marry in.'

21. **fugacia** 'swift,' cf. 4, 46.

23—4. **tenebris obortis** 'with a film of darkness upon my eyes,' cf. *lacrimis obortis*, 8, 109. The preposition *ob* conveys the idea of covering and obstruction. **succiduo** 'sinking beneath me.' Cf. *M.* 10, 458 *Poplite succiduo genua intremuere, fugitque Et color et sanguis.*

25. **Iphiclus**, father of Protesilaus and king of Phylace. **Acastus**, father of Laodamia. The latter is usually described as son of Pelias, and one of the Argonauts; but it has been questioned whether some other hero of this name is not meant.

29. **ut rediit animus**: Ovid twice in these epistles (see 9, 141) uses the final syllable of the 3rd pers. perf. of *eo* long. -*it* in the perfect was originally long, and is so often used by Plautus; Ennius however generally makes it short; Virgil also usually makes it short, though occasionally availing himself of the ancient usage, *e.g. G.* 2, 211 *At rudis enituit impulso vomere campus. Aen.* 8. 363 *Alcides subiit, haec illum regia cepit.* And Ovid confines the use mostly to the compounds of *eo.* Cf. *Am.* 3, 8, 17 *qua periit aliquis potes hanc contingere dextram?* See Professor Nettleship, 'Appendix to Conington's Virgil,' Vol. 3.

31—2. Cf. Ballad in Percy's 'Reliques,'

There sall nae mantle cross my back
Na kaim gae in my hair,...

. . . .

Sin' the lowlands o' Holland
Hae twinn'd my love and me.

For **praebere pectendos**, cf. 2, 141.

33—4. 'As the Bacchanals (cf. 4, 47) whom Bacchus is believed to have touched with his vine-wreathed thyrsus, so I roam hither and thither (**huc illuc**) wheresoever the frenzy has driven me.' **Bicorniger** 'Bacchus,' represented sometimes under the form of a bull. Thus in Eur. *Bacch.* 1159 Pentheus guided by Bacchus goes to his death ταῦρον προηγητῆρα συμφορᾶς ἔχων.

hasta: the Bacchanals carried a spear wreathed with vine and other green boughs, cf. *Am.* 3, 15—17 *Corniger increpuit thyrso graviore Lyaeus*, and *Met.* 3, 666—7 *Ipsa racemiferis frontem circumdatus uvis Pampineis agitat velatam frondibus hastam.*

35. **matres Phylaceides** 'the matrons of Phylace,' the town of Protesilaus, from which Laodamia is writing.

37—40. For the tenses of these verbs, see on 2, 99. **scilicet** expresses indignant irony, see on 4, 21.

41. **qua possum** 'as far as I can,' or 'the only way I can,' cf. 10, 135. **squalore**: *i.e.* 'with mourning robes.' The dictionaries give many instances, *e.g.* Cic. *Ver.* 5, 48 *aspicite, judices, squalorem sordesque sociorum.*

43. **Dyspari** 'ill-omened Paris,' for the old reading *Dux Pari*, from Hom. *Il.* 3, 39 Δύσπαρι, εἶδος ἄριστε, γυναιμανὲς, ἠπεροπευτά. Such a play on a name may be compared with that on 'Helen' in Aeschyl. *Ag.* 671 ἑλέναυς, ἕλανδρος, ἑλέπτολις.

45. **Taenariae**: *i.e.* 'Spartan,' from the promontory Taenarum (Cape Matapan) in Laconia, see sup. 1, 46. The Spartan wife is of course Helen. **vellem** 'I could have wished.'

48. **flebilis** 'a cause of tears,' cp. Horace, *Od.* 1, 24, 9 *multis ille bonis flebilis occidit.* Menelaus is *flebilis ultor*, as the mover of a war which must give many mothers and wives cause to weep for their slain, *bella matribus detestata*, Hor. *Od.* 1, 1, 24.

50. **det**: *i. e.* dedicate his arms in the temple of Jupiter, as a thank-offering for his safe return. Cf. *Tr.* 4, 8, 21 *Miles ut emeritis non est satis utilis annis Ponit ad ambiguos quae tulit arma deos.* Such offerings were called in Greek ἀναθήματα: an instance of such an one in the Homeric warriors is that of Euphorbus, whom Pythagoras declared to have possessed the same soul as himself, and proved it by taking down his shield from the temple wall; a story referred to by Hor. *Od.* 1. 28, 10, sq. **Reduci Jovi** '*to Jupiter Redux*,' *i.e.* the god who brings back.

51. **subiit** 'has occurred to my mind,' cf. infr. 123.

53. **Tenedos:** an island off the shore of the Troad, cf. *Aen.* 2, 21 *Est in conspectu Tenedos notissima fama Insula.*

For the rivers **Simois** and **Xanthus**, see 1, 33; and 5, 30. **Ide:** Ovid has *Ida* in 5, 138; *Iden* in 5, 73, where see note.

58. **quique suo...opes** 'And as one would who was carrying on his person the wealth of Troy,' cf. 8, 14. Cp. Shaksp., As you Like it, 2, 7 'The city woman bears the cost of Princes on unworthy shoulders.' Hy. VIII. i. 1, 83, 'O, many have broke their backs by laying manors on them For this great journey.' **ferret:** the subj. with *qui* restricting a general statement, 'the sort of person who.' Roby § 1692. For the visit of Paris to Sparta, see on 5. 41.

60. **pars quota** 'how large a portion of the resources of his kingdom is in each prince's train.' **quotus** 'what fraction of,' is generally used to mean 'how small a fraction?' But as it is a perfectly neutral word, there is no reason why it should not mean the one as well as the other. *quotus* is for instance perfectly neutral in the phrase *quotus esse velis rescribe* (Hor. *Ep.* 1, 5, 30), 'write word how many you wish to be at dinner,' lit. 'what fraction (large or small) of your company you wish to be.' And Ovid elsewhere uses it for 'how large a proportion,' cf. *M.* 7, 522 *Et quota pars illi rerum periere mearum*, 'How large a part of my power perished in them!' It is entirely against all sense for Laodamia to say 'Paris came laden with wealth, and with how small a portion of his kingdom.' I cannot therefore agree either with Palmer or Ramsay in their explanations, which indeed I scarcely understand. **quemque** refers to the various chieftains we may suppose to have been in the train of Paris.

61. **consors Ledaea gemellis:** Helen and Clytemnestra were born from one egg, Castor and Pollux from the other, of Leda. **consors gemellis** 'sister to the twins.' *Consors* is a favourite word with Ovid, and he uses it of various relationships beside that of wife or husband, *e.g.* in *M.* 8, 444 *consorti sanguine* is 'with the blood of the brother,' as also in 13, 663 *consortia pectora.* Above we have had (3, 47) *consortes generisque necisque*, of brothers. But the peculiarity here is the construction of *consors* with the dative, which I do not think can be paralleled in Ovid.

62. **haec Danais posse nocere puto** 'these are the things which I think may damage the Greeks,' *i.e.* wealth and splendour, which she says are able *nocere* 'to be prejudicial' to the Greeks, by taking their fancy and so eventually leading to the war.

63—7. These lines are in the same spirit as those in 1, 13—16. But the writer has forgotten that Laodamia living in Thessaly was not likely to have heard the conversation of Paris in Sparta. **nescio quem**: see on 7, 124. 3, 78. According to Loers it expresses the vagueness of the information; but the *Paris dixit* implies that she heard it from Paris himself.

68. **multos Hectoras**, 'many men as dangerous as Hector.' Shakespeare *Rich. III.*: 'I think there be six Richmonds in the field.' Loers quotes Suet. *Caes.* 1 *Caesari multos Marios inesse.* Troilus and Cress. 5, 5. 'There is a thousand Hectors in the field.'

71. **fas est** 'if it is the will of fate,' cf. *Tr.* 3, 5, 27 *seu temere expecto sive id contingere fas est.*

76. **viro**: dat. of agent after gerund, see on 2, 115.

77. **pugna vivere** 'struggle to keep alive.' In 3, 25 we have *pugnas ne;* in *Rem.* 122 *pugnat ire. pugna* is used here in a kind of double meaning: (1) join in the battle, (2) struggle to do so and so.

86. 'My tongue stopped for fear of the bad omen.' A chance word, that might be interpreted into meaning misfortune, fear or failure, would be of evil omen in beginning a journey.

88. Another bad omen in commencing any business or journey was to stumble on the threshold. Hence, says Professor Ramsay, a bride was always carried over the threshold, both on leaving her father's, and entering her husband's, house. He quotes *Am.* 1, 12, 3,—on receiving an unfavourable answer from his mistress:

Omina sunt aliquid,—modo cum discedere vellet,
Ad limen digitos restitit icta Nape.
Missa foras iterum limen transire memento
Cautius; atque alte sobria ferre pedem.

Tibullus 1, 3, 19 *Oh! quotiens ingressus iter; mihi tristia dixi Offensum in porta signa dedisse pedem.*

89—90. *i.e.* she tries to avert the evil omen, by assuming that it is a good one.

91. **animosus** 'full of spirit,' implying 'too full for safety.' Cf. 8, 1.

92. **fac** 'see that this fear of mine is all given to the winds.' The winds and waves are the Poet's receptacle for all that is vain and false, see on 2, 25.

93. **sors** 'the oracle.' As one way of consulting an oracle was by drawing lots, *sors* came to mean, at any rate in poetry, any oracular response. Cf. *F.* 2, 713 *Consulitur Phoebus. Sors est ita reddita: 'Matri Qui dederit princeps oscula, victor erit.'*

94. **Troada**: the feminine adjective *Troas* occurs again below v. 137. Cf. *Lemnias* 6, 139.

96. **strenuus**, like *animosus* above v. 91, means 'too active for safety.' The word is connected with *στρῆνος*, and perhaps our 'strength,' 'strong.'

97. **mille**: used indefinitely for a large number. Cf. *Aen.* 2, 98 *quos...non anni domuere decem non mille carinae.*

98. **iam fatigatas** 'when they have already been well worked by other people's oars.' So *M.* 8, 825 *dentemque in dente fatigat* 'he works one tooth on another,' *i.e.* with no food between them.

101. **remoque veloque** 'speed on your ship with oar and sail together,' *i.e.* make all possible haste. As a rule rowing would only go on when sailing was impossible. Cf. *Rem.* 789 *Illo Lotophagos, illo Sirenas in antro Esse puta: remis adice vela tuis.* For the use of oars where sailing becomes dangerous or impossible see *Aen.* 3, 207 *vela cadunt, remis insurgimus*, and *ib.* 563 *Laevam cuncta cohors remis ventisque petivit.* The expression became proverbial; cp. Cic. Fam. 12, 25 *inde ventis remis in patriam omni fastinatione properavi.* Plaut. Asin. 1, 3, 5 *Remigiis velisque quantum poteris festina et fuge.*

104. **dolor**, 'a source of sorrowful anxiety.' Loers quotes *Tr.* 3, 3, 17 *Te loquor absentem, te vox mea nominat unam, Nulla venit sine te nox mihi, nulla dies.*

107. **aucupor** 'I snatch eagerly at,' cf. 9, 41. **mendaces**: she calls her sleep *mendax*, because in it she enjoys an imaginary interview with her husband.

110. 'Ah! why in your words is there many a mournful sound?' Ovid sometimes uses *venit* as little more than equivalent to *fit*, see 4, 26. **querella** is here equivalent to *verbum triste.*

[Palmer has transformed the line thus, *cur venit, a verbis muta, querella latens?* 'Why does a dark complaint, unexpressed in words, reach my ears?' How indeed could it, if unexpressed? If *querella latens* must stand, owing to the corruption *tens* in P., it would still be wrong to read *muta:*

and it should perhaps be translated 'an undercurrent of sadness' or 'lamentation.' However I think there is little or no reason for any further change than that of Madvig. P. may be 'the only MS. of any value,' yet the unanimity of all others shows a unity of tradition which is worth something.]

111. **simulacra...adoro**: 'I propitiate the phantoms of the night.' For *simulacra* see on 10, 95. The object of this propitiation was to obviate the evil effects of a dream. For this purpose there were several solemn observances, such as dipping three times in water. See Arist. *Ran.* 1339 *θέρμετε δ' ὕδωρ ὡς ἂν θεῖον ὄνειρον ἀποκλύσω.* *Aen.* 8, 67 *Nox Aenean somnusque reliquit. Surgit et aetheriā spectans orientia Solis Lumina, rite cavis undam de flumine palmis Sustinet, ac talis effundit ad aethera voces.* Persius 2, 15 *Tiberino in gurgite mergis Mane caput bis terque, et noctem flumine purgas?* Propert. 4, 10, 13 *Ac primum pura somnum tibi discute lympha.*

112. **fumo meo**, *i.e.* a sacrifice from me. **Thessalis**: fem. adj. from Thessalus. Cp. *Argolis* (6, 81), *Sithonis* (2, 6), *Aetolis* (9, 131), *Tantalis* (8, 122).

113—4. Laodamia says that her tears falling on the fire of the altar had the same effect as the wine which was usually employed to extinguish the embers, and which had the effect of making them blaze up, and then go out.

115. **quando**: see on 1, 11.

116. **languida a laetitia mea**, 'faint from sheer joy,' cf. *a somno languida* 10, 9. For **solvar**, *i.e.* 'relax my embrace,' see supr. 12. For the position of *ipsa* see 9, 96. 12, 18.

120—1. **narrantia verba**=*verba narrantis*, cf. 11, 69 *precantia verba.*

in his: sc. *osculis.*

122. **promptior** 'more fluent.' *F.* 4, 310 *ad rigidos promptaque lingua senes.*

123—4. **subit...subeunt** 'occur to my mind,' see supr. 51.

cadit: cf. 9, 42.

126. **invitis aquis** 'though the sea forbids,' cf. 2, 100 *pelago negante,* referring to the detention of the fleet at Aulis.

127—8. 'Which of you would wish to sail *home* against a contrary wind? And to venture *from home* when a storm at sea forbids it?' The emphasis is on *in patriam* and *a patria.*

129. **suam ad urbem**, *i.e.* Troy, the walls of which were said to have been built by Neptune and Apollo; cf. 3, 151 *Neptunia Pergama.*

132. 'That delay is caused not by random accident, but by God.' *Casus* and *numinis* are subjective genitives, to both of which *mora* belongs.

134. **vertite vela**, *i.e.* sail back home, cf. 10, 149.

Inachiae 'Argive' and then generally 'Greek.' *Inachus* son of Oceanus was said to have been first king of Argos. See 14, 23, 105.

135. **omen**: see 86.

137. **Troasin**: dat. plur. of Troas (supr. 94). Cf. *Lemniasin A. A.* 3, 672. **sic** 'as they will,' see on 12, 157.

138. **conspicient** 'will have a full view of.'

140. **barbara**, *i.e.* Trojan, non-Hellenic. See on 1, 26.

144. **referas** 'take care that you bring back these arms to dedicate to Jupiter Redux,' see supr. 50. **fac referas**: see on 2, 66, supr. 92.

147. **haec**, *i.e.* the bride. **exuit**: for the construction of this verb see on 9, 111.

151. **diverso in orbe** 'in a different part of the world,' *Tr.* 3, 1, 26 *longinquo referam lassus ab orbe pedem.*

152—158. For this part of the legend see introduction to this Epistle. Palmer says that it is 'unspeakably silly.' But has he not done something to create the silliness which he derides by translating *cera* 'a doll'? It is in fact the word used for a likeness or image, generally, it is true, of the departed; but still if done in the lifetime there is no reason for supposing that it should be on the footing of a mere doll. Such 'images' were sometimes coloured and made with considerable art, *Tr.* 2, 521 *prisca virorum Artifici fulgent corpora picta manu:* and were successful as likenesses, Mart. 7, 44 *Maximus ille tuus, Ovidi, Caesonius hic est, Cujus adhuc vultum vivida cera tenet.* See Rich, *Dict. of Antiq.* 'Cera.' That these *cerae* were used as portraits of lovers is also shown by *Rem.* 732, where Ovid refers to this legend, *Si potes et ceras remove: quid imagine muta Carperis? hoc periit Laodamia modo.*

159. **mea numina**. Cf. *F.* 2, 842 *perque tuos Manes qui mihi numen erunt.*

161—2. **ut** = *utinam:* a use which seems not Ovidian, but which is more commonly found in solemn formulas of cursing, etc. *e.g.* Ter. *Haut.* 810 *ut di te perduint.*

'And by that head, which I pray I may see grow white with hoary locks, which I pray that you may be able to bring back home yourself,' *i.e.* not have sent back, mere ashes in the funeral urn. The lines, especially the second, are exceedingly weak, not to say (with Palmer) absurd.

166. 'If you care for me, take care of yourself.'

XIV.

HYPERMNESTRA LYNCEO.

Aegyptus and Danaus were twin sons of Belus, king of Egypt. The former had fifty sons, the latter fifty daughters. Aegyptus wished his sons to marry their cousins. Danaus however had been warned by an oracle that he would perish by the hands of a son-in-law. He therefore with his daughters fled to Argos. The sons of Aegyptus pursued them thither; and Danaus at last yielded to their wishes, but gave each of his daughters a sword with which he bade them kill their respective husbands. All obeyed except the eldest, Hypermnestra, who spared her husband Lynceus. For this her father threw her into prison. She was tried by an Argive tribunal, and acquitted; and her father afterwards forgave her and united her to Lynceus. From her prison she writes this letter to Lynceus.

[The longest account of this fable which we possess, and which could have been in Ovid's hands, is that in Apollodorus, book 2. The main incident is given by him in these words, *αἱ δὲ κοιμώμεναι τοὺς νυμφίους ἀπέκτειναν πλὴν Ὑπερμνήστρας, αὐτὴ δὲ Λυγκέα διέσωσε πάρθενον αὐτὴν φυλάξαντα.* It has been rendered memorable to us by one of Horace's most successful Odes (3, 11), and bis words have evidently been in Ovid's mind.

Una de multis face nuptiali
Digna perjurum fuit in parentem
Splendide mendax, et in omne virgo
Nobilis aevum.

Surge, quae dixit juveni marito,
Surge; ne longus tibi somnus, unde
Non times, detur: socerum et scelestas
Falle sorores;

Quae velut, nactae vitulos leaenae,
Singulos eheu! lacerant: ego illis
Mollior, nec te feriam, neque intra
Claustra tenebo.

Me pater saevis oneret catenis,
Quod viro clemens misero peperci:
Me vel extremos Numidarum in agros
Classe releget.

I, pedes quo te rapiunt et aurae
Dum favet nox et Venus; i secundo
Omine, et nostri memorem sepulchro
Sculpe querelam.]

1. **mittit**: sc. *epistolam.* **Hypermnestra**: the final -*a* follows the quantity of the Greek.

6. **rea** 'an accused person:' this probably refers to the legend (not mentioned in Apollodorus, but in Pausanias 2, 19, 6) of Hypermnestra having been tried and acquitted by an Argive court. See introd.

9—10. **igne**: referring to the lighted nuptial torches, the sanctity of which she had not violated, and which she says her father may use for her funeral pyre. An association of ideas before noticed, vid. on 2, 120. 6, 45. 12, 140. **sacris**: *i.e.* the marriage rites, see 2, 120.

11. **non bene** 'with no good purpose,' *i.e.* wherewith to murder my husband treacherously. **ensem**: attracted from the ablative to the case of its relative *quem.*

iugulet: jugulari is to *cut* the throat, as opposed to stabbing, *M.* 12, 484 *medio jugulaberis ense, Quandoquidem mucro est hebes.*

14. **non est, quam piget esse piam** 'she is not pious who is sorry for being so.' A good action which one repents of ceases to be a good action. Just as 'deliberate moral choice' beforehand is needed, according to the philosopher, to constitute a good action. *piam* and *pia* are equally admissible as Latin, and *piam* is preferable both from considerations of prosody and authority.

16. **hic eventus** 'this result,' *i. e.* remorse.

17. **admonitu** 'recollection,' cf. 9, 135.

18. **orsa** 'what I had just begun,' *i.e.* the writing of this letter. The passive participle of *ordior* occurs again in *Ad Liviam* 210 *Tristia quum medius rumperet orsa dolor*, see on 12, 169 for these participles.

20. **de caede non sibi facta** 'about a murder which she did not commit.' **sibi**: the dative of agent, cf. 2, 115 and index. **putes**: subjunctive with restrictive relative, cf. 13, 58. 'The woman whom you believe capable of murdering her husband, shrinks from even writing about a murder which she did not commit.'

23. 'At the very beginning of night, when one does not know whether to call it the beginning of night or the end of day.' Aeschylus (*Cho.* 55) calls this border-land *μεταίχμιον σκότου.* Cf. Shakespeare, 'How goes the night?' 'Almost at odds with morning, which is which.'

23. **Inachides**: 'descendants of Inachus,' *i.e.* 'we daughters of Danaus.' Inachus was the mythical ancestor of the family (13, 134), which claimed to be descended thus: Inachus, Io, Epaphus, Libya, Belus, Danaus.

Pelasgi: Pelasgus according to Aeschylus was the king of Argos when the Danaids arrived there, *Suppl.* 248—9 *ἐμοῦ δ' ἄνακτος εὐλόγως ἐπώνυμον γένος Πελασγῶν τήνδε καρποῦται χθόνα.* Apollodorus however calls him Gelanor. But *Danaus* and *Pelasgus* are mythical personages whose names arise from those of the ancient inhabitants of the Peloponnesus—the Danai and Pelasgi—who by the usual inversion of mythology are said to derive their appellation from those kings.

24. **socer**: *i.e.* Aegyptus. Palmer quotes Euripides from Aristoph. *Ran.* 1207 to show that Aegyptus according to some legends accompanied his sons: *Αἴγυπτος ὡς ὁ πλεῖστος ἔσπαρται λόγος σὺν παισὶ πεντήκοντα ναυτίλῳ πλάτῃ Ἄργος κατασχών.* The two lines seem to infer that Pelasgus is entertaining the sons of Aegyptus and that the brides are brought home to their husbands in his palace; whereas in Aeschylus it is the daughters of Danaus who are entertained and protected by Pelasgus.

26. **in invitos focos**: the epithet which belongs to the Gods transferred to their altars. This marriage she means was contrary to the will of heaven.

27—8. **Hymen Hymenaee**: cf. 12, 143. **Iovis conjux** 'Juno pronuba,' cf. 6, 43. **urbe sua**: Argos, of which Juno was the tutelary deity.

29. **comitum clamore frequentes**, sc. *clamoribus comitum frequentium celebrati*, 'amidst the shouts of thronging comrades:' cf. 12, 143.

30. **madidas**: *i.e.* with unguents. A mark of their dissoluteness, cf. *M.* 3, 544—6 *Quem neque bella juvant, nec tela, nec usus equorum, Sed madidi murra crines mollesque coronae.*

34. **securum per Argos.** The Latins used the word Argos (1) as a neuter indeclinable, *aptum dicet equis Argos*, Hor. *Od.* 1, 7, 9, (2) as a plural in the oblique cases, *dulces reminiscitur Argos*, Virg. *Aen.* 10, 782. *Ecce autem Inachiis sese referebat ab Argis Saeva Jovis conjunx*, ib. 7, 286, cf. Varro, *L. L.* 9, 89 *itaque dicimus* **hic Argus** *cum hominem dicimus, cum oppidum Graecanice* **hoc Argus**, *cum Latine* **Argei**.

36. **tamen** refers to *videbar*, 'nay, I not only thought I heard, I actually had heard them.'

quodque verebar erat 'and what I was dreading might happen, was actually happening.'

39—40. Cf. 10, 139 *corpus ut impulsae segetes aquilonibus horret*, and *Amor.* 1, 7, 53 *Exanimis artus et membra trementia vidi, Ut cum populeas ventilat aura comas.*

42. 'And the wine I had given you was the wine of sleep.' The use of soporifics was well known to the ancients, cf. *F.* 4 547 *abstinet alma Ceres somnique papavera causas Dat tibi cum tepido lacte bibenda, puer.* The genitive *soporis* is doubtless bold, and I am inclined to think that some emendation may be wanted, though for more reasons than one I cannot accept Palmer's.

46. **reccidit** (cf. *Rem.* 610) arises from the reduplicated perfect *cecidit*. The syllable *re* is long either from the doubling of the consonant, or on the principle of compensation for a lost syllable, cp. *repperi* for *re-peperi*, *rettuli* for *re-tetuli*. **male sublato** 'scarcely raised,' cf. 4, 23.

51—2. **laniata**: cf. 7, 175. **purpureos**: as being a princess, cf. 5, 88. **exiguo sono** 'in a whisper,' abl. of quality with epithet.

56. **faciunt ad** 'tender woman's hands are not fit to use cruel weapons,' cf. 6, 128; also *facere cum aliquo*. *A. A.* 3, 762. By exactly the same idiom we might say 'Soft hands don't *do* for cruel weapons.'

57. **quin age**: Roby § 1617.

58. **omnibus**: dat. of agent, see above, v. 20. For Ovid's use of ablative of agent without *ab* (which it is possible to consider this) see index.

59. **aliquam** 'any,' emphatic.

61—2. **aut**, referring to alternative implied in previous lines. 'Can I be capable of committing such a murder, or can they be said to deserve it?' Cf. 10, 111. 12, 13.

'Have they deserved death for occupying their uncle's realms, which after all would have had to be given to sons-in-law of another family,' *i.e.* if these men who are of our own blood had not taken them. The emphasis is on *externis*, and Hypermnestra seems to argue that after all the sons of Aegyptus, by marrying their cousins, have saved the realm from going out of the family. A trisyllable at the end of the pentameter is not used elsewhere in the earlier poems of Ovid; but we should not therefore be too hasty in rejecting the line, when we consider that it is a licence which Ovid's predecessors often took, and which he afterwards allowed himself.

63—64. 'Even if they have deserved death, how have we deserved to burden ourselves with so dreadful a pollution as their blood?'

65. **quid mihi**, 'what have I to do with a sword?' *Am.* 1, 7, 27 *quid mihi vobiscum, caedis sceleris que ministrae?* *Tr.* 2, 1 *quid mihi vobiscum est, infelix cura, libelli?* *F.* 2. 101 *quid tibi cum gladio?* Cf. 6, 47, and Mayor on Pliny Ep. 3, 9, 27. **quid bellica tela puellae** 'what have weapons of war to do with a girl?' a less common but perfectly intelligible phrase.

67. **sua verba** 'the words which called them forth,' or 'which suited them.'

73. **surge age, Belide**: from Horace, *Surge quae dixit juveni marito, surge, ne longus tibi somnus, unde non times, detur*, etc.

Belide, voc. of *Belides*, cf. *Achille* (3, 25 etc.), *Aesonide* (6, 109), *Alcide* (9, 75). Lynceus is grandson of Belus; see introduction.

modo here and in v. 1 seems to mean 'but lately alive,' joined closely with *fratribus*.

77. **tu fugis, ipsa moror**, present for future or imperative, expressing instant and eager action, see on 2, 20.

79—80. **ex caede** 'after the slaughter.' **dinumerat** 'counts one by one,' *i.e.* carefully. **summa** 'the full tale,' cf. 2, 56.

81. **cognatae mortis** 'of the death of his kinsmen,' cf. 4, 138, *cognato nomine*. **iacturam**: properly, 'a throwing away,' hence, any 'loss.'

82. **facti sanguinis parum esse** 'that there had not been enough blood shed.' Loers quotes Livy 2, 30 *plus sanguinis ibi factum*, see also ib. 35, 51 *sanguinem usquam factum audire*.

83. **a patriis pedibus** 'from my father's feet,' at which I had thrown myself as a suppliant.

84. **haec** 'such as this!' see 8, 53 and index.

85. **scilicet** 'the truth is that.' **ex illo** 'from that time.'

86. **quo**: Madvig would read **quom**=*ex quo tempore*, cf. Ter. *Haut.* 54 and note.

ex homine 'from a woman.' She now refers to the story of *Io*, her ancestress (see v. 23), and declares that Juno's wrath with the family has lasted since her time.

ex bove facta dea 'from a heifer became a goddess,' *i.e.* Isis, see Paley on *F.* 5, 620.

89—90. **liquidi parentis**: Io was daughter of the River-god Inachus. **non sua** 'that did not naturally belong to her.' Jupiter turned her into a heifer to escape the jealousy of Juno, who first set Argus to watch her, and when he was killed, tormented her with a gadfly.

93. **umbra** 'in your shadow,' *i.e.* reflected on the water. For *umbrae* of shadows cast by objects, cf. *M.* 3, 144 *jamque dies medius rerum contraxerat umbras*.

94. **factos ad** 'made to correspond,' *i.e.* four feet, instead of two.

95. **pelex** 'rival,' cf. 9, 121. **sorori** 'by Juno,' dat. after gerund, see 13, 76.

98. **arma**: *i.e.* her horns.

99—100. 'And you, who lately were so rich as to seem worthy even of Jupiter, now lie naked on the bare ground.' Loers quotes *M.* 4, 261 *Sedit humo nuda nudis incompta capillis*.

101. **cognata flumina**: kin to her as daughter of the river Inachus.

103. **Io.** The first syllable of Io is long in Greek, and in Ovid elsewhere except *Ibis* 624, see on 62.

105—6. **Inachi**, vocative of feminine patronymic *Inachis*, see on 13, 43.

eadem sequeris: 'you fly from this heifer which you see reflected; but what you fly from is yourself; you are at once the guide and the guided.'

107—8. Io was said to have been restored to her proper shape on the banks of the Nile, and there to have brought forth her son Epaphus.

portus: for the 'mouths' of a river see *Am.* 2, 13, 9 *Quaque celer Nilus late delapsus in alveo Per septem portus in maris exit aquas.* **exuit**, see 13, 147. **pelicis**, see v. 95.

109—110. Hypermnestra now reverts from the Episode of Io to her own case. 'Why should I tell of these remote events which I only know from tradition? The events of my own life-time supply me with abundant subject for lamentation.'

quorum mihi cana senectus auctor 'of which hoar antiquity is my informant.' **cana senectus** may be a general term for antiquity, *i.e.* the records of antiquity; or for *cani senes* the old men who have handed down the traditions. **ultima** 'remote,' of past time. Loers quotes *Aen.* 7, 49 *sanguinis ultimus auctor.* **anni mei** 'my years' for 'the events of my years,' just as *tempora* means 'the state of the times' or 'the events of the times.'

111—2. **pater patruusque**: Danaus and Aegyptus. **ultimus orbis**, 'a remote part of the world,' see 13, 151.

113—4. **ille**, Aegyptus. **inops**, cf. 6, 162. **cum sene** 'with our old father Danaus.'

116. **fratrum** 'my cousins,' *fratres patrueli*, cf. 8, 28.

117—118. She means that her forty-nine sisters also perished. Of this we hear nothing from any other source. In fact Apollodorus states that by Jupiter's order they were purified by Minerva and Mercury, and were all given as prizes at gymnastic games.

120. 'What is to be done with a guilty woman, when I am held guilty for a praiseworthy action?' **rea agar** are to be taken together, lit. 'am accused of a noble deed.' **laus** = *laudabile factum*, cf. 8, 55.

121—122. 'The hundredth of a family of brothers and sisters.' She counts her male cousins and her sisters as all on the same footing as regards relationship.

123. **sororis** 'cousins,' as *frater*, above, v. 116.

124. 'And if you deserve to have all the favours I have done you,' *i.e.* in saving your life.

125—6. 'Either help me, or (if you must) abandon me to death, but at any rate see that my body is duly burnt.' *que* couples *adde* closely with *dede;* she does not ask Lynceus to abandon her to death, but puts the two alternatives, 'either help me, or *if* you let me die, give me due funeral rites.'

furtivis 'secret,' because Danaus, in his anger against her, would prevent it.

127. **sepeli**, *i.e.* bury the urn which contains my ashes.

128. **sculptaque**: Ovid is thinking of Horace again, *et nostri memorem sepulchro sculpe querelam.*

129. **pretium**, cf. 84.

131—2. **libet**: 'I should like to write more, but my hand is wearied with the weight of my chain.' **vires** 'my bodily strength.'

INDEX OF PROPER NAMES.

GENERAL INDEX.

Cambridge:
PRINTED BY J. & C. F. CLAY,
AT THE UNIVERSITY PRESS.

www.ingramcontent.com/pod-product-compliance
Lightning Source LLC
Chambersburg PA
CBHW030356270326
41926CB00009B/1134

* 9 7 8 3 3 3 7 1 8 6 8 2 1 *